Instructor's Manual, Test Bank, & Resource Integrator

to accompany

PUBLIC SPEAKING FOR COLLEGE & CAREER

Ninth Edition

by
HAMILTON GREGORY
Asheville-Buncombe Technical Community College

Boston   Burr Ridge, IL   Dubuque, IA   Madison, WI   New York   San Francisco   St. Louis
Bangkok   Bogotá   Caracas   Kuala Lumpur   Lisbon   London   Madrid   Mexico City
Milan   Montreal   New Delhi   Santiago   Seoul   Singapore   Sydney   Taipei   Toronto

Instructor's Manual, Test Bank, & Resource Integrator to accompany
PUBLIC SPEAKING FOR COLLEGE & CAREER
Hamilton Gregory

Published by McGraw-Hill, an imprint of The McGraw-Hill Companies, Inc., 1221 Avenue of the Americas, New York, NY 10020.
Copyright © 2010 by The McGraw-Hill Companies, Inc.

1 2 3 4 5 6 7 8 9 0 WDD/WDD 0

ISBN 978-0-07-729568-4
MHID   0-07-729568-4

www.mhhe.com

*Teachers have a gift for giving:
it drives them with the same
irrepressible drive that drives others
to create a work of art or a market
or a building.*

A. BARTLETT GIAMATTI
FORMER PRESIDENT, YALE

Contents

Introduction

This manual is designed as a tool for instructors who use *Public Speaking for College & Career* as a text.

I do not believe that there is one, true way to conduct a public speaking class. I have seen creative, successful instructors use many different approaches. (And I suspect that what works for one instructor may not work for another.) With this in mind, I have tried to present a variety of options in this manual. These options are based on my own experience and on techniques that I have gleaned over the years from colleagues who teach the course in various parts of the nation.

Whatever approach you use, it is a good idea to map out your entire course in advance and let students know on the first day what will be expected of them. Many of them are apprehensive, and a detailed syllabus will help build their confidence in you and help them calm their fears. In the pages that follow, I have provided some suggestions on what to consider in developing a syllabus. I have also examined the issues of students' stage fright and the debate over whether to videotape student speeches. In addition, I have provided over a dozen different evaluation forms that can be used by instructors and/or students. A special section in this manual discusses how instructors can videotape and use speeches that are aired on the C-SPAN public-affairs television network.

For the 19 chapters of the text, this manual includes the following:

Chapter Objectives and Resource Integrator: The basic goals of each chapter are written in the form of behavioral objectives. Resources are listed for each objective, as well as for the chapter as a whole. Resources include exercises and videos of speeches.

Key to Review Questions: Answers are provided for the review questions that appear at the end of each chapter in the text.

Building Critical-Thinking Skills: Guidelines are given for interpreting the questions that appear at the end of each chapter in the text.

Worksheets and Handouts: In some chapters, ready-to-reproduce worksheets or handouts are provided for further work, or to guide students in the preparation of their speeches.

Activities: Students can be given speech assignments or other activities to sharpen their skills.

Objective Tests: In the Test Bank in this manual, four tests (Forms A, B, C, and D) for each chapter are provided so that you can quickly and easily verify whether students have studied and retained information in the text. The tests are ready to print. Form A is a true-false test, Forms B and C use multiple-choice questions, and Form D has short-answer questions. For all tests, answer keys are provided. Forms A, B, C, and D are sufficiently different to permit one test to be used as the class test and the others as makeup tests for absentees.

Essay Questions: Essay questions are provided for each chapter. These questions, of course, can be added to the objective tests or used separately.

If you have any suggestions on how I can improve any part of the text or the supplements, I would appreciate your writing to me at the address below:

Hamilton Gregory
P.O. Box 8447
Asheville, N.C. 28814

Or you can e-mail me at:
    hamiltongregory@charter.net

Thanks for your support and suggestions.

Supplements

Speech Videos DVD
High resolution versions of all of the videos that accompany this book -- full-length speeches and speech excerpts – have been placed on a DVD as an option for instructors. Because they are high resolution, the videos are ideal for viewing on a large screen in a classroom or auditorium.

Instructor's Resource DVD-ROM
A rich assortment of teaching aids is offered on the Instructor's Resource DVD-ROM, including:

Instructor's Manual, Test Bank, and Resource Integrator. This supplement provides numerous resources for both novice and experienced instructors, including dozens of ready-to-reproduce worksheets and forms for classroom use, tips for videotaping classroom speeches, sample course outlines, speech evaluation forms, chapter resources, and test items. A special feature in the manual is a Resource Integrator that describes textbook features, activities, and multimedia materials that are relevant to each chapter.

Test Bank. A computerized test bank is provided in both Windows and Mac format. In addition, the DVD-ROM contains Word files of four ready-to-reproduce tests for each chapter: Form A has true-false questions; Forms B and C have multiple-choice questions; and Form D contains short-answer questions.

Chapter Highlights on PowerPoint. Well-illustrated PowerPoint slides highlight key points in each chapter in the book. Instructors can choose a version that has no videos or a version that includes video clips (speech excerpts) and "Lessons from the Movies" (see below). The program is designed to reflect the correct way to create slides. As a result, many of the slides have graphics but no words, so the instructor will need to use the accompanying scripts to provide narration.

"Building an Outline." A PowerPoint presentation shows students how to organize their ideas in an outline. A sample outline is constructed step-by-step so that students can see the process applied to a speech.

"Lessons from the Movies." This feature includes 10 narrated stories that use still shots from Hollywood films such as *Mona Lisa Smile* (Julia Roberts) to illustrate various principles of effective public speaking, such as the need to know your listeners' knowledge level as you prepare a speech.

Teaching Public Speaking Online. Sam Zahran of Fayetteville Technical Community College is the author of "Teaching Public Speaking Online with *Public Speaking for College & Career*." The guide is designed to help instructors develop and implement online public speaking courses using the pedagogical resources found in the text and supplements.

Classroom Performance System. *eInstruction: The Classroom Performance System (CPS)* is a wireless response system that allows instructors to receive immediate feedback from students. CPS units include easy-to-use software for instructors' use in creating questions and assessments and delivering them to students. The units also include individual wireless response pads for students' use in responding. Suggested questions are offered. CPS also runs alongside the PowerPoint slides that supplement the text. For further details, go to www.mhhe.com/einstruction.

Connect Public Speaking

The Instructor's Section of connectpublicspeaking.com includes all of the supplements listed above under Instructor's Resource DVD-ROM. Contact your McGraw-Hill representative for a password.

Instructor's Resource DVD-ROM

This DVD-ROM is available from your McGraw-Hill representative. Contents include:

- Instructor's Manual with Resource Integrator
- Chapter Tests: Four ready-to-reproduce tests for each chapter in Microsoft Word Document format: Form A has true-false questions; Forms B and C have multiple-choice questions, and Form D contains short-answer questions.
- Computerized Test Bank (Windows and Macintosh)
- Chapter Highlights PowerPoint slides – one version is *with* videos, the other version *without* videos (NOTE: The scripts that accompany the slides are required because some of the slides have photos, but no text.)
- *Teaching Public Speaking Online with Public Speaking for College & Career* by Sam Zahran, Fayetteville Technical Community College
- "Building an Outline" PowerPoint program
- "Lessons from the Movies"—10 narrated stories that use still shots from Hollywood films such as *Mona Lisa Smile* (Julia Roberts) to illustrate various principles of effective public speaking. Here is an overview:

Chapter	Movie	Topic
Chapter 1 (Introduction to Public Speaking)	*A Beautiful Mind*	Interference
Chapter 2 (Controlling Nervousness)	*Krippendorf's Tribe*	Preparation
Chapter 3 (Listening)	*Kate and Leopold*	Multi-Tasking
Chapter 3 (Listening)	*My Best Friend's Wedding*	Cell Phones
Chapter 4 (Audience)	*Mona Lisa Smile*	Audience Analysis
Chapter 9 (Presentation Aids)	*The Business of Strangers*	Murphy's Law
Chapter 11 (Introductions & Conclusions)	*Four Weddings and a Funeral*	Concluding with a Quotation
Chapter 13 (Wording the Speech)	*Erin Brockovich*	Crude Language
Chapter 14 (Delivery)	*Philadelphia*	Nonverbal Communication
Chapter 17 (Persuasive Strategies)	*The Man Who Shot Liberty Valence*	Credibility

Sample Speeches

Full speeches and video clips of speech excerpts are available in two formats:

1. Speech Videos DVD – high-resolution versions that are ideal for projecting onto a screen in a classroom or auditorium.

2. Speech Videos – low-resolutions versions available at connectpublicspeaking.com.

The full-length speeches include four sets of "needs improvement" and "model" speeches for purposes of comparison: Speeches 5 and 6, "Animal Helpers," Speeches 9 and 10, "How to Make Avocado Salsa," Speeches 12 and 13, "Detox," and Speeches 14 and 15, "Bicycle Helmets."

On *Connect Public Speaking*, most of the speeches are accompanied by audio introductions, critical-thinking questions, printable outlines, and on-screen, scrolling outlines.

Full Speeches

Speech 1   Scars and Bruises (Self-Introduction)

With humor and grace, Christine Fowler tells of the misadventures she experienced while growing up. This speech can be used with:

- Chapter 1 (Introduction to Public Speaking) to provide a good model of a speech introducing oneself to the class.

- Chapter 14 (Delivering the Speech) to illustrate a friendly delivery.

- Chapter 18 (Special Types of Speeches) to exemplify effective use of self-deprecating humor.

Speech 2   The Four-Day Work Week – Pros and Cons (Informative Speech)

Felipe Dieppa reports that many companies, schools, and agencies are converting to a four-day, 10-hour work week, and he explores the pluses and minuses of the plan. The speech can be used with:

- Chapter 5 (Selecting Topic, Purpose, and Central Idea) to show a good topic, specific purpose, and central idea.

- Chapter 6 (Finding Information) to show the value of using solid research to make a speech credible and interesting.

- Chapter 9 (Presentation Aids) to illustrate the use of a poster.

- Chapter 11 (Introductions and Conclusions) to point out an engaging opener and a good summary at the end.

- Chapter 14 (Delivering the Speech) to illustrate animated delivery and vocal variety.

- Chapter 15 (Speaking to Inform) to demonstrate objective reporting in an informative speech.

Speech 3   One Slip – and You're Dead (Informative Speech)

Natalia Payne defines the extreme sport known as "free solo climbing." She makes good use of narratives as she paints a portrait of two climbers. The speech can be used with:

- Chapter 5 (Selecting Topic, Purpose, and Central Idea) to show a good topic, specific purpose, and central idea.

- Chapter 6 (Finding Information) to show the value of using books and e-mail interviews for research.

- Chapter 8 (Supporting Your Ideas) to illustrate the power of narratives.

- Chapter 9 (Presentation Aids) to demonstrate the value of dramatic photos in PowerPoint slides.

- Chapter 11 (Introductions and Conclusions) to point out an engaging opener and a good summary at the end.

- Chapter 14 (Delivering the Speech) to illustrate enthusiasm in delivery.

- Chapter 15 (Speaking to Inform) to show how a speaker can make a topic interesting to the audience.

Speech 4   Wedding Crashers (Informative Speech)

Dave Reed uses an e-mail survey to answer the question: Has a Hollywood movie inspired a wave of copycat wedding crashings throughout the United States? The speech can be used with:

- Chapter 5 (Selecting Topic, Purpose, and Central Idea) to show a good topic, specific purpose, and central idea.

- Chapter 6 (Finding Information) to show the value of using articles and interviews to make a speech credible and interesting.

- Chapter 11 (Introductions and Conclusions) to point out an engaging opener and a good summary at the end.

- Chapter 14 (Delivering the Speech) to illustrate animated delivery and vocal variety.

Speech 5   Animal Helpers I (Informative: Needs Improvement)

This video shows a student who fails to do her homework and gives information that everyone already knows. Her delivery is poor, and she displays a mediocre visual aid too quickly. (All of her mistakes are listed in the commentary box on the CD screen.) This speech can be used with:

- Chapter 1 (Introduction to Public Speaking) to illustrate the seven elements of the speech communication process, especially interference (which is created when the speaker displays a visual aid that is too small to be seen).

7

- Chapter 4 (Reaching the Audience) to illustrate a speaker who fails to offer listeners new and interesting material.

- Chapter 5 (Selecting Topic, Purpose, and Central Idea) to show lack of focus.

- Chapter 6 (Finding Information) to show the lamentable results of failing to do adequate research.

- Chapter 14 (Delivering the Speech) to demonstrate ineffective delivery.

- Chapter 15 (Speaking to Inform) to illustrate the wrong way to inform.

Speech 6   Animal Helpers II (Informative: Improved Version)

Brianne Berkson delivers a much-improved speech, energetically giving interesting information that her audience probably doesn't know. This video can be used with:

- Chapter 4 (Reaching the Audience) to illustrate a speaker who provides listeners with meaningful content.

- Chapter 5 (Selecting Topic, Purpose, and Central Idea) to show a good topic, specific purpose, and central idea.

- Chapter 6 (Finding Information) to show the value of using solid research to make a speech credible and interesting.

- Chapter 7 (Evaluating Information & Avoiding Plagiarism) to point out that the speaker avoids far-out, dubious claims of animal feats that are frequently reported on the Internet.

- Chapter 11 (Introductions and Conclusions) to point out an engaging opener and a good summary at the end.

- Chapter 14 (Delivering the Speech) to illustrate animated delivery and vocal variety.

- Chapter 15 (Speaking to Inform) to show a model informative speech.

Speech 7   Humanoid Robots (Informative Speech)

Joe Haupt gives an update on what humanoid robots can do today and what they are likely to do in the future. This video can be used with:

- Chapter 4 (Reaching the Audience) to illustrate a speaker who provides listeners with meaningful content.

- Chapter 5 (Selecting Topic, Purpose, and Central Idea) to show a good topic, specific purpose, and central idea.

- Chapter 6 (Finding Information) to show the value of using solid research to make a speech credible and interesting.

- Chapter 8 (Visual Aids) to illustrate effective PowerPoint slides.

- Chapter 10 (The Body of the Speech) to show the chronological pattern of organization.

- Chapter 14 (Delivering the Speech) to illustrate animated delivery and vocal variety.

- Chapter 15 (Speaking to Inform) to show a model informative speech.

Speech 8   Indian Weddings (Informative)

Preeti Vilkhu, who had recently married a man chosen by her parents, explains the wedding customs of India. This speech can be used with:

- Chapter 4 (Reaching the Audience) to demonstrate sensitivity to cultural differences (she shows respect for American views that are contrary to Indian customs).

- Chapter 5 (Selecting Topic, Purpose, and Central Idea) to show a speaker who chooses a topic from her own experience.

- Chapter 9 (Presentation Aids) to point out the use of overhead transparencies and objects (cloth).

- Chapter 15 (Speaking to Inform) to show an informative speech that provides new and interesting information not known by the audience.

Speech 9   How to Make Avocado Salsa (Informative: Needs Improvement)

This video shows a student who gives a clumsy, poorly prepared demonstration. (All of his mistakes are listed in the commentary box on the CD screen.) This speech can be used with:

- Chapter 14 (Delivering the Speech) to demonstrate ineffective delivery.

- Chapter 15 (Speaking to Inform) to illustrate the wrong way to demonstrate a process.

Speech 10   How to Make Avocado Salsa (Informative: Improved Version)

Nick Amick shows how to prepare and deliver a demonstration speech that is interesting and well-presented. This video can be used with:

- Chapter 4 (Reaching the Audience) to illustrate a speaker who provides listeners with meaningful content.

- Chapter 5 (Selecting Topic, Purpose, and Central Idea) to show a good topic, specific purpose, and central idea.

- Chapter 11 (Introductions and Conclusions) to point out an engaging opener and a good summary at the end.

- Chapter 14 (Delivering the Speech) to illustrate a lively, conversational style.

- Chapter 15 (Speaking to Inform) to show a model demonstration speech.

Speech 11   How to Hide Valuables (Demonstration)

Burch Wang provides an excellent demonstration. He speaks with friendliness and energy, using gestures well. His speech can be used with:

- Chapter 9 (Presentation Aids) to show effective use of photos on PowerPoint slides.

- Chapter 11 (Introductions and Conclusions) to point out the use of a provocative narrative at the beginning and a good summary at the end.

- Chapter 14 (Delivering the Speech) to illustrate dynamic extemporaneous speaking, with good use of gestures and notes.

- Chapter 15 (Speaking to Inform) to show a good process speech.

Speech 12   Detox I (Persuasive: Needs Improvement)

Steven Kaplan urges his listeners to detoxify their bodies, but he fails to verify research information and he ends up misleading the audience. The speech can be used with:

- Chapter 7 (Evaluating Information and Avoiding Plagiarism) to show the dangers of finding misinformation on the Internet and accepting it as fact.

- Chapters 16 and 17 (persuasion) to illustrate ineffective persuasion.

Speech 13   Detox II (Persuasive: Improved Version)

Steven Kaplan redeems himself after giving an awful speech (above). He uses impressive research to convince his listeners that their bodies do NOT need detoxification. The speech can be used with:

- Chapter 7 (Evaluating Information and Avoiding Plagiarism) to show how a researcher can use critical thinking to detect and reject unverified claims on the Internet.

- Chapter 8 (Support Materials) to show good use of support materials such as expert testimony.

- Chapter 11 (Introductions and Conclusions) to point out an interesting introduction and a strong clincher at the end.

- Chapter 14 (Delivering the Speech) to illustrate good delivery.

- Chapters 16 (Speaking to Persuade) to provide a model of a dynamic persuasive speech.

- Chapter 17 (Persuasive Strategies) to show use of sufficient evidence.

Speech 14   Bicycle Helmets I (Persuasive: Needs Improvement)

This video demonstrates the folly of boring, tedious PowerPoint slides that are read aloud. The delivery is stiff and fast, and the speaker shows no regard for his listeners. The speech can be used with:

- Chapter 4 (Reaching the Audience) to illustrate a speaker who fails to connect with his listeners.

- Chapter 9 (Presentation Aids) to spotlight hard-to-read PowerPoint slides and the wrong way to present them.

- Chapter 14 (Delivering the Speech) to demonstrate a monotone voice and a dull, hurried delivery.

- Chapters 16 and 17 (persuasion) to illustrate ineffective persuasion.

Speech 15   Bicycle Helmets II (Persuasive: Improved Version)

Michael Maraviglia offers a well-developed, vastly improved version of the bicycle helmet speech, speaking with passion and using visuals correctly. The speech can be used with:

- Chapter 4 (Reaching the Audience) to illustrate a speaker who uses an audience questionnaire in preparing his speech and then refers to the results in the speech itself, and to illustrate a speaker who is audience-centered.

- Chapter 8 (Support Materials) to show good use of support materials such as examples, testimony, and statistics.

- Chapter 11 (Introductions and Conclusions) to point out an intriguing introduction and a strong challenge at the end.

- Chapter 14 (Delivering the Speech) to illustrate good delivery.

- Chapters 16 (Speaking to Persuade) to provide a model of a dynamic persuasive speech.

- Chapter 17 (Persuasive Strategies) to show use of ample evidence.

Speech 16   The Deadliest Natural Disaster (Persuasive)

Kimberly Villanueva uses the motivated sequence to try to reach her listeners and encourage them to take action. This speech can be used with:

- Chapter 6 (Finding Information) to show a speaker who has made good use of research in preparing her speech.

- Chapter 8 (Support Materials) to show good use of support materials such as examples, testimony, and statistics.

- Chapter 9 (Presentation Aids) to illustrate the use of large, vivid posters.

- Chapter 11 (Introductions and Conclusions) to point out provocative questions at the beginning and a good summary and challenge in the conclusion.

- Chapter 14 (Delivering the Speech) to illustrate a conversational style of delivery.

- Chapters 16 (Speaking to Persuade) to provide a model of the motivated sequence.

Speech 17   Native American Crafts (Persuasive)

Ian Federgreen uses the problem-solution pattern in a well-researched, passionately delivered speech about the injustice of counterfeit crafts. This speech can be used with:

- Chapter 2 (Controlling Nervousness) to show a speaker who enters his speech with nervous tension, but stays in control and is confident because he has prepared well and because he focuses his energies on reaching the audience.

- Chapter 5 (Selecting Topic, Purpose, and Central Idea) to show that a speaker can choose a topic from current events and then fully research it.

- Chapter 6 (Finding Information) to show a speaker who has obviously carried out extensive research in preparing his speech.

- Chapter 8 (Support Materials) to show good use of support materials such as examples, testimony, and statistics.

- Chapter 9 (Presentation Aids) to illustrate the use of photos on PowerPoint slides.

- Chapter 11 (Introductions and Conclusions) to point out an interesting attention-getter at the beginning and a powerful challenge at the end.

- Chapter 14 (Delivering the Speech) to exemplify a speaker who has a strong desire to communicate with his audience.

- Chapter 16 (Speaking to Persuade) to provide a model of the problem-solution pattern.

Speech 18   Inmates and Tomatoes (Persuasive Speech – Motivated Sequence)

Is it possible that solving a problem in jails can provide food for low-income families? Nicole Sudhaus uses the motivated sequence skillfully to show the creative solution to a problem. This video can be used with:

- Chapter 6 (Finding Information) to illustrate effective research.

- Chapter 8 (Support Materials) to show good use of support materials such as examples, testimony, and statistics.

- Chapter 11 (Introductions and Conclusions) to point out an excellent introduction and conclusion.

- Chapter 14 (Delivering the Speech) to illustrate a conversational style of delivery.

- Chapters 16 (Speaking to Persuade) to provide a model of the motivated sequence.

Speech 19   Are You Being Overcharged? (Persuasive Speech – Motivated Sequence)

Laura Valpey uses the five steps of the motivated sequence skillfully to show how Americans can avoid being cheated at the checkout counter. This video can be used with:

- Chapter 6 (Finding Information) to show a speaker who has made good use of research in preparing her speech.

- Chapter 8 (Support Materials) to show good use of support materials such as examples, testimony, and statistics.

- Chapter 9 (Presentation Aids) to illustrate the use of PowerPoint slides.

- Chapter 11 (Introductions and Conclusions) to point out provocative questions at the beginning and a good conclusion.

- Chapter 14 (Delivering the Speech) to illustrate a conversational style of delivery.

- Chapters 16 (Speaking to Persuade) to provide a model of the motivated sequence.

Speech 20   Would You Vote for Aardvark? (Persuasive speech – Problem-Solution)

Turron Kofi Alleyne explains a problem—some elections are won by candidates simply because their names appear on the top of the ballot—and offers a solution. This video can be used with:

- Chapter 6 (Finding Information) to show a speaker who has done extensive research.

- Chapter 8 (Support Materials) to show good use of support materials such as hypothetical examples, testimony, and statistics.

- Chapter 9 (Presentation Aids) to illustrate the use of homemade PowerPoint slides.

- Chapter 11 (Introductions and Conclusions) to show the effective use of an intriguing introduction and a humorous conclusion.

- Chapter 12 (Outlining) to show a catchy title.

- Chapter 16 (Speaking to Persuade) to provide a model of the problem-solution pattern.

Speech 21   Too Much of a Good Thing (Persuasive speech – Problem-Solution)

Arlene Chico Lugo explains the problem of overdosing on "safe" medicines, and provides a solution. This video can be used with:

- Chapter 6 (Finding Information) to show a speaker who has obviously carried out extensive research in preparing her speech.

- Chapter 8 (Support Materials) to show good use of support materials such as examples, testimony, and statistics.

- Chapter 9 (Presentation Aids) to illustrate the use of posters.

- Chapter 11 (Introductions and Conclusions) to show the effective use of a catchy introduction and a conclusion that echoes the introduction.

- Chapter 16 (Speaking to Persuade) to provide a model of the problem-solution pattern.

Speech 22   Three Celebrity Heroes (Tribute)

Amy Casanova offers a creative and fascinating tribute to three celebrities who are unselfish heroes. This speech can be used with:

- Chapter 1 (Introduction to Public Speaking) to demonstrate that preparing and giving a speech can be a rewarding personal experience and a delight to the listeners.

- Chapter 6 (Finding Information) to show a speaker who enriches her speech by doing extensive research.

- Chapter 8 (Support Materials) to show good use of narratives.

- Chapter 10 (The Body of the Speech) to point out the smooth use of transitions.

- Chapter 13 (Wording the Speech) to exemplify the artful use of language.

- Chapter 14 (Delivering the Speech) to illustrate an enthusiastic, conversational manner of speaking.

- Chapter 18 (Special Types of Speeches) to provide a model of the speech of tribute.

Video Clips

Chapter 4	4.1	Analyzing the Audience
Chapter 4	4.2	Helping Listeners Who Speak English as a Second Language
Chapter 5	5.1	Choosing a Topic
Chapter 5	5.2	Conveying the Central Idea
Chapter 6	6.1	Using Books as Sources
Chapter 6	6.2	Conducting E-Mail Interviews
Chapter 7	7.1	Giving Credit to Sources
Chapter 8	8.1	Using a Vivid Image
Chapter 8	8.2	Using an Example
Chapter 8	8.3	Making a Contrast
Chapter 8	8.4	Using an Analogy
Chapter 8	8.5	Using Testimony
Chapter 8	8.6	Using Statistics

A valuable feature on all the videos is closed captioning, accessed by clicking on the "CC" icon. Closed captioning is helpful not only for viewers with hearing disabilities, **but also for students who speak English as a second language.** The captions help to ensure that each speaker's words are understood.

Connect Public Speaking

Visit connectpublicspeaking.com and take a look at the resources that are available for instructors. Also note the student resources, which include:

Practice Tests

To help students prepare for classroom tests, *Connect Public Speaking* includes a practice test for every chapter, with 15 multiple-choice and 15 true-false questions. If they choose an incorrect answer, they are given an immediate explanation of their mistake and invited to try again.

Key-Term Flashcards

A deck of electronic flashcards for each chapter is a helpful tool for studying key terms and preparing for exams. This software application manages the text's glossary by chapter and allows students to create customizable "decks" of key terms.

Glossary

An alphabetical glossary of all text terms and their definitions is a handy resource for study and review.

Topic Helper

To help students come up with a topic for their next speech, *Topic Helper* lists hundreds of potential subjects.

Checklist for Preparing and Delivering a Speech

This list of steps not only helps students manage the preparation of their classroom speeches, but it also provides a valuable guide for speeches that they may be asked to give in career and community settings.

Outline Exercises

By dragging and dropping parts of a scrambled outline into a properly sequenced outline, students can practice outlining with actual content, and become skilled at outlining five types of speeches: informative, persuasive, demonstration, speech of tribute, and self-introduction. These exercises are based on nine different speech outlines.

Outlines

Most of the speeches on video are accompanied by full outlines that can be viewed and printed out.

Outline Tutor

Outline Tutor helps students organize their material in outline format. This interactive program shows the various parts of an outline and makes it easy to insert content into the appropriate sections of the outline.

PowerPoint Design Tips

Basic principles of good design are explained in this tutorial.

WEBLINKS

Internet addresses in the text may change or even disappear, so readers may visit WEBLINKS at connectpublicspeaking.com to find updates listed by page number.

Supplementary Readings

Various articles, many of which appeared in earlier editions in a booklet, cover topics that the book does not have space to include. Some examples:

- "Speech Phobia" – In Chapter 2 of the text, students are advised to read this article if they need extra help in dealing with stage fright.

- "Speaking in Front of a Camera" – This feature gives tips on how to speak effectively when on TV or in a videotaped program.

Interactive Exercises

By doing exercises and checking the correct answers, students can consolidate their learning of various skills, such as creating purpose statements.

Research Aids

Four tables in the text have been adapted for connectpublicspeaking.com, and will be kept up-to-date:

1. Internet Search Tools

2. Electronic Search Options

3. Where to Find Materials

4. Evaluations of Web sites

Classroom Performance System

eInstruction: The Classroom Performance System (CPS) is a wireless response system that allows instructors to receive immediate feedback from students. *CPS* units include easy-to-use software for instructors' use in creating questions and assessments and delivering them to students. The units also include individual wireless response pads for students' use in responding. Suggested questions are offered. *CPS* also runs alongside the PowerPoint slides that supplement the text. For further details, go to www.mhhe.com/einstruction.

Free Resources

Video-Sharing Sites

Sites such as YouTube (youtube.com) offer speeches and speech excerpts that can be viewed in the classroom. As long as the instructor uses such videos only for instructional purposes in an educational setting, there are no copyright restrictions.

C-SPAN

Educators have permission to make videos of speeches delivered on C-SPAN, the public-affairs cable TV network, and use them in the classroom. C-SPAN concentrates on national political issues, especially as reflected in the proceedings of both houses of the United States Congress and in political debates and interviews.

C-SPAN speeches can provide instructors with both positive and negative examples. While some of the speeches are models of careful organization and skillful delivery, others provide samples of what not to do in an oral presentation. Some speakers, especially government officials, read monotonously from tedious manuscripts that are loaded with clichés, euphemisms, and bureaucratic jargon.

Because you can rarely know in advance whether a speech is going to provide examples of the teaching points you want to make, I don't recommend using a live C-SPAN speech in the classroom (except of course for ceremonial situations such as a President's inaugural address). It is safer to tape the speech and then decide whether to use it in the classroom.

Here is the verbatim, official copyright policy of C-SPAN:

> C-SPAN (Cable Satellite Public Affairs Network) hereby grants educators associated with degree-granting educational institutions this license containing the right to tape any C-SPAN-produced program without receiving prior permission from the network, so long as the copying is for in-classroom use and not for sale, distribution, or any political purpose. As public domain material, the video coverage of the floor proceedings of the U.S. House of Representatives and the U.S. Senate is not subject to this license, and as such, may also be similarly used for educational purposes.
>
> The terms of this license constitute a liberal copyright policy that allows educators to record C-SPAN-produced programs (at school or at home) for later use. Such programs may be retained in perpetuity for future in-classroom use.
>
> No license fee shall be due for using C-SPAN as an educational resource so long as such use is made in accordance with the terms of this license.

For up-to-date information on C-SPAN programs, visit this Web site:

www.c-span.org

Old C-SPAN programs can be procured via the Web site.

Class Policies

Here are some important issues in determining policies for a public speaking class:

What kinds of speeches and/or group projects should be required?

There is a rich diversity of speech assignments in American colleges and universities. Below are some of the more popular types of assignments. Some instructors assign specific types; others stipulate only a broad category, such as informative or persuasive. For the final classroom speech, some instructors permit students to choose any kind they wish.

Icebreaker Speeches
>Speech of Self-Introduction
>Speech Introducing a Classmate
>Pet Peeve Speech
>"I Believe" Speech
>(For a discussion of these types, see Chapter 1 of this manual.)

Informative Speeches
>Informative Speech
>Informative Speech with Visual Aids
>Definition Speech
>Description Speech
>Process (or Demonstration) Speech
>Explanation Speech
>Book Analysis
>Personal Experience Speech
>(For a discussion of these types, see Chapter 15 of this manual.)

Persuasive Speeches
>Persuasive Speech
>Speech to Influence Thinking
>Speech of Refutation
>Speech to Motivate Action
>Speech Using the Motivated Sequence
>Speech Using Problem-Solution Pattern
>(For a discussion of these types, see Chapter 16 of this manual.)

Special Speeches
>Entertaining (or After-Dinner) Speech
>Speech of Introduction
>Speech of Presentation
>Speech of Acceptance
>Speech of Tribute
>Inspirational Speech
>(For a discussion of these types, see Chapter 18 of this manual.)

Impromptu Speeches
    Impromptu Speech
    Oral Evaluation of Class Speeches
    (For a discussion of these types, see Chapter 14 of this manual.)

Group Projects
    Problem-Solving Group Project
    Team Presentation
    Symposium
    Panel Discussion
    (For a discussion of these types, see Chapter 19 of this manual.)

What method of delivery should be required of students?

Most instructors require the extemporaneous method of delivery for most or all speeches because that is the method most frequently used in business, professional, and technical careers.

Some instructors assign impromptu speeches to give students experience in "thinking on their feet." Other instructors avoid this kind of speech because they think the stress is counterproductive for beginning speakers; they prefer that impromptu speeches be assigned in advanced speech classes.

How many speeches should be required of each student?

The number of required speeches will depend upon how many students you have, how long the term is, and how much lecturing you plan to do. One of the goals of *Public Speaking for College and Career* is to cover all the necessary preparation steps in such detail that you can minimize your lecturing, if you so desire, and provide maximum time for student speeches. Some instructors like their students to give six or seven short speeches, while others prefer students to give only three or four medium-length or long speeches.

What time limits should be imposed on speeches?

Time limits vary widely from school to school, and from instructor to instructor. Many instructors like to start off with fairly short speeches (such as 2-3 or 3-5 minutes) in the beginning of the course and then work up to longer speeches (such as 5-7, 6-8, 7-10, or 8-10 minutes). There are two important variables that will determine what length you set for classroom speeches: How many students are in the class? How many speeches will you require of each student?

The question-and-answer period is usually not included in the timing because its length is beyond the student's control.

Should students be penalized for going under or over time limits?

Some people are oblivious to how much time elapses when they speak in public. They blithely inflict one-hour speeches on audiences when they have been asked to limit themselves to five minutes. If they are informed later of their time, they are truly shocked—they swear that surely no more than five or ten minutes elapsed. To insure that your students develop a sense of time, you may want to penalize them not only for going over the time limit, but for going under as well. Going under the limit can be a problem if they are participating in a videotaped or televised program and they "run out" of material before the show is over.

Because practice time at home may differ from delivery time in the classroom, most instructors give a latitude of a minute or two on either side of the target time. If, for example, you wanted your students to speak for 7 minutes, it is reasonable and fair to give 6 minutes as the minimum and 8 as the maximum. Some instructors give an even more generous cushion of time; for example, for a 6-minute speech, they stipulate a minimum of 4 and a maximum of 8.

How can you penalize the student? Some instructors deduct five points from the speech grade for going under or over the time limits. Other instructors deduct five points for *every minute* under or over.

Should visual aids be required?

I recommend that visual aids be required for most speech assignments because (1) they are almost mandatory in business and professional presentations today, and (2) they help speakers communicate effectively with persons who speak English as a second language or who have auditory or learning disabilities.

If visual aids are merely recommended, students tend not to use them; if they are required, however, students are forced to think of possibilities, and often come up with creative visuals.

Some students will point out, quite rightly, that certain speeches do not lend themselves to sophisticated visual aids such as charts and videos. For these speeches, a poster listing the main points would suffice.

Should a question-and-answer period be held for each speech?

Many instructors recommend a question-and-answer period for each speech because (1) it gives the speaker immediate feedback from the audience, (2) it gives listeners a chance to clarify confusing issues and ask about omitted material, (3) it gives the speaker valuable experience in interacting on an improvised basis with an audience, and (4) question-and-answer periods are standard procedure in most of the speeches that a student will give in his or her career.

What if a student is not asked any questions?

Some speeches elicit no comments or questions from student listeners. Since this sometimes makes a speaker feel that his or her speech was not very interesting to the audience, you may want to tell your students that getting no questions is not necessarily a sign of disapproval or rejection—it can mean that the speaker has covered his or her topic so well that nothing occurs to the listeners to ask.

Some instructors look over each student's outline in advance and write down at least one question to ask the student in case none of the classmates speak up. This, of course, insures that each student gets at least one question.

Should the question-and-answer period have a time limit?

In some speeches, listeners get deeply involved and are bubbling with good questions; it seems cruel to arbitrarily cut off the discussion. On the other hand, a Q-&-A period on an exciting topic cannot be allowed to consume most of the class period and crowd out other speeches. The best approach may be to build a generous allotment of time for the Q-&-A period into your schedule, cut off the questions when the time limit is reached, and then—if any leftover time exists after all scheduled speeches have been delivered—come back to the speaker and continue with the Q-&-A period if any listeners are still interested.

How many speeches should be scheduled per class period?

It is difficult to fit speeches snugly into a time slot. Let's say you have a 50-minute class and you plan to have five 6-minute speeches per day, with time in between for question-and-answer periods and peer evaluations. On some days, you may have several speakers who go beyond the time limit, so you can't include all the speeches. On other days, you may have only three of the five speakers to show up, and their speeches elicit no questions at all from the audience. You end up with 20 minutes of idle time.

In deciding how many speeches to schedule per class, here are some suggestions:

1. Remember that everything takes longer than you think it will. When you are mapping out your schedule, it is easy to allot a certain number of minutes per speech, but in the reality of the classroom, things always seem to take longer: key speakers are late in getting to class; some speakers exceed their time limits; some speakers take a long time to set up or put away their visual aid . . . The solution is to leave a generous cushion of time for every scheduled event. It is better to have some time left over than to fail to have enough time for all speeches.

2. Have "filler" activities for days when speeches are finished earlier than expected. You may want to have a backlog of mini-lectures and films, or you may want to spend the time discussing problems that have arisen in the most recent speeches. Some instructors use leftover time by having a discussion of items in the end-of-chapter exercises in the text.

3. Schedule make-up days. Inevitably some speakers will fail to appear on their speech day. And sometimes, despite your best efforts, you are unable to fit all speeches into the schedule. So, you need to have a makeup day, for every set of speeches, built into the schedule. (Note: In order to discourage cuts, some instructors do not allow students to make up missed speeches; other instructors allow make-ups but penalize the student by lowering the speech grade one level—for example, dropping a B to a C.)

Should speakers know the exact date of their speech?

Instead of telling everyone in the class to be ready to speak on certain days, you may want to inform each student (far in advance) of the exact day his or her speech is to be given. This helps students control their anxiety. It also helps them do a better job of listening (if they don't know when they are to speak, they may not pay attention to classmates' speeches because of the gnawing thought, "Oh no, am I next?").

How should the order of speakers be determined?

I have found it helpful to organize a class arbitrarily into groups at the beginning of the course—Group A, Group B, etc. Then I vary the order in which the groups speak. Group A, for example, is assigned the first day in the first round of speeches, but Group B is assigned the first day in the second round, Group C the first day in the third round, and so on.

Within each group, how should the order of speakers be determined on speech day? Here are three alternatives: (1) You can announce the order of speakers in advance (to help students do a better job of listening, as mentioned in the section above). (2) You can assign speaking order at random. (3) You can ask for volunteers; some students like to go first or second to "get it over with." Those who do not volunteer for a slot can be assigned at random.

Instructor Peggy Ryan has an effective way of determining the order of speakers in a 3-hour class. Right before class, she puts sign-up numbers on the board (1, 2, 3, etc.) with a blank space beside every number. As students arrive, they write their name next to whatever number they prefer. Thus, the one who puts his or her name next to "9" is the ninth speaker. If the last student to arrive sees only one spot left—#2, say—then he or she is the second speaker.

How can students be encouraged to attend class?

In some courses, class attendance is not terribly important, because material missed in class can be studied in the textbook. But a public speaking class is different; it works best when most students show up every time, especially when speeches are given. Speakers need a full audience in order to get maximum experience from speechmaking. And since listening is an important component of a public speaking class, students need to be in class to sharpen their evaluation and listening skills.

Here are some ways to encourage attendance:

1. In talking to the class at the beginning of the course, stress the reasons why class attendance is so important. (Make sure you repeat your message later to any students who were absent.) One instructor says, "I tell students that if they cut class on the day their classmates are speaking, they are being terribly rude—they are saying, in effect, '*Your* speech is not worth my time.' In other words, I appeal to their sense of civility and fairness to their peers."

2. Provide incentives. If your school permits such a policy, you can make a promise like this on your course syllabus: "Students with an A average and no more than four hours of absences will be exempt from the final exam. Students with a B average and no more than two hours of absences will be exempt from the final exam." This kind of policy is often a strong incentive for students to attend regularly.

3. Quiz students on the class speeches. Knowing that they will be tested on the content of their classmates' speeches provides some students with a strong motivation to attend.

4. Provide penalties for absences. Some instructors deduct points from the final grade for more than 2 or 3 cuts. Other instructors drop students from class if they miss more than a certain number of hours. (Note: Some colleges and universities, acting on the basis of

state law or legal interpretations, do not allow instructors to use absences as a factor in figuring grades.)

What rules should be established for the course?

Though each instructor will devise rules for his or her unique situation, some sample guidelines that you may want to consider including in your class policy are shown in the Sample Syllabus in this manual.

Should outlines be required?

Most instructors require outlines because if they don't, students will either not do an outline at all or they will construct a flimsy one. Outlines are difficult for many students, and they need a lot of advice as they construct them. Though they may grumble at the time, by the end of the course almost all students say they were glad they were forced to do outlines.

I require students to do their outlines in parts over a two-week period, and turn in each part and get it approved before proceeding to the next part. I developed this procedure because of some disasters that occurred when I first began teaching this course: in those days, I did not require outlines to be turned in until the hour of the student's speech. Much to my dismay, I discovered that some students would put off all work until a few hours before their speech. Some of them (I was told) would desperately throw together an outline in the parking lot a short time before class. The results, predictably, were terrible speeches.

The two outlining options contained in SpeechMate CD—Outline Tutor and the Microsoft Word outline template—prompt students to include all parts and to place them in the correct order. Before students reach the final stage of outlining, I encourage them to use one of the preliminary techniques discussed at the end of Chapter 10. Using stick-on slips to experiment with the order of material is popular with my students.

Should students be allowed to change their outlines?

Instructors differ on whether outline changes are acceptable. Some allow students to make any changes they wish as they go through the preparation stages. In other words, students are permitted to throw out their topic and start over; they are permitted to revise their outline and speaking notes—even if they are doing so five minutes before speech time. The advantage of this approach is that it underscores the idea that an outline is a flexible device that is designed to help speakers organize their thoughts, not a cruel, pedagogical instrument designed to force rigidity and dampen creativity.

If you follow this approach, you may want to assure students that when they give a speech, you will not sit in the back of the room and hold their outline in one hand and see if they meticulously follow it. You may want to point out that in some cases, they may need to make adjustments while they are speaking. For example, if they see quizzical or confused expressions on their listeners' faces when they make a particular point, they should insert an extra explanation to try to clarify the point.

Should students be required to turn in their speaking notes?

Some instructors require that notes be turned in after a speech—so that a speaker reveals whether he or she used a sensible system. If a clumsy note system seemed to cause problems in the speech, the instructor can show the student how to improve his or her notes for future speeches.

Other instructors, who do not take up notes, usually act on the assumption that if the student delivers a speech well, it really doesn't matter what system of notes he or she used.

Should students evaluate their peers?

When students evaluate each other's speeches, they develop listening and evaluation skills that are valuable for any communicator in our society. The speaker also benefits: he or she gets a variety of helpful responses from many different perspectives.

Should the evaluation be oral or written?

Oral Evaluations. Two advantages of oral evaluations are (1) students get impromptu speaking experience, and (2) if they are chosen at random after the speech, the entire class is super-alert as listeners since everyone realizes that he or she may be the one selected. Disadvantages include (1) evaluations are uneven—some speakers get good, helpful evaluations, while others get weak, ineffective evaluations, and (2) this procedure takes up a lot of class time.

If you use oral evaluations, you may want to require your evaluators to use a checklist or you may want to assign (in advance) certain areas to analyze, such as the introduction or support materials.

Written Evaluations. The most popular form of peer evaluation is the written critique sheet. Some instructors have all listeners use the checklist to evaluate every speech that is given. Other instructors select only a few student evaluators per speech.

You may want to use evaluation forms contained in this manual.

When students use evaluation sheets to evaluate each other, you may want to tell them to *not* write their names on the sheets (because anonymity encourages candor). [Note: Occasionally you may get a smart-aleck who writes sarcastic or hurtful remarks under the cloak of anonymity. Sometimes these remarks can be quite destructive to the self-esteem and morale of the student being attacked. To prevent this (fortunately rare) occurrence, you can have all students write their names on the tops of the evaluation sheets, but at the same time, promise to cut off the names before you give the sheets to the speaker.]

Here are two options you may want to consider for the return of peer evaluations:

Option #1: Speakers receive evaluations soon after the speech.

When speakers get peer evaluations sheets right after the speech or at the end of the period, they get quick feedback.

Suggestion: To protect their anonymity, peer evaluators should not be asked to pass their sheets to the student speaker. Instead they can pass the sheets to you and then you can shuffle them before handing them to the speaker.

Option #2: Speakers receive evaluations a few days later.
You may want to take up peer evaluation sheets and then give them to the speakers a few days later. This has the advantage of letting you see how peer evaluators are faring and if they need guidance.

Note of caution: If you keep evaluations for a few days, some students may think that you are planning to use them to figure the speaker's grade, so they may be tempted, out of kindness, to rank a speaker higher than they normally would. To avoid this, tell the students explicitly that peer evaluations are strictly for the benefit of the speaker and will play no part in your grading system.

How can students be taught to evaluate their peers effectively?

To get maximum benefit from the peer evaluation system, students should be trained to use the peer evaluation sheet before they get involved in their first evaluation of a classmate. You can go over the peer evaluation form in class step-by-step and discuss each part. One effective method discussed in this manual is to give a speech to your class and have the students evaluate you.

Students can get some good tips on evaluating speeches from the section entitled "Speech Evaluations" in Chapter 3 of the text.

Should students applaud each speaker?

Whether to permit or encourage applause at the end of each speech is a matter for each instructor to decide. Some instructors avoid applause because it might disturb neighboring classrooms. I have tried both ways—and I have discovered that students (as speakers and as listeners) overwhelmingly favor applause. Whatever policy is adopted, it is a nice touch for the instructor to say warmly, "Thank you, [speaker's name]," when the question-and-answer period is over and it is time for the student to sit down. This helps make the student feel appreciated.

Should the instructor give oral critiques?

Instead of or in addition to written critiques, some instructors give oral critiques of student speeches, either at the end of each speech or at the end of the class period. Some instructors give the critique in front of the entire class so that other students can profit from the comments; other instructors dismiss class a few minutes early and give critiques to each speaker privately in order to avoid any embarrassment.

The oral critique in front of the entire class has two main advantages: It gives immediate feedback to the student, and it provides examples—for the rest of the class—of what to do and what not to do. The disadvantages, however, are that it is time-consuming, it can easily become repetitious, and a student who has just given a speech may be in too much emotional turmoil to listen attentively and receptively to a critique.

Giving Your Own Speech

Consider giving a speech and having students evaluate you. Such a speech provides your students with a good model for speechmaking and it lets them get familiar with the evaluation form(s) they will be using during the course. It provides some additional dividends: (1) By seeing your willingness to expose yourself to criticism, you underscore the idea that everyone should welcome feedback in order to sharpen communication skills. (2) You are able to learn of errors or problems in your presentation that you were unaware of. For example, students recently gave me valuable feedback on a distracting mannerism that had crept into my delivery—I had apparently developed the unconscious habit of continually straightening my tie while speaking.

Here is the way one instructor presents her own speech:

1. Early in the course, she passes out the evaluation form that students will be using to critique each other, and carefully goes over each part.

2. She announces that she will give a speech in the way that she expects students to give theirs. "After my speech is over," she says, "I will give you time to fill in the evaluation sheet. This will be anonymous. I will have a student collect these and shuffle them, so that I will not know who wrote what."

3. She sits down and has a student introduce her. She gets out of her seat, walks to the lectern, and gives her speech.

4. After the speech, she has a question-and-answer period, gives time for evaluation, and then has a student collect and shuffle the forms.

5. She passes out a copy of the outline and speaking notes that she used for her speech and goes over them, pointing out key features. This serves as good review of the basic principles of outlining and making notes.

On end-of-the-course evaluations of the class, she reports, most students rank her model speech as one of the most helpful parts of the entire course.

Fear of Public Speaking

Should a public speaking instructor refrain from mentioning the issue of fear of speaking (or, as it is variously called, stage fright, speech fright, or communication apprehension)? After all, if you talk about nervousness, aren't you creating a problem that would not otherwise exist?

From research literature, the following conclusions can be drawn[1]:

1. Stage fright is a problem that afflicts most students, to one degree or another, regardless of whether the instructor talks about it.

2. Showing students how to control their nervousness prevents some students from dropping out of the course, and helps almost all students keep their anxiety at a manageable level.

3. Talking about stage fright apparently does not cause students to acquire fears they otherwise never would have thought about.

Another important issue: *some students have a low or moderate level of stage fright in speaking to their peers in the public speaking classroom, but develop debilitating anxiety when they must speak to groups in their careers.* This is a phenomenon that was described to me frequently as I interviewed business and professional leaders for the text. For example, a middle-aged physician told me that she had no trouble giving oral reports in college and medical school, but developed an extreme fear of public speaking several years after she became a doctor. (Incidentally, many actors aren't overly bothered by stage fright until they reach middle age, according to Stephen Aaron's *Stage Fright: Its Role in Acting* [University of Chicago Press, 1986]; late in his career, the celebrated thespian Laurence Olivier developed such a severe case of stage fright that it nearly forced him into an early retirement.) Assigning Chapter 2 of the text will give your students "preventive medicine" for their careers. By understanding the psychology and physiology of stage fright, they may be able to avoid future crises.

Teaching Suggestions

Here are some suggestions for helping your students with stage fright:

1. Assign Chapter 2 (Controlling Nervousness) early in the course and have a follow-up discussion on the subject in class. You may want to assign Chapter 2 and announce a quiz on the chapter to be given at the beginning of the next class. After the quiz, you can go over the answers as a way of covering the highlights of Chapter 2.
    After a thorough discussion of stage fright, I tell my students that I will not talk about it again in the classroom (though I welcome private chats with any student who has trouble

---

[1] Philip M. Ericson and John W. Gardner, "Two Longitudinal Studies of Communication Apprehension and Its Effects on College Students' Success," *Communication Quarterly*, Spring 1992, pp. 127-137; James C. McCroskey, Steven Booth-Butterfield, and Steven K., Payne, "The Impact of Communication Apprehension on College Student Retention and Success," *Communication Quarterly*, Spring, 1989, pp. 100-107; Lynne Kelly, "Implementing a Skills Training Program for Reticent Communicators," *Communication Education*, April 1989, pp. 85-101.

coping with this problem). I do this to underscore one of the points in Chapter 2: in a speech, it is best not to refer to your nervousness, either through jokes or apologies. Instead, concentrate on getting your ideas across to the audience, and your nervousness will recede to the background. What I am trying to say to students, in effect, is: Nervousness is a problem; let's understand it, learn to deal with it; but then let's put our attention where it belongs—on reaching the audience.

2.   Give students a comprehensive syllabus and schedule on the first day of class. Detail how many speeches they must give, what kind of speeches, and your rules for preliminary materials (such as outlines). Let them know by what criteria you will grade them. Seeing that you have carefully planned the course will reassure the students and take away some of their phantom fears of the "great unknown."

3.   Have low-key icebreaker exercises at the beginning of the course to let students get to know each other. One such exercise is the speech of self-introduction. If you plan to require group work, you may want to have it at the beginning of the course so that students can work with their peers and have the experience of presenting their ideas as part of a group—a less fearful event than giving a speech as an individual.

4.   Consider having a unit on oral interpretation of literature (see articles in the *Supplementary Readings* section of connectpublicspeaking.com) early in the course. Oral readings give students a chance to use their voices dramatically and expressively in a situation that is less fear-inducing than giving a speech.[2]

5.   Provide a hospitable classroom atmosphere. Show students that you are sympathetic with the difficulties of the inexperienced speaker. In the early assignments, go heavy on praise and light on criticism. You may want to give no grades for early assignments, or if you do give grades, to have them count less proportionately than later grades.

Speech Phobia

For most students, the thorough coverage given to stage fright in Chapter 2 should be adequate. But a few students will need more. These are the men and women who suffer from speech phobia, a crippling fear that is as powerful as the phobic fear of heights or snakes. Their phobia is stage fright magnified ten times. I cannot overstate the terror that these students experience; some of them sign up for public speaking because it's a required course and then drop out on the eve of their first speech; some of them take every other course required for graduation, then drop out of school rather than take public speaking. I know one such student who attended three different colleges, dropping out of all three on the threshold of graduation because of her phobia. "At one college," she said, "the course was called Oral Communication, but I dreaded it so much that I called it Oral Humiliation." Some of these phobics go through life avoiding any occasion to speak in public; they steer clear of any profession that requires speechmaking; they give up promotions if the new position would require giving a speech.

To help these students, here are some suggestions:

---

[2] Heidi M. Rose, Andrew S. Rancer, and Kenneth C. Crannell, "The Impact of Basic Courses in Oral Interpretation and Public Speaking on Communication Apprehension," *Communication Reports*, Winter 1993, pp. 54-60.

1. Identify them. On the first day of class, I recommend announcing that you will be discussing and/or assigning a chapter on stage fright, a fear that is experienced by most speakers, but that you will not go over (in class) the kind of fear that is so extreme that the person needs special, individual help. "If you fall into this category," I tell my students, "please do not drop this course. You can be helped. Please come by my office and talk to me personally." It is important to make a statement on the first day of class because some phobics, when they ascertain that yes, indeed, they will be required to give speeches, disappear. They never again come to class.

2. After a discussion or test on Chapter 2 (Controlling Nervousness), let students know about the "Speech Phobia" article on connectpublicspeaking.com.

3. When phobic students come to your office, make sure they have already read the "Speech Phobia" article. If they haven't, give them a printout and tell them to come back to see you again, regardless of whether the article helped them. If they have already read it, proceed to the next step.

4. Offer sympathy and support. Ask how you can help. For example, would it be helpful for you to arrange for the student to give a practice speech to a small group before the date of their real, graded speech? (See the "Speech Phobia" article for details.)

5. If, despite the handout and your support and advice, a student is too fearful to continue taking the class, try to put him or her in touch with someone on campus or in the community who has experience in dealing with phobias. Incidentally, some health-insurance programs pay for treatment. Social Phobia, of which the most common type is extreme stage fright, is recognized by the American Psychiatric Association as a treatable psychological problem. It is classified in *Diagnostic and Statistical Manual of Disorders* under Anxiety Disorders. Many psychiatrists and psychologists specialize in treating this problem, sometimes inside psychiatric hospitals but most often on an outpatient basis. They report a high success rate in helping patients overcome this phobia.[3]

6. If you can keep phobics in school and in public speaking class, you will have the satisfaction of helping human beings in distress and you will play a part in lowering your school's rate of attrition.

---

[3] William Anixter, M.D., Medical Director, Mountain Psychiatric Center, and Robert C. Carson, and others, *Abnormal Psychology and Modern Life*, eighth edition (Glenview, Illinois: Scott, Foresman & Co., 1988).

Special Problems

What can the instructor do when a student speaker panics and sits down abruptly without finishing the speech?

Dr. William Anixter, a psychiatrist who specializes in speech phobia, recommends letting the student stay seated so that he or she has a chance to "calm down and regroup." Meanwhile, Dr. Anixter says, the instructor can explain to the class what's happening: a surge of adrenaline has immobilized the student. "Point out that after four to five minutes, the adrenaline will subside [to a manageable level] if the speaker avoids thinking negative things."

After a period of calm, the instructor can try to gently coax the speaker into trying his or her speech again. In some cases, the instructor may want to postpone the speech until the next class period.

What can the instructor do when a student "freezes" at the lectern and can't start (or continue) a speech?

One technique that some instructors have used successfully is to "interview" the student—that is, ask questions about the subject matter of the speech to draw the student out. For example, if a student's speech concerned saving whales from destruction, the instructor could ask, "Is the whale population being depleted?" and "Who is responsible for the destruction of whales?" As the student answers these questions, he or she might get "unfrozen" and able to proceed with the speech.

A delightful example of this technique was related by Anna Cox Brinton in a biography of William Bacon Evans, a Quaker educator.

At a Quaker conference at Cape May, New Jersey, a delegate named Jimmy Stevens was chosen by his classmates to report on youth activities to an audience of hundreds of people. When he was introduced, he stood before the crowd, but was so frightened he could not utter a word. A long silence ensued. Jimmy tried to speak, but words failed to come forth. "The hush throughout the auditorium grew painful," said Brinton.

Then, in the front row, "so close that Jimmy could see the kindly eyes and cheerful expression," William Bacon Evans rose. "Very quietly, but in a voice clear enough to be heard in the farthest corner of the huge auditorium, he began to speak." Employing the old-fashioned Quaker usage of the second-person singular, he said, "What is thy name?" Brinton continues the story:

> All was still. Then, haltingly, the answer came: "James Stevens."
>
> When William Bacon Evans spoke again, he was speaking for all who were present. "Where does thee live?" There was an atmosphere of peace just in the way the words were spoken.
>
> "In Philadelphia," slowly came the feeble reply.
>
> "May I ask how old thee is?"
>
> Again there was a quiet waiting. "Fourteen," finally came the answer. This time the voice was stronger. It was not a disturbed silence now—just a patient waiting.

31

"What group has thee been attending here at the conference?"

Again there was a long silence. Then came the reply, this time with more assurance: "Junior High."

It was at this point that William Bacon Evans knew that Jimmy was ready. "And what did thee come to tell us?"

There followed a good report. In concluding what he had to say, Jimmy turned to William Bacon Evans. "Thank you," he said, simply.[4]

---

[4] Anna Cox Brinton, *The Wit and Wisdom of William Bacon Evans*, (Wallingford, Pennsylvania: Pendle Hill Publications, 1966), pp. 41-42.

Videotaping Speeches

Should you videotape your students' speeches? Here are arguments that I have heard instructors make on both sides of this issue:

Arguments FOR Videotaping

1. Many students love seeing themselves on video, and learn a great deal about how to improve their delivery.

2. Video allows students to see themselves as others see them. In other words, they gain a truly objective perspective.

3. Video permits endless replays for close examination of problems.

4. Students who think that their nervous symptoms are blatantly obvious to the audience are pleasantly surprised to see that their trembling hands and knocking knees are not visible to the camcorder (and thus not to the audience).

5. If instructors use video as aids in evaluating speeches, the tapes free them from scribbling comments during a speech; they can direct their full attention to the live presentation. Also, the video can be viewed several times so that instructors can make sure they are being fair in their grading.

6. Instructors and students can evaluate the video privately to discuss areas that need improvement.

Arguments AGAINST Videotaping

1. For the inexperienced speaker, videotaping adds extra stress on top of an already heavy burden of worry and fear.

2. It takes too much time to play back speeches. If one round of student speeches takes four hours of class time, then replaying all the speeches will obviously take the same amount of time.

3. Video causes the students to become self-conscious, rather than audience-conscious. In other words, it makes them shift their focus from their audience to themselves.

4. Some students become dispirited when they see themselves on video. "I didn't know I looked so fat," moaned one student. "Oh, I sound terrible," lamented another. Some students claim that video is a source of humiliation that adds to their lack of confidence.

Videotaping Options

Here are some options that various instructors have chosen:

Option #1: Do not videotape any speeches in the basic public speaking class. Instead, use videotape in later courses with advanced students who need to polish their delivery techniques.

Option #2: Make videotaping optional. The virtue of this system is that you offer students a choice. The major drawback is that some students do not become aware of the fun and value of videotaping unless they are obliged to participate; once they see themselves on videotape, they are often glad they had the opportunity.

Option #3: Use videotaping only in low-key, informal, ungraded exercises. Here are some sample exercises:

- To develop vocal variety, students can read or recite a dramatic poem, a passage from a play, or a segment of a famous speech. Or they can recite teacher-supplied sentences in a variety of ways, such as angry, sad, happy, fearful, and sarcastic. (These sentences could be pulled at random from the morning newspaper or the yellow pages of the telephone directory.)

- To develop eye contact and other nonverbal communication skills, students can stand up for one minute without notes and tell an interesting story or pretend that they are a politician appealing for votes or act as a TV person (weather reporter, actor in a commercial, news anchor).

One advantage of this option is that students get to appear on video in a low-pressure situation. The instructor can even encourage students to "ham-it-up" in order to loosen up and break through their shell of self-consciousness. Because these exercises are short, they often permit the instructor to play back the videotape in the same class period.

Option #4: Videotape each student's first speech and last speech. This gives the student a chance to see how far he or she progressed from the beginning of the course to the end.

Option #5: Videotape most or all of the student speeches. A separate videocassette could be used for each student, so that each succeeding speech is added to the same tape. Or a separate videocassette could be used for each class.

Equipment for Videotaping

If you will be doing more than occasional videotaping, I recommend that you ask your department to purchase a video system. Here is what I consider the ideal setup:

1. Wireless microphone

   Believe it or not, using a remote microphone is the most important element in producing a quality videotape of a speech. It enables the speaker's voice to come through loud and clear, rather than soft and distant. I recommend the Azden WMS-PRO Two-Mic System. (If your school's purchasing department cannot get an educational rate, you can purchase it for $143.95 from B & H Photo/Video in New York City, www.bhphotovideo.com). (Unlike many NYC video dealers who use the infamous bait-and-switch con game, B&H is honest and reliable.)

Here's how the system works: The student wears a tiny, clip-on lavaliere microphone (the kind often seen on TV), which is connected by cord to a small transmitter about the size of a cigarette pack. The transmitter can be clipped to a belt or slipped into a pocket. (I went to a fabric shop and bought a few long strips of heavy cloth of different colors, so that if a student has nothing to which to clip the transmitter, he or she can use one of the strips of cloth as a primitive, but effective belt.) The transmitter does not have to be visible; in other words, if students want to put it in a back pocket or clip it to their belt near the small of their back, it will still transmit without any problem.

The transmitter transmits radio signals to a receiver that you plug into your camcorder. The Azden model has two FM frequencies; it doesn't matter which you use—just make sure that the transmitter and receiver are tuned to the same frequency! The Azden system includes a small earphone, which is very important as a monitoring device, to make sure that the speaker has not accidentally turned off his or her transmitter. It is a good idea to listen on the earphone right before the speaker starts speaking. (You can ask him or her to say "Testing-one-two-three" or rub a finger across the microphone.)

The Azden model I recommend also has an optional handheld mike, which you can use for small-group work and TV-style interviews.

The system is powered by two 8-volt batteries. Long-lasting alkaline batteries can give you at least 7 hours of service. They probably can deliver even longer service, but I usually put in fresh batteries after 7 hours just to make sure I don't run out of power during a student's speech.

Incidentally, while students in my classes sometimes grumble about having to be videotaped, none of them have ever complained about getting themselves "wired" for a speech. I guess television has made the process seem like a natural part of life.

Tell students the clip-on microphone can be placed anywhere on their chest; then they can forget about it. They don't need to direct their voice towards it, because it is very powerful in picking up sounds (even if the "bulb" of the mike is pointing downward).

2. Camcorder

Your school's audiovisual department can advise you on the best models of camcorders. Any of the popular formats—VHS, digital, 8mm, Hi8, S-VHS-C, VHS-C, and S-VHS—will serve you well.

One important feature to consider is the zoom lens on the camcorder: Do you need a lens that will fill the frame with a speaker's head from far away? Do you need a lens that will take good close-up shots of small objects like jewelry? To choose a camcorder that has a zoom lens suitable for your needs, you should try out several models until you find one that is perfect for you.

3.   Video Tripod with Fluid Head

For videotaping speeches, you can achieve steadiness by using a sturdy tripod and a fluid head. (The head is the thingamajig that provides a mount for the camcorder and offers a handle for panning. A *fluid* head permits you to pan quickly and smoothly). I recommend the Bogen Tripod Model 3046 (cost: $129.95 at B&H; see phone number above) and the Bogen 3160 XL Fluid Head (cost: $59.00 at B&H).

Reassuring Students and Getting Permission

A side benefit of videotaping speeches is that the instructor can use videos in later classes to illustrate teaching points. However, I recognize that some students do not like being videotaped and they hate the idea of anyone else viewing the video. Therefore, early in the course, when I show for the first time a video of a student speech for instructional purposes, I tell the class that I will videotape their speeches but I give this reassurance: "I will never use a video of you without getting your written permission."

At the end of the course, I have a form that I distribute to all students. On it, I ask,

Regarding your first informative speech, may I have your permission to show a videotape of it to other classes? Yes No

. . . and so on. I get permission for each separate speech because sometimes students will grant permission for one speech but not for another. At the bottom of the sheet is space for the student's signature. This form is obviously a legal safeguard, but it is primarily designed to respect students' wishes.

Tips for Videotaping

1.   Have an audiovisual technician or a skilled student volunteer handle all aspects of the videotaping, so that you are free to concentrate on listening to and evaluating student speeches.

2.   I recommend that the camcorder be positioned on a tripod and left in one place (because if the camcorder operator moves about the room for various shots, this distracts both the speaker and the listeners). If your operator is skilled at filming, he or she should be encouraged to zoom in for a close-up of the face occasionally. If you are forced to operate the equipment by yourself, position the camcorder and tripod in the back of the room or off to one side, set the lens on a wide panoramic view of the lectern and surrounding area, and then set the tape to run continuously, without operator interference.

3.   Unfortunately, videotape makes most people look 10-15 pounds heavier than they really are. (Now you know why you hated those family reunion videos!) This effect can be minimized, however, if you position the camcorder slightly higher than your subjects' faces. In other words, shoot down rather than up or straight on.

4.   Advise student speakers to ignore the camcorder. In other words, their true audience is the people in front of them, not the camcorder.

36

5.   Make sure the audiovisual technician understands his or her role—to be unobtrusive, non-directive, and undistracting.

6.   If you are doing the videotaping yourself, here are some recommendations:

   •   Keep the video rolling throughout the class; I know that this wastes tape, but it prevents you from worrying about starting and stopping and it prevents you from occasionally having the recording button off when you think it's on.

   •   When you zoom in and out, do so gently, slowly.

   •   If you're using a remote microphone, keep the audio on for the entire class (for the same reason cited for the camcorder).

   •   Use an earphone or "earbud" to verify that the audio system is connected and working.

7.   If speakers will be using a clip-on microphone, tell students in advance that they should avoid wearing anything that is crinkly, such as a nylon jogging suit. Such attire makes a rustling sound that is picked up by the microphone as a distracting noise. Also suggest that students wear a belt or a sweater or shirt with pockets—so that the transmitter can be easily clipped on or slipped into a pocket.

8.   You may want to consider having your students buy their own videocassettes. Then, when you videotape, you can put each student's speeches on his or her own videocassette (rather than mixing them together with speeches of classmates), thus giving the student a permanent record of the speeches and a means for self-improvement. This is an especially good approach if you are making videotaping optional: students can bring their own tapes to class whenever they want their speeches to be videotaped. An alternative would be to have a separate cassette for each student; then, at the end of the course, sell cassettes to those students who want them. In the case of cassettes that go unsold, they can be recycled the next time you teach the course. One disadvantage of this system is the inconvenience of loading a different cassette into the recorder before each speech.

9.   If you are able to sit with each student privately and play back his or her speech, this would be an ideal way to point out strengths and weaknesses. If time does not permit such an arrangement, you may want to let the student check out the cassette and take it to a viewing place, such as an audiovisual room on campus, for a private viewing. Since many students do not know how to evaluate themselves effectively, you may want to encourage or assign students to view the tape with trained evaluators (such as graduate assistants) or with fellow students who can point out strengths as well as weaknesses.

Grading

Here are some issues involving how to grade students in a public speaking class:

How should students be graded?

Grading is a tough issue. On the one hand, we instructors feel the need to give low grades to students who deliver poor speeches; on the other hand, we want to provide a supportive, positive atmosphere in which all of our students experience as much success as possible in order to gain confidence for their careers.

A public speaking class is unlike most other classes in that a student's self-esteem is heavily involved. In a speech, his or her ego is exposed and vulnerable: a low grade can be a deflating experience. A "D" on a math exam might be inconsequential; a "D" on a speech can be devastating. Even though we are, of course, evaluating the speech and not the speaker's character and worth as a human being, the student nevertheless may believe, "I have been evaluated and I have been found to be deficient."

How, then, to grade? Each instructor must decide this issue based on his or her own perspective and philosophy. For whatever value they may hold, here are some questions to consider as you work out your own policy:

1. **What aspects of the course do you wish to give the most weight?** Do you want the content of speeches to count more than delivery—or about the same? Do you want some aspects of delivery to count more than other aspects? Do you want all speeches to carry equal weight? Or do you want to give greater weight to the major speeches in the latter part of the course?

2. **Do you plan to grade preliminary work such as outlines?** Some instructors give separate grades for outlines; some give points for outlines in the final grade for a particular speech; some don't grade outlines but deduct points from the speech grade if an outline is late; still others don't grade outlines at all.

A good case can be made on both sides of the issue of whether to grade outlines. The instructors who give points for outlines say that students need the threat of grades hanging over them in order to do their best work. Furthermore, they say that including outlines in the grading scheme is fair to those students who may spend hours developing a superb outline, but give a ragged, nervous delivery that undermines the worth of their material. A high grade on the outline will compensate for a low grade on the speech itself. Besides, these instructors say, if students can learn to construct good outlines, they have learned the most important skills in a public speaking class—their delivery will improve with experience.

On the other hand, the instructors who don't grade outlines say that an outline is a means to an end, not an end in itself, and therefore students should be graded only on their finished product—the speech itself. In community speeches, they point out, a person is judged entirely on his or her speech—the audience never sees the outline.

3. **Should students have input on grades?** In addition to evaluating their peers, some students are allowed to grade each other—or at least contribute a fraction of a grade.

Instructors who use this system say that its advantage is that students feel that they are getting a broader (and perhaps fairer) system of grading than can be provided by the instructor alone. On the other hand, instructors who do not use this method say that its disadvantage is that many students are relatively inexperienced in evaluating, and may give undeserved grades (either high or low).

4. **Should you grade a speech immediately after it is delivered?** Some instructors fill in an evaluation/grading sheet during and immediately following a student's speech, and then hand it to the student a few minutes later or at the end of the period. This method has the obvious advantage of giving the student immediate feedback—a valuable principle of effective learning. A potential disadvantage is that the instructor may find it hard to assess many variables and write cogent, helpful comments while under the pressure of time.

   Other instructors grade the student's speech hours later and return the evaluation/grading sheet at the next class period. This method has the advantage of letting the instructor give extra thought to the evaluation, and if an audiotape or videotape has been made of the speech, the instructor has a chance to reassess certain parts of the speech. The disadvantage is that time has elapsed, and other speeches have occurred in the meantime, and the instructor may have forgotten certain features.

   Some instructors combine these two methods—that is, they evaluate students on the spot, using a pencil to record impressions, but instead of returning the evaluations soon afterward, they keep them and review them later to see if their original assessments still seem fair and accurate. If they need to make changes, they can erase their first comments and write in new ones.

Suggestions

1. Whatever grading system you use, announce it at the beginning of the course. This will give students a clear picture of what is most important in the course. And it will give them a sense of security to know that you have worked out in advance all the details of grading and evaluation.

2. See the section "Speech Evaluations" in Chapter 3 of the text for suggestions on evaluation.

Should students be graded on knowledge of the textbook?

Some instructors give no tests at all, relying on speeches alone to determine the student's grade. A good case can be made for this approach: if a student delivers an excellent speech, it doesn't really matter how well (or whether) he or she read the textbook. However, there are two good reasons why students should be held accountable for reading the textbook: (1) there are ideas and tips in the textbook that are important to the student (especially for his or her future career) but which may not necessarily involve the immediate classroom speeches, and (2) a student should do much better on speeches if he or she is required to read the text; in other words, while a student may be able to barely reach a passing grade on his or her speeches without reading the textbook, he or she may be able to give good speeches if forced to read the text.

Though many instructors believe that a student should be tested and graded on the text, they feel that these grades should represent a small fraction of the total grade. For them, the actual speeches are more important than textbook knowledge. The instructor might want to work out a proportion such as this:

Classroom speeches	6/8
Average of quizzes	1/8
Final exam	1/8

Should students be tested on each textbook chapter assigned?

Many students read textbook chapters only if they know they will be tested on them. So you may want to test on all chapters that are assigned. You can use the ready-to-reproduce tests provided in the back of this manual or you can give several multi-chapter tests, clipping together the tests as they are already printed, or preparing a fresh test by choosing a few questions from each chapter test.

The chapter tests in this manual are designed to cover all the important points of each chapter, so they make a good device for reviewing. In other words, after the tests are graded, you can go over them with the entire class as a way of reiterating key points.

Sample Course Outlines

How an instructor structures this course depends, of course, on such variables as number of students, time limits of speeches, and number of speeches required. The samples below show possible arrangements for a one-semester course and for a one-quarter course.

Outline for a 15-Week Semester

Class	Activity
1	Introduction to the Course
2	Principles of Speech Communication (Chapter 1)
3	Controlling Nervousness (Chapter 2)
4	Listening (Chapter 3)
5	Speech I (Icebreaker Speech)
6	Speech I (Icebreaker Speech)
7	Reaching the Audience (Chapter 4)
8	Selecting Topic (first half of Chapter 5)
9	General Purpose, Specific Purpose and Central Idea (second half of Chapter 5)
10	Finding Information (Chapter 6)
11	Evaluating Information & Avoiding Plagiarism (Chapter 7)
12	Support Material (Chapter 8)
13	Presentation Aids (Chapter 9)
14	The Body of the Speech (Chapter 10)
15	Introductions and Conclusions (Chapter 11)
16	Outlining (Chapter 12)
17	Informative speaking (Chapter 15)
18	Outlines due for Speech II
19	Delivery (Chapter 14)
20	Speech II

21	Speech II
22	Speech II
23	Speech II
24	Language and Style (Chapter 13)
25	Outlines due for Speech III
26	Persuasive Speeches (Chapter 16)
27	Persuasive Strategies (Chapter 17)
28	Speech III
29	Speech III
30	Speech III
31	Speech III
32	Outlines due for Speech IV
33	Special Types of Speeches (Chapter 18)
34	Speech IV
35	Speech IV
36	Speech IV
37	Speech IV
38	Speaking in Groups (Chapter 19)
39	Outlines due for Speech V
40	Discussion of Job Interviews (see articles in *Supplementary Readings* on connectpublicspeaking.com)
41	Speech V (or group presentation)
42	Speech V (or group presentation)
43	Speech V (or group presentation)
44	Speech V (or group presentation)
45	Final Exam

Outline for a 10-Week Quarter

Class	Activity
1	Introduction to the Course
2	Principles of Speech Communication (Chapter 1)
3	Controlling Nervousness (Chapter 2)
4	Listening (Chapter 3)
5	Speech I (Icebreaker Speech)
6	Speech I (Icebreaker Speech)
7	Reaching the Audience (Chapter 4)
8	Selecting Topic (first half of Chapter 5)
9	General Purpose, Specific Purpose and Central Idea (second half of Chapter 5)
10	Finding Information (Chapter 6)
11	Evaluating Information & Avoiding Plagiarism (Chapter 7)
12	Support Material (Chapter 8)
13	Presentation Aids (Chapter 9)
14	The Body of the Speech (Chapter 10)
15	Introductions and Conclusions (Chapter 11); Outlining (Chapter 12)
16	Informative speaking (Chapter 15)
17	Outlines due for Speech II
18	Delivery (Chapter 14)
19	Speech II
20	Speech II
21	Speech II
22	Speech II
23	Persuasive Speeches (Chapter 16); Persuasive Strategies (Chapter 17)
24	Outlines due for Speech III
25	Language and Style (Chapter 13)
26	Speech III
27	Speech III
28	Speech III
29	Speech III
30	Final Exam

Sample Syllabus

Public speaking courses can be taught in many different ways. Here is a sample of one instructor's syllabus.

PUBLIC SPEAKING

(instructor's name)   (phone number)

COURSE OBJECTIVES: This course is designed to introduce you to the basic principles of effective public speaking. Emphasis is placed on preparation for speeches (audience analysis, research, outlining, etc.). You will be required to give five speeches.

TEXT: *Public Speaking For College and Career*, 9th edition, by Hamilton Gregory (McGraw-Hill)
connectpublicspeaking.com

ATTENDANCE: Regular attendance is expected. See Ground Rules below.

DROP RULES: If you miss more than 7 hours of class, you will be dropped from the course.

EXAM EXEMPTIONS: You will not be required to take the final exam if you have an A average and not more than 3 hours of absences OR if you have a B average and no absences.

OFFICE HOURS: My office is Room 207 in this building. Office hours are M-W-F, 10-11; Tues.-Thurs., 9-10. If these hours aren't convenient, I can make arrangements to see you another time. Call the above number to make an appointment.

TESTS: Tests will cover information from class lectures, videos, and the textbook (including Tips for Your Career and other highlighted features). If you are absent, you should get notes from a fellow student who was present during the class you missed.

GRADING POLICY:

Speech I	1/6
Speech II	1/6
Speech III	1/6
Speech IV	1/6
Speech V	1/6
Average of quizzes	1/12
Final exam	1/12

SPEECH ASSIGNMENTS:

1. **Introductory speech** (2-4 minutes). This speech will not be graded. If you speak over 6 minutes, time will be called.

2. **Speech I—Informative speech** (about 6 minutes). An outline must be submitted in advance. See Speech Evaluation Sheet for an explanation of the possible penalties. The minimum time is 4 minutes; the maximum time is 8 minutes.

3. **Speech II—Informative speech using visual aids** (about 6 minutes). An outline must be submitted in advance. See Speech Evaluation Sheet for an explanation of the possible penalties. Minimum time: 4 minutes; maximum time: 8 minutes.

4. **Speech III—Persuasive speech using visual aids** (about 6 minutes). An outline must be submitted in advance. See Speech Evaluation Sheet for an explanation of the possible penalties. The minimum time is 4 minutes; the maximum time is 8 minutes.

5. **Speech IV—Entertaining speech** (about 5 minutes). An outline must be submitted in advance. See Speech Evaluation Sheet for an explanation of the possible penalties. The minimum time is 3 minutes; the maximum time is 7 minutes.

6. **Speech V—Speech of your choice** (about 6 minutes). An outline must be submitted in advance. See Speech Evaluation Sheet for an explanation of the possible penalties. Minimum time: 4 minutes; maximum time: 8 minutes

GROUND RULES:

1. **Class attendance on speech days is mandatory, even if you are not scheduled to speak.** Part of the course is learning to listen intelligently and to evaluate speeches. When you skip your fellow students' speeches, you are being rude to them, saying, in effect, "Your speech is not worth my time."

2. Your outline should be legible—either typed or written neatly.

3. You may **not** read any part of your speech (except for a brief quotation). You should rely only on brief notes contained on either a single piece of paper or on index cards. (You will not be required to turn in your notes.)

4. You must provide a question-and-answer period at the end of your speech. (If no one asks a question, don't feel bad; it doesn't necessarily mean that you gave a poor speech. Perhaps you covered all the points, and there's nothing left to ask about.)

5. If you are not prepared to speak on the day scheduled, stand ready to speak at the next class period. You will not, however, go first. The people scheduled for that day will go first; then, if there is time, you will speak.

6. You **must** give all assigned speeches in order to get a passing grade for this course. Thus if you are absent at the end of this term and do not give your final speech, you will be required to give it to another public speaking class next term.

Problems & Possible Solutions

Perennial problems crop up in most public speaking classes, including my own. Most of the possible solutions below have been suggested by users of *Public Speaking for College and Career*, and I gratefully pass along these ideas to other instructors:

Problem: How can the instructor assign the speech-preparation chapters in the textbook before students give their first speeches and still have time to include all required speeches? (This time-bind is especially difficult for instructors who teach under the quarter system.)

Possible Solutions: Suggestion 1: If your class meets for only one hour, you can try this: Assign ungraded self-introduction speeches early in the course, but instead of having all of them delivered in one or two class periods, spread them out over many days. This will leave you enough time to have chapter quizzes every day. For example, on Monday have a few self-introduction speeches during the first part of class and give a quiz on Chapter 5 toward the end of class; on Wednesday return the Chapter 5 quizzes, answer any questions about them, have a few self-introduction speeches, and give a quiz on Chapter 6 . . . and so on.

Suggestion 2: Cover only "indispensable" chapters early in the course. One instructor handles the time problem by assigning crucial chapters early in the course, and then covering other chapters after the first speeches begin. The contents of some chapters are covered in class; students who are absent for a discussion must read the relevant chapter and take a test on it. This insures that all students are exposed to the important points of the course.

Here is the sequence of her assignments:

- To give students an overview of speech preparation and delivery, go over "Quick Guide to Public Speaking" (in Chapter 1) or "Checklist for Preparing and Delivering a Speech" (which appears on SpeechMate CD).

- In class, discuss the benefits of a public speaking course (absentees must read Ch. 1, "Introduction to Public Speaking," and take a test on it).

- Ch. 2, "Controlling Nervousness"—Out-of-class reading; give test

- Ch. 5, "Selecting Topic, Purpose, & Central Idea"—Out-of-class reading; give test

- In class, discuss types of informative speeches (absentees must read Ch. 15, "Speaking to Inform" and take a test on it).

- Ch. 6, "Finding Information"—Out-of-class reading; give test

- Ch. 8, "Supporting Your Ideas"—Out-of-class reading; give test

- Ch. 9, In class, discuss visual aids (absentees must read Ch. 9, "Presentation Aids" and take a test on it).

- Ch. 10, "The Body of the Speech"—Out-of-class reading; give test

- Ch. 11, "Introductions and Conclusions"—Out-of-class reading; give test

- Ch. 12, "Outlining the Speech"—Out-of-class reading; give test
- Ch. 14, "Delivering the Speech"—Out-of-class reading; give test

Later in the course, after the speeches are in progress, she assigns the other chapters that she wants to cover.

Problem: Some students are weak in outlining and organizational skills, primarily because they fail to study sample outlines, such as those provided at the end of chapters 12, 15, and 16 in the text. How can we force such students to scrutinize model outlines?

Possible Solution: Try these activities:
- Draw students' attention to Fig. 5.3 on p. 95 in the text, Figures 12.1 and 12.3 in Chapter 12 of the text, and Outline Tutor (available from connectpublicspeaking.com).

- In class go over the "Building an Outline" transparency program (available in this manual or as a PowerPoint slide program). The program shows the step-by-step construction of an informative speech outline and a persuasive speech outline.

- Evaluation Sheet E-21, "Evaluation of Sample Outline" (in the Evaluation Forms section of this manual), can be used to force students to go over a sample outline. The worksheet can be done in class and then discussed; the instructor may want to call on individuals at random for their answers to particular questions.

- If students need more models than those provided in the text, use sample speeches and outlines available at connectpublicspeaking.com.

Problem: As their first major speech approaches, some students feel overwhelmed and can't seem to pull themselves together. They cut class and eventually drop the course.

Possible Solution: Early in the course, discuss the article, "How to Prepare a Speech Without Feeling Overwhelmed" (in the *Supplementary Readings* on connectpublicspeaking.com). Some students, who have never systematically broken a large academic task into small pieces, are glad to have the "tools" provided by the "Checklist for Preparing and Delivering a Speech" on connectpublicspeaking.com. Also point out the section in Chapter 10 of the text called "Simplifying the Process"; these flexible strategies help students see that creating a speech should be a methodical, bit-by-bit process rather than a sit-down-and-do-it-all-at-once torment.

Problem: In the early stages of the course, some students have trouble grasping the relationship between the outline, the speaking notes, and the speech as delivered. They mistakenly think that the outline is a script that should be

47

read at the lectern.

Possible Solution: Fig 12.1 in the text (p. 237), was designed to overcome this problem. Several times early in the course you may want to draw students' attention to this graphic and discuss it, so that they can get a clear picture of the sequence.

Problem: Some students fail to include all parts of the outline. This hurts the quality of their speech.

Possible Solution: Use special forms to encourage (even coerce) students to include all parts:

- Connectpublicspeaking.com has an Outline Tutor.

- "Outline Template" in *Supplementary Readings* (on connectpublicspeaking.com) can be used for preliminary outlines.

- Sheet E-1, Checklist for Revising an Outline (in the Evaluation Forms section of this manual) can be used to make a critique of an outline.

- Sheet E-2, Checklist for Revising an Outline (in the Evaluation Forms section of this manual) is just like E-1 except that it adds a system for grading the outline.

Problem: Some students do poorly on chapter tests even though they claim to have studied diligently.

Possible Solution: Some instructors have found that the cause of this problem is giving tests on several chapters at once, so they recommend testing on only one chapter per class period. Students seem to do a better job of retaining information from the textbook when they are assigned only one chapter at a time than when they are assigned two or three at a time. (This strategy may not always be possible for instructors who have the time problem discussed above.)

Problem: Students create visual aids that are unattractive or not highly visible to all members of the audience.

Possible Solution: Discuss in class these sections in Chapter 9: pages 180-192 and pages 189-195.

Problem: Some students point out that half of their instructor's evaluation form covers delivery, and yet the text devotes only one chapter to delivery.

Possible Solution: When I am asked about this, I respond by saying, "Yes, the coverage in the text is lopsided, but here's why: preparation is more difficult (for most people) than delivery, and most students need much more guidance in preparation (choosing a topic, devising a central idea, developing an outline) than in delivery. Besides, delivery skills improve as a person actually delivers speeches and receives feedback—precisely what occurs in this course."

Problem:	For student evaluations of their classmates' speeches, a short form is needed for quick feedback.
Possible Solution:	Try Evaluation Form E-3 in this manual. It doesn't cover every aspect of speechmaking, but anything not listed can be mentioned at the bottom of the page under either "What were the speaker's major strengths?" or "In what areas does he or she need improvement?" In my classes, I stress that students must fill in at least a few words under both questions.
Problem:	Some students don't study "Tips for Your Career" and other highlighted material in the text because they think these items are marginal or optional.
Possible Solution:	Mention in the syllabus and in your first-day orientation that these items are highlighted because they cover important issues, and will appear in chapter tests.
Problem:	Some students fail portions of the course because they don't know key rules.
Possible Solution:	Early in the course, I give my students a true-false quiz on the syllabus and rules for speeches, and then I go over the answers. This test may seem silly, but it works! A student cannot say—later in the course—"But I didn't know visual aids were required."

The Quest for Jobs

The *Supplementary Readings* on connectpublicspeaking.com include these articles on job searches:

- Job Interviews

- Frequently Asked Questions

- Letter of Application

- Résumé

In my classes, I try to squeeze in one hour for a discussion of job interviews, and then I suggest the handouts for outside reading. (I don't have to use quizzes as a weapon to coerce reading—in this one area, students are highly motivated to read on their own!)

Because most students are exposed to this subject in other classes, I am sometimes tempted to skip it, but on end-of-the-course evaluations, many students rate the job interviews discussion as one of the most valuable parts of the course.

Sometimes I think that these handouts merely state obvious information that everyone knows, but then I talk to human-resources managers who tell me that most job applicants continue to make the same old self-defeating blunders: showing up in jeans for an interview at a corporation, volunteering the fact that they were fired from their last job, whining about the injustices of their most recent boss, giving tedious 15-minute answers to simple questions, and so on.

Evaluation Forms

Here are some evaluation forms that you can use as they are, or of course you can modify them to suit your needs. The sheet number for each form is in the upper left corner.

E-1—Checklist for Revising an Outline

This form can be used to give a systematic evaluation of preliminary outlines. Note that space is provided for comments on items not covered in the checklist. (In Chapter 12 of this manual, see Sheets 12.1 and 12.2 for outline formats and see Sheet 12.7 for a grade form for outlines.)

E-2—Checklist for Revising an Outline

Identical in content to E-1, this form adds a grading scale in the left-hand margin. For each item on the outline, the student can be given a certain number of points out of 5, 10, or 25. If he or she omits an item from the outline, a score of zero can be given. At the end of the form is a box in which the instructor can place the total number of points. The form also has a check-off place at the top of page 1 for those instructors who want to indicate whether the outline was turned in on time or late.

E-3—Speech Evaluation

This form is designed for students to use in evaluating each other's speeches. It was created at the suggestion of several instructors who wanted a short form that students could fill in quickly.

E-4—Evaluation

This sheet can be used by the instructor to evaluate student speeches. A key—sheet E-7—can be stapled to this form or it can be reproduced on the back side. Both the form and the key can be distributed to the students at the beginning of the course so they will know precisely by what standards they will be judged.

E-5—Evaluation

This sheet is identical to E-4, except that space for time penalties is included. A key—sheet E-7—can be stapled to this form or it can be reproduced on the back side. Both the form and the key can be distributed to the students at the beginning of the course so they will know precisely by what standards they will be judged.

E-6—Evaluation

This sheet is identical to E-4, except that 8 penalties are included. A key—sheet E-7—can be stapled to this form or it can be reproduced on the back side. Both the form and the key can be distributed to the students at the beginning of the course so they will know precisely by what standards they will be judged. [Note: The reason for the harsh penalty for not showing up at all on speech date (10 points versus only 5 for showing up unprepared) is to discourage a student from saying, "Well, I'm not prepared to give my speech today, so I'll just cut class." He or she needs to come to class, of course, to be part of the audience.]

E-7—Key to Evaluation Form

This key explains the terminology used in forms E-4, E-5, and E-6. If students receive this key early in the course, they will have a handy guide on exactly what standards will be used by the instructor in his or her evaluation. The key can be stapled to one of the above forms or reproduced on the back side. (The instructor can circle or underline guidelines that the student needs to heed.)

E-8—Evaluation

This form is similar to E-6 except that it includes separate slots for Visual Aids under Content and for Using Visual Aids under Delivery.

E-9—Key to Evaluation Form

This key, which can accompany form E-8, is similar to E-7 except that it reflects the emphasis given to visual aids on form E-8.

E-10—Evaluation

This form is similar to E-8 except that it puts greater emphasis on credibility and on expressiveness.

E-11—Key to Evaluation Form

This key accompanies form E-10.

E-12—Speech Evaluation

This is a form that students can use to evaluate each other's speeches. It is a standard form that can be used with most types of speeches.

E-13—Speech Evaluation—Central Idea

This form is a variation of sheet E-12. It asks the evaluator to state the central idea of the speech—a good way to see if the speaker has presented the speech well and/or if the evaluator has listened well.

E-14—Evaluation—Speech with Visual Aids

This is another variation on form E-12. This time the emphasis is on how well the student used visual aids.

E-15—Evaluation—Informative Speech

This version of the peer evaluation form has questions at the bottom to give feedback on how informative the speech was for the listener.

E-16—Evaluation—Persuasive Speech

This form is similar to form E-15 except that it gauges how persuasive the student's speech was for the listener.

E-17—Speech Evaluation

This two-page form is quite different from all the preceding ones in that it does not require a response for each line. Its virtue is that it forces students to pay attention to the checklist instead of just idly putting all 5's on the sheet. Its drawback is that it takes longer to complete than the above evaluations.

E-18—Evaluation of a Speech

This two-page evaluation form is similar to the others, except that it uses a "yes" or "no" evaluation scheme.

E-19—Central Idea

With this handout, students can be required to fill in the central idea for each speech they hear in the classroom. This can be graded, or the students can be asked to keep it for later quizzes. They can be told, "You will be quizzed on the central ideas of the speeches delivered in class. This form can be used to record the central ideas as you listen to your fellow students' speeches." If you quiz on the central idea, you may not want to expect the students to match names with ideas (for example, "What was John Doe's central idea?"). Instead, you can give true-false questions (T F John Doe argued that the Olympics should not permit professional athletes to compete) or multiple-choice questions (John Doe argued that (a) ___, (b) ___, (c) ___, or (d) ____.)

E-20—Oral Reading

This form can be used to evaluate oral readings. (See also the Supplementary Reading, "Oral Interpretation of Literature.")

E-21—Evaluation of Sample Outline

To force students to study sample outlines (as found in the text and on connectpublicspeaking.com, you can pass out this sheet and assign a sample outline. You might want to do this in class and take up the papers to make sure that all items are filled in.

Name_____

Checklist For Revising An Outline

Please note the items checked and revise your outline accordingly.

Outline format
_____You need to use the correct outline format.
_____You need to use complete sentences.
_____Other: _____

Audience Analysis & Adaptation
_____You need to show sensitivity to audience demographics (age, sex, educational level, racial and ethnic background, religion, and economic and social status).
_____You need to make your subject matter interesting to the audience.
_____You need to consider the knowledge level of the audience.
_____You need to consider the attitudes of the audience.
_____Other: _____

Title
_____Add a title.
_____Make your title more interesting.
_____Other: _____

General Purpose
_____Add a general purpose.
_____General purpose is inappropriate for this speech.
_____Other: _____

Specific Purpose
_____Add a specific purpose.
_____Specific purpose should begin with an infinitive.
_____Specific purpose should include a reference to your audience.
_____Specific purpose needs to be limited to one major idea.
_____Specific purpose needs to be more precise.
_____Specific purpose is too broad.
_____Specific purpose is too technical.
_____Specific purpose is inappropriate for this audience.
_____Other: _____

Central Idea
_____Add a central idea.
_____Central idea is unclear.
_____Central idea is too broad.
_____Other: _____

Introduction
_____Add attention material.
_____Add orienting material.
_____Attention material is unlikely to grab listeners' attention and interest.
_____Orienting material needs to preview the body of the speech.
_____You need to give adequate background information.
_____You need to establish your credibility.
_____Other: _____

Transition between Introduction and Body
_____Add a transition.
_____Your transition needs to be more graceful.
_____Other: _____

Body
_____The body of the speech is poorly organized.
_____You have too many main points.
_____The following main points are unclear: _____
_____The following main points need to support the central idea: _____
_____Main points _describe_ your plan, rather than _assert_ an idea.
_____You risk overwhelming your listeners with too much information.
_____Provide stronger support for the following point(s): _____
_____Use visual aids for the following point(s): _____
_____The following words are inappropriate, unclear or inaccurate:
_____Other: _____
_____Other: _____

Transitions between Main Points
_____Add transitions between the following main points: _____
_____Transitions need to be more graceful.
_____Other: _____

Transition between Body and Conclusion
_____Add a transition.
_____Transition needs to be more graceful.
_____Other: _____

Conclusion
_____Add a conclusion.
_____You need to summarize your key points.
_____You need to reinforce the central idea with a clincher.
_____Do not put a new main point in the conclusion.
_____Add an appeal for action.
_____Other: _____

Bibliography
_____Add a bibliography.
_____Bibliographical entries are written incorrectly.
_____Other: _____

Visual Aids
_____Add a list of visual aids.
_____Other: _____

Other Comments:

Checklist For Revising An Outline

Please note the items checked and revise your outline accordingly.

/5   **Outline Format**
_____You need to use the correct outline format.
_____You need to use complete sentences.
_____Other: _____

/5   **Audience Analysis & Adaptation**
_____You need to show sensitivity to audience demographics (age, sex, educational level,
     racial and ethnic background, religion, and economic and social status).
_____You need to make your subject matter interesting to the audience.
_____You need to consider the knowledge level of the audience.
_____You need to consider the attitudes of the audience.
_____Other: _____

/5   **Title**
_____Add a title.
_____Make your title more interesting.
_____Other: _____

/5   **General Purpose**
_____Add a general purpose.
_____General purpose is inappropriate for this speech.
_____Other: _____

/5   **Specific Purpose**
_____Add a specific purpose.
_____Specific purpose should begin with an infinitive.
_____Specific purpose should include a reference to your audience.
_____Specific purpose needs to be limited to one major idea.
_____Specific purpose needs to be more precise.
_____Specific purpose is too broad.
_____Specific purpose is too technical.
_____Specific purpose is inappropriate for this audience.
_____Other: _____

/5   **Central Idea**
_____Add a central idea.
_____Central idea is unclear.
_____Central idea is too broad.
_____Other: _____

/10 **Introduction**
_____Add attention material.
_____Add orienting material.
_____Attention material is unlikely to grab listeners' attention and interest.
_____Orienting material needs to preview the body of the speech.
_____You need to give adequate background information.
_____You need to establish your credibility.
_____Other: _____

/5   **Transition between Introduction and Body**
_____Add a transition.
_____Your transition needs to be more graceful.
_____Other: _____

/25   **Body**
_____The body of the speech is poorly organized.
_____You have too many main points.
_____The following main points are unclear:
_____The following main points fail to support the central idea:
_____Main points _describe_ your plan, rather than _assert_ an idea.
_____You risk overwhelming your listeners with too much information.
_____Provide stronger support for the following point(s):
_____Use visual aids for the following point(s):
_____The following words are inappropriate, unclear or inaccurate:
_____Other: _____
_____Other: _____

/5   **Transitions between Main Points**
_____Add transitions between the following main points:
_____Transitions need to be more graceful.
_____Other: _____

/5   **Transition between Body and Conclusion**
_____Add a transition.
_____Transition needs to be more graceful.
_____Other: _____

/10   **Conclusion**
_____Add a conclusion.
_____You need to summarize your key points.
_____You need to reinforce the central idea with a clincher.
_____Do not put a new main point in the conclusion.
_____Add an appeal for action.
_____Other: _____

/5   **Bibliography**
_____Add a bibliography.
_____Bibliographical entries are written incorrectly.
_____Other: _____

/5   **Visual Aids**
_____Add a list of visual aids.
_____Other: _____

Other Comments:

/100

Speech Evaluation

Speaker's name _____

CONTENT	Poor	Fair	Average	Good	Excellent
• topic interesting?	1	2	3	4	5
• central idea made clear?	1	2	3	4	5
• introduction interesting?	1	2	3	4	5
• body of speech well-organized?	1	2	3	4	5
• support materials adequate?	1	2	3	4	5
• visual aids effective?	1	2	3	4	5
• transitions smooth?	1	2	3	4	5
• conclusion effective?	1	2	3	4	5

DELIVERY	Poor	Fair	Average	Good	Excellent
• good eye contact?	1	2	3	4	5
• speaking rate okay?	1	2	3	4	5
• voice clear and loud enough?	1	2	3	4	5
• sounded conversational?	1	2	3	4	5
• avoided *uh, um, okay*?	1	2	3	4	5
• gestures adequate?	1	2	3	4	5
• posture good?	1	2	3	4	5
• used notes well?	1	2	3	4	5
• showed enthusiasm?	1	2	3	4	5

What were the speaker's major strengths?

In what areas does he or she need improvement?

Other comments:

Evaluation

Speaker's name _____

CONTENT	Absent	Poor	Fair	Average	Good	Excellent
A. Topic	0	1	2	3	4	5
B. Central Idea	0	1	2	3	4	5
C. Interest Level	0	1	2	3	4	5
D. Adaptation to Audience	0	1	2	3	4	5
E. Introduction	0	1	2	3	4	5
F. Body	0	1	2	3	4	5
G. Support Material	0	1	2	3	4	5
H. Transitions	0	1	2	3	4	5
I. Conclusion	0	1	2	3	4	5
J. Language	0	1	2	3	4	5

DELIVERY

	Absent	Poor	Fair	Average	Good	Excellent
A. Approach & Beginning	0	1	2	3	4	5
B. Eye Contact	0	1	2	3	4	5
C. Speaking Rate	0	1	2	3	4	5
D. Expressiveness	0	1	2	3	4	5
E. Clarity & Volume	0	1	2	3	4	5
F. Gestures & Movement	0	1	2	3	4	5
G. Posture & Poise	0	1	2	3	4	5
H. Use of Notes (& Visuals)	0	1	2	3	4	5
I. Enthusiasm	0	1	2	3	4	5
J. Ending & Departure	0	1	2	3	4	5
Sub-totals:	___	___	___	___	___	___

Time: _____

GRADE: ___

COMMENTS:

Evaluation

Speaker's name _____

CONTENT	Absent	Poor	Fair	Average	Good	Excellent
A. Topic	0	1	2	3	4	5
B. Central Idea	0	1	2	3	4	5
C. Interest Level	0	1	2	3	4	5
D. Adaptation to Audience	0	1	2	3	4	5
E. Introduction	0	1	2	3	4	5
F. Body	0	1	2	3	4	5
G. Support Material	0	1	2	3	4	5
H. Transitions	0	1	2	3	4	5
I. Conclusion	0	1	2	3	4	5
J. Language	0	1	2	3	4	5

DELIVERY

	Absent	Poor	Fair	Average	Good	Excellent
A. Approach & Beginning	0	1	2	3	4	5
B. Eye Contact	0	1	2	3	4	5
C. Speaking Rate	0	1	2	3	4	5
D. Expressiveness	0	1	2	3	4	5
E. Clarity & Volume	0	1	2	3	4	5
F. Gestures & Movement	0	1	2	3	4	5
G. Posture & Poise	0	1	2	3	4	5
H. Use of Notes (& Visuals)	0	1	2	3	4	5
I. Enthusiasm	0	1	2	3	4	5
J. Ending & Departure	0	1	2	3	4	5
Sub-totals:	___	___	___	___	___	___

Time: _____

COMMENTS:

Raw score: ___

Minus penalties: ___

Going under time minimum: ___

Going over time maximum: ___

FINAL GRADE: ___

Evaluation

Speaker's name _____

CONTENT	Absent	Poor	Fair	Average	Good	Excellent
A. Topic	0	1	2	3	4	5
B. Central Idea	0	1	2	3	4	5
C. Interest Level	0	1	2	3	4	5
D. Adaptation to Audience	0	1	2	3	4	5
E. Introduction	0	1	2	3	4	5
F. Body	0	1	2	3	4	5
G. Support Material	0	1	2	3	4	5
H. Transitions	0	1	2	3	4	5
I. Conclusion	0	1	2	3	4	5
J. Language	0	1	2	3	4	5

DELIVERY						
A. Approach & Beginning	0	1	2	3	4	5
B. Eye Contact	0	1	2	3	4	5
C. Speaking Rate	0	1	2	3	4	5
D. Expressiveness	0	1	2	3	4	5
E. Clarity & Volume	0	1	2	3	4	5
F. Gestures & Movement	0	1	2	3	4	5
G. Posture & Poise	0	1	2	3	4	5
H. Use of Notes (& Visuals)	0	1	2	3	4	5
I. Enthusiasm	0	1	2	3	4	5
J. Ending & Departure	0	1	2	3	4	5
Sub-totals:	___	___	___	___	___	___

Time: _____

Raw score: ___

COMMENTS:

Minus penalties: ___

FINAL GRADE: ___

Penalties:
___ Specific purpose statement late: –5
___ Central idea & main points late: –5
___ Tentative outline late: -5
___ Final outline late: -5
___ Unprepared to speak on date scheduled: -5
___ Not showing up at all on speech date: -10
___ Going under time minimum: -5
___ Going over time maximum: -5
*There is no penalty if you let the instructor know
(ahead of time if possible) of a legitimate excuse
(illness, death in the family, etc.)

Key To Evaluation Form

CONTENT

A. Topic: Choose a topic that is appropriate for your audience and narrow it to fit comfortably in the time allotted.

B. Central Idea: Make your central idea clear to the audience. Make sure that your entire speech serves to develop, explain, reinforce, or prove the central idea.

C. Interest Level: Make your speech interesting and appealing to every member of the audience. Avoid boring listeners with obvious material that everyone already knows.

D. Adaptation to the Audience: Adapt your ideas, language, and delivery to the needs, interests, and desires of your audience.

E. Introduction: Grab the attention of your listeners and make them want to listen to the rest of your speech. Prepare them for the body of the speech (by stating the central idea and/or previewing the main points). Give any background information or definitions that listeners would need in order to understand the speech. Establish your credibility: If you got your information from your own experience, explain your expertise and involvement; if you got your information from other sources, explain their trustworthiness (unless you plan to do so during the body of the speech).

F. Body: State your main points clearly and make sure that they back up the central idea. The body should be well-organized and easy to follow.

G. Support Material: Provide adequate support (such as examples, narratives, and statistics) to explain or prove the main points, but refrain from overwhelming the audience with too many facts or technical details. Your support material should be clear, interesting, and credible. If visual aids are used as support material, they should help the audience understand and remember key points.

H. Transitions: Make smooth transitions from one part of the speech to another.

I. Conclusion: Indicate (by words or by tone of voice) when you are approaching the end of your speech. Give a strong ending that smoothly wraps up the speech and reinforces the central idea.

J. Language: Use words that are clear, accurate, grammatically correct, and understandable to your audience. Never use language that is offensive or inappropriate.

DELIVERY

A. Approach & Beginning: When you are called to speak, get out of your seat without sighing or mumbling, walk confidently to the front of the room, spend a few moments standing in silence (this is a good time to arrange your notes and get your first sentences firmly in mind), and then look directly at the audience as you begin your speech.

B. Eye Contact: Look at all parts of the audience, glancing down at your notes only occasionally. Avoid staring at a wall or the floor; avoid looking out a window.

C. Speaking Rate: Speak at a rate that makes it easy for the audience to absorb your ideas—neither too slow nor too fast. When appropriate, use pauses.

D. Expressiveness: Your voice should sound as animated and as expressive as it does when you carry on a conversation with a friend.

E. Clarity & Volume: Pronounce words distinctly and speak loud enough so that all listeners can clearly hear you. Avoid verbal fillers such as *uh, um, okay, ya know*.

F. Gestures and Movement: If it's appropriate, use gestures to accompany your words. Make them naturally and gracefully, so that they add to, rather than distract from, your message. You may move about during your speech, as long as your movements are purposeful and confident—not random and nervous. Refrain from jingling keys or coins, riffling note cards, or doing anything that distracts the audience.

G. Posture & Poise: Stand up straight. Try to be comfortable, yet poised and alert. Avoid leaning on the lectern or slouching on a desk.

H. Use of Notes (& Visuals): Glance at your notes only occasionally to pick up the next point. Don't read them or absent-mindedly stare at them. (If visual aids are used, they should be presented smoothly. Don't "talk" to aids or let them distract listeners from your message.)

I. Enthusiasm: Don't simply go through the motions of "giving a speech." Your whole manner—eyes, facial expression, posture, voice—should show enthusiasm for the subject. You should seem genuinely interested in communicating your ideas to the audience.

J. Ending & Departure: Say your conclusion, pause a few moments, and then ask—in a sincere tone of voice—"Are there any questions?" Don't give the appearance of being anxious to get back to your seat (by pocketing your notes or by taking a step toward your seat).

Evaluation

Speaker's name _____

CONTENT	Absent	Poor	Fair	Average	Good	Excellent
A. Topic	0	1	2	3	4	5
B. Central Idea	0	1	2	3	4	5
C. Adaptation to Audience	0	1	2	3	4	5
D. Introduction	0	1	2	3	4	5
E. Body	0	1	2	3	4	5
F. Support Material	0	1	2	3	4	5
G. Visual Aids	0	1	2	3	4	5
H. Transitions	0	1	2	3	4	5
I. Conclusion	0	1	2	3	4	5
J. Language	0	1	2	3	4	5
DELIVERY						
A. Approach & Beginning	0	1	2	3	4	5
B. Eye Contact	0	1	2	3	4	5
C. Speaking Rate	0	1	2	3	4	5
D. Voice	0	1	2	3	4	5
E. Gestures & Movement	0	1	2	3	4	5
F. Posture & Poise	0	1	2	3	4	5
G. Use of Notes	0	1	2	3	4	5
H. Use of Visuals	0	1	2	3	4	5
I. Enthusiasm	0	1	2	3	4	5
J. Ending & Departure	0	1	2	3	4	5
Sub-totals:	___	___	___	___	___	___

Time: _____

COMMENTS:

Raw score: ___

Minus penalties: ___

FINAL GRADE: ___

Penalties:
__ Specific purpose statement late: −5
__ Central idea & main points late: −5
__ Tentative outline late: -5
__ Final outline late: -5
__ Unprepared to speak on date scheduled: -5
__ Not showing up at all on speech date: -10
__ Going under time minimum: -5
__ Going over time maximum: -5
*There is no penalty if you let the instructor know (ahead of time if possible) of a legitimate excuse (illness, death in the family, etc.)

Key To Evaluation Form

CONTENT

A. Topic: Choose a topic that is appropriate for your audience and narrow it to fit comfortably in the time allotted.

B. Central Idea: Make your central idea clear to the audience. Make sure that your entire speech serves to develop, explain, reinforce, or prove the central idea.

C. Adaptation to the Audience: Adapt your ideas, language, and delivery to the needs, interests, and desires of your audience. Make the speech interesting and appealing to all listeners. Avoid boring them with obvious material that everyone already knows.

D. Introduction: Grab the attention of your listeners and make them want to listen to the rest of your speech. Prepare them for the body of the speech (by stating the central idea and/or previewing the main points). Give any background information or definitions that listeners would need in order to understand the speech. Establish your credibility: If you got your information from your own experience, explain your expertise and involvement; if you got your information from other sources, explain their trustworthiness (unless you plan to do so during the body of the speech).

E. Body: State your main points clearly and make sure that they back up the central idea. The body should be well-organized and easy to follow.

F. Support Material: Provide adequate support (such as examples, narratives, and statistics) to explain or prove the main points, but refrain from overwhelming the audience with too many facts or technical details. Your support material should be clear, interesting, and credible.

G. Visual Aids: Each visual should help the audience understand and remember key points.

H. Transitions: Make smooth transitions from one part of the speech to another.

I. Conclusion: Indicate (by words or by tone of voice) when you are approaching the end of your speech. Give a strong ending that smoothly wraps up the speech and reinforces the central idea.

J. Language: Use words that are clear, accurate, grammatically correct, and understandable to your audience. Never use language that is offensive or inappropriate.

DELIVERY

A. Approach & Beginning: When you are called to speak, get out of your seat without sighing or mumbling, walk confidently to the front of the room, spend a few moments standing in silence (this is a good time to arrange your notes and get your first sentences firmly in mind), and then look directly at the audience as you begin your speech.

B. Eye Contact: Look at all parts of the audience, glancing down at your notes only occasionally. Avoid staring at a wall or the floor; avoid looking out a window.

C. Speaking Rate: Speak at a rate that makes it easy for the audience to absorb your ideas—neither too slow nor too fast. When appropriate, use pauses.

D. Voice: Your voice should sound as animated and as expressive as it does when you carry on a conversation with a friend. Pronounce your words distinctly and speak loud enough so that all listeners can clearly hear you. Avoid verbal fillers such as *uh*, *um*, *okay, ya know*.

E. Gestures and Movement: If it's appropriate, use gestures to accompany your words. Make them naturally and gracefully, so that they add to, rather than distract from, your message. You may move about during your speech, as long as your movements are purposeful and confident—not random and nervous. Refrain from jingling keys or coins, riffling note cards, or doing anything that distracts the audience.

F. Posture & Poise: Stand up straight. Try to be comfortable, yet poised and alert. Avoid leaning on the lectern or slouching on a desk.

G. Use of Notes: Merely glance at your notes occasionally to pick up the next point. Don't read them or absentmindedly stare at them.

H. Use of Visuals: Present visuals smoothly. Do not "talk" to aids or let them distract listeners from your message.

I. Enthusiasm: Don't simply go through the motions of "giving a speech." Your whole manner—eyes, facial expression, posture, voice—should show enthusiasm for the subject. You should seem genuinely interested in communicating your ideas to the audience.

J. Ending & Departure: Say your conclusion, pause a few moments, and then ask—in a sincere tone of voice—"Are there any questions?" Don't give the appearance of being anxious to get back to your seat (by pocketing your notes or by taking a step toward your seat).

Evaluation

Speaker's name _____

CONTENT	Absent	Poor	Fair	Average	Good	Excellent
A. Topic & Central Idea	0	1	2	3	4	5
B. Adaptation to Audience	0	1	2	3	4	5
C. Credibility	0	1	2	3	4	5
D. Introduction	0	1	2	3	4	5
E. Body	0	1	2	3	4	5
F. Support Material	0	1	2	3	4	5
G. Visual Aids	0	1	2	3	4	5
H. Transitions	0	1	2	3	4	5
I. Conclusion	0	1	2	3	4	5
J. Language	0	1	2	3	4	5

DELIVERY						
A. Approach & Beginning	0	1	2	3	4	5
B. Eye Contact	0	1	2	3	4	5
C. Speaking Rate	0	1	2	3	4	5
D. Expressiveness & Enthusiasm	0	1	2	3	4	5
	0	1	2	3	4	5
E. Voice: Clarity & Fluency	0	1	2	3	4	5
F. Gestures & Movement	0	1	2	3	4	5
G. Posture & Poise	0	1	2	3	4	5
H. Use of Notes	0	1	2	3	4	5
I. Use of Visuals	0	1	2	3	4	5
J. Ending & Departure						

Sub-totals: ___ ___ ___ ___ ___ ___

Time: _____

COMMENTS:

Raw score: ___

Minus penalties: ___

FINAL GRADE: ___

Penalties:
___ Specific purpose statement late: –5
___ Central idea & main points late: –5
___ Tentative outline late: -5
___ Final outline late: -5
___ Unprepared to speak on date scheduled: -5
___ Not showing up at all on speech date: -10
___ Going under time minimum: -5
___ Going over time maximum: -5
*There is no penalty if you let the instructor know (ahead of time if possible) of a legitimate excuse (illness, death in the family, etc.)

Key To Evaluation Form

CONTENT

A. Topic & Central Idea: Choose a topic that is appropriate for your audience and narrow it to fit comfortably in the time allotted. Make your central idea clear to the audience. Make sure that your entire speech serves to develop, explain, reinforce, or prove the central idea.

B. Adaptation to the Audience: Adapt your ideas, language, and delivery to the needs, interests, and desires of your audience. Make the speech interesting and appealing to all listeners. Avoid boring them with obvious material that everyone already knows.

C. Credibility: In the introduction and/or body, show that your material is reliable. If you got your information from your own experience, explain your expertise and involvement; if you got your information from other sources, explain their trustworthiness.

D. Introduction: Grab the attention of your listeners and make them want to listen to the rest of your speech. Prepare them for the body of the speech (by stating the central idea and/or previewing the main points). Give any background information or definitions that listeners would need in order to understand the speech.

E. Body: State your main points clearly and make sure that they back up the central idea. The body should be well-organized and easy to follow.

F. Support Material: Provide adequate support (such as examples, narratives, and statistics) to explain or prove the main points, but refrain from overwhelming the audience with too many facts or technical details. Your support material should be clear, interesting, and credible.

G. Visual Aids: Each visual should help the audience understand and remember key points.

H. Transitions: Make smooth transitions from one part of the speech to another.

I. Conclusion: Indicate (by words or by tone of voice) when you are approaching the end of your speech. Give a strong ending that smoothly wraps up the speech and reinforces the central idea.

J. Language: Use words that are clear, accurate, grammatically correct, and understandable to your audience. Never use language that is offensive or inappropriate.

DELIVERY

A. Approach & Beginning: When you are called to speak, get out of your seat without sighing or mumbling, walk confidently to the front of the room, spend a few moments standing in silence (this is a good time to arrange your notes and get your first sentences firmly in mind), and then look directly at the audience as you begin your speech.

B. Eye Contact: Look at all parts of the audience, glancing down at your notes only occasionally. Avoid staring at a wall or the floor; avoid looking out a window.

C. Speaking Rate: Speak at a rate that makes it easy for the audience to absorb your ideas—neither too slow nor too fast. When appropriate, use pauses.

D. Expressiveness & Enthusiasm: Your voice should sound as animated and as expressive as it does when you carry on a conversation with a friend. Don't simply go through the motions of "giving a speech." Your whole manner—eyes, facial expression, posture, voice—should show enthusiasm for the subject. You should seem genuinely interested in communicating your ideas.

E. Voice: Clarity & Fluency: Pronounce your words distinctly and speak loud enough so that everyone in the audience can clearly hear you. Avoid verbal fillers such as *uh, um, ah, er, okay, ya know.*

F. Gestures and Movement: If it's appropriate, use gestures to accompany your words. Make them naturally and gracefully, so that they add to, rather than distract from, your message. You may move about during your speech, as long as your movements are purposeful and confident—not random and nervous. Refrain from jingling keys or coins, riffling note cards, or doing anything that distracts the audience.

G. Posture & Poise: Stand up straight. Try to be comfortable, yet poised and alert. Avoid leaning on the lectern or slouching on a desk.

H. Use of Notes: Glance at your notes occasionally to pick up the next point. Don't read them or absent-mindedly stare at them.

I. Use of Visuals: Present visuals smoothly. Do not "talk" to aids or let them distract listeners from your message.)

J. Ending & Departure: Say your conclusion, pause a few moments, and then ask—in a sincere tone of voice—"Are there any questions?" Don't give the appearance of being anxious to get back to your seat (by pocketing your notes or by taking a step toward your seat).

Speech Evaluation

Speaker's Name_____

Scale: 1=poor 2=fair 3=average 4=good 5=excellent (Put N if the item is not applicable for this particular speech.)

Introduction

___The speaker grabbed my attention.

___The opening remarks made me want to listen to the rest of the speech.

___The speaker adequately prepared me for the body of the speech (by stating the central idea and/or previewing the main points.

Body

___The central idea and main points were clear and understandable.

___The speaker provided adequate support (such as examples, narratives, and statistics) to develop or prove the main points.

___The speaker refrained from overwhelming me with too many facts or technical details.

___The speech was well-organized and easy to follow.

___The speaker made smooth transitions from one idea to another.

___The speaker's language was clear, accurate, and appropriate.

Conclusion

___The speaker indicated (by words or tone of voice) that he or she was approaching the end of the speech.

___The speaker gave a strong ending that smoothly wrapped up the speech and reinforced the central idea.

Delivery

___The speaker avoided going too fast in the opening of the speech.

___The speaker seemed truly interested in communicating his or her ideas.

___The speaker maintained good eye contact.

___The speaker used notes effectively.

___The speaker appeared poised and confident.

___Gestures were used effectively.

___The speaker spoke at an ideal rate (neither too slow nor too fast).

___The speaker's voice was animated, conversational, and easy to listen to.

___The speaker spoke distinctly and loud enough for everyone to hear.

___The speaker avoided distracting mannerisms (such as jingling coins).

___The speaker avoided too much movement (pacing, etc.).

___The speaker avoided verbal fillers (such as *uh, um, er, ah, okay, ya know*).

___The speaker used pauses effectively.

Visual Aids (if applicable)

___Visual aids were simple, clear, and vivid.

___Visual aids were relevant and appropriate.

___Visual aids were adequately explained.

Overall Impressions

___The speech was interesting.

___The speaker seemed well-prepared.

___The remarks seemed well-adapted to this particular audience.

What were the speaker's major strengths?

In what areas does he or she need improvement?

Other Comments:

Speech Evaluation—Central Idea

Speaker's Name_____

Scale: 1=poor 2=fair 3=average 4=good 5=excellent (Put N if the item is not applicable for this particular speech.)

Introduction

___The speaker grabbed my attention.

___The opening remarks made me want to listen to the rest of the speech.

___The speaker adequately prepared me for the body of the speech (by stating the central idea and/or previewing the main points.

Body

___The central idea and main points were clear and understandable.

___The speaker provided adequate support (such as examples, narratives, and statistics) to develop or prove the main points.

___The speaker refrained from overwhelming me with too many facts or technical details.

___The speech was well-organized and easy to follow.

___The speaker made smooth transitions from one idea to another.

___The speaker's language was clear, accurate, and appropriate.

Conclusion

___The speaker indicated (by words or tone of voice) that he or she was approaching the end of the speech.

___The speaker gave a strong ending that smoothly wrapped up the speech and reinforced the central idea.

Delivery

___The speaker avoided going too fast in the opening of the speech.

___The speaker seemed truly interested in communicating his or her ideas.

___The speaker maintained good eye contact.

___The speaker used notes effectively.

___The speaker appeared poised and confident.

___Gestures were used effectively.

___The speaker spoke at an ideal rate (neither too slow nor too fast).

___The speaker's voice was animated, conversational, and easy to listen to.

___The speaker spoke distinctly and loud enough for everyone to hear.

___The speaker avoided distracting mannerisms (such as jingling coins).

___The speaker avoided too much movement (pacing, etc.).

___The speaker avoided verbal fillers (such as *uh, um, er, ah, okay, ya know*).

___The speaker used pauses effectively.

Visual Aids (if applicable)

___Visual aids were simple, clear, and vivid.

___Visual aids were relevant and appropriate.

___Visual aids were adequately explained.

Overall Impressions

___The speech was interesting.

___The speaker seemed well-prepared.

___The remarks seemed well-adapted to this particular audience.

_____

What was the central idea of the speech?

What were the speaker's major strengths?

In what areas does he or she need improvement?

Other Comments:

EVALUATION—SPEECH WITH VISUAL AIDS

Speaker's Name_____

Scale: 1=poor 2=fair 3=average 4=good 5=excellent (Put N if the item is not applicable for this particular speech.)

Introduction

___The speaker grabbed my attention.

___The opening remarks made me want to listen to the rest of the speech.

___The speaker adequately prepared me for the body of the speech (by stating the central idea and/or previewing the main points.

Body

___The central idea and main points were clear and understandable.

___The speaker provided adequate support (such as examples, narratives, and statistics) to develop or prove the main points.

___The speaker refrained from overwhelming me with too many facts or technical details.

___The speech was well-organized and easy to follow.

___The speaker made smooth transitions from one idea to another.

___The speaker's language was clear, accurate, and appropriate.

Conclusion

___The speaker indicated (by words or tone of voice) that he or she was approaching the end of the speech.

___The speaker gave a strong ending that smoothly wrapped up the speech and reinforced the central idea.

Delivery

___The speaker avoided going too fast in the opening of the speech.

___The speaker seemed truly interested in communicating his or her ideas.

___The speaker maintained good eye contact.

___The speaker used notes effectively.

___The speaker appeared poised and confident.

___Gestures were used effectively.

___The speaker spoke at an ideal rate (neither too slow nor too fast).

___The speaker's voice was animated, conversational, and easy to listen to.

___The speaker spoke distinctly and loud enough for everyone to hear.

___The speaker avoided distracting mannerisms (such as jingling coins).

___The speaker avoided too much movement (pacing, etc.).

___The speaker avoided verbal fillers (such as *uh, um, er, ah, okay, ya know*).

___The speaker used pauses effectively.

Visual Aids

___Visual aids were simple, clear, and vivid.

___Visual aids were relevant and appropriate.

___Visual aids were adequately explained.

___The visuals helped me to understand and remember the speaker's points.

___The speaker did not let visuals distract from the message.

___The visual aids were presented smoothly.

___Speaker did not "talk" to the visual aids.

___Right amount of visual aids were used.

Overall Impressions

___The speech was interesting.

___The speaker seemed well-prepared.

___The remarks seemed well-adapted to this particular audience.

_____

What were the speaker's major strengths?
In what areas does he or she need improvement?
Other Comments:

EVALUATION—INFORMATIVE SPEECH

Speaker's Name_____

Scale: 1=poor 2=fair 3=average 4=good 5=excellent (Put N if the item is not applicable for this particular speech.)

Introduction

___The speaker grabbed my attention.

___The opening remarks made me want to listen to the rest of the speech.

___The speaker adequately prepared me for the body of the speech (by stating the central idea and/or previewing the main points.

Body

___The central idea and main points were clear and understandable.

___The speaker provided adequate support (such as examples, narratives, and statistics) to develop or prove the main points.

___The speaker refrained from overwhelming me with too many facts or technical details.

___The speech was well-organized and easy to follow.

___The speaker made smooth transitions from one idea to another.

___The speaker's language was clear, accurate, and appropriate.

Conclusion

___The speaker indicated (by words or tone of voice) that he or she was approaching the end of the speech.

___The speaker gave a strong ending that smoothly wrapped up the speech and reinforced the central idea.

Delivery

___The speaker avoided going too fast in the opening of the speech.

___The speaker seemed truly interested in communicating his or her ideas.

___The speaker maintained good eye contact.

___The speaker used notes effectively.

___The speaker appeared poised and confident.

___Gestures were used effectively.

___The speaker spoke at an ideal rate (neither too slow nor too fast).

___The speaker's voice was animated, conversational, and easy to listen to.

___The speaker spoke distinctly and loud enough for everyone to hear.

___The speaker avoided distracting mannerisms (such as jingling coins).

___The speaker avoided too much movement (pacing, etc.).

___The speaker avoided verbal fillers (such as *uh, um, er, ah, okay, ya know*).

___The speaker used pauses effectively.

Visual Aids (if applicable)

___Visual aids were simple, clear, and vivid.

___Visual aids were relevant and appropriate.

___Visual aids were adequately explained.

Overall Impressions

___The speech was interesting.

___The speaker seemed well-prepared.

___The remarks seemed well-adapted to this particular audience.

How informative was the speech? (check one) ___I already knew everything the speaker said. ___I learned many new things. ___I learned a few new things.

What were the speaker's major strengths?

In what areas does he or she need improvement?

Other Comments:

EVALUATION—PERSUASIVE SPEECH

Speaker's Name_____

Scale: 1=poor 2=fair 3=average 4=good 5=excellent (Put N if the item is not applicable for this particular speech.)

Introduction

___The speaker grabbed my attention.

___The opening remarks made me want to listen to the rest of the speech.

___The speaker adequately prepared me for the body of the speech (by stating the central idea and/or previewing the main points.

Body

___The central idea and main points were clear and understandable.

___The speaker provided adequate support (such as examples, narratives, and statistics) to develop or prove the main points.

___The speaker refrained from overwhelming me with too many facts or technical details.

___The speech was well-organized and easy to follow.

___The speaker made smooth transitions from one idea to another.

___The speaker's language was clear, accurate, and appropriate.

Conclusion

___The speaker indicated (by words or tone of voice) that he or she was approaching the end of the speech.

___The speaker gave a strong ending that smoothly wrapped up the speech and reinforced the central idea.

Delivery

___The speaker avoided going too fast in the opening of the speech.

___The speaker seemed truly interested in communicating his or her ideas.

___The speaker maintained good eye contact.

___The speaker used notes effectively.

___The speaker appeared poised and confident.

___Gestures were used effectively.

___The speaker spoke at an ideal rate (neither too slow nor too fast).

___The speaker's voice was animated, conversational, and easy to listen to.

___The speaker spoke distinctly and loud enough for everyone to hear.

___The speaker avoided distracting mannerisms (such as jingling coins).

___The speaker avoided too much movement (pacing, etc.).

___The speaker avoided verbal fillers (such as *uh, um, er, ah, okay, ya know*).

___The speaker used pauses effectively.

Visual Aids (if applicable)

___Visual aids were simple, clear, and vivid.

___Visual aids were relevant and appropriate.

___Visual aids were adequately explained.

Overall Impressions

___The speech was interesting.

___The speaker seemed well-prepared.

___The remarks seemed well-adapted to this particular audience.

_____

How persuasive was the speech? (check only one) ___I agreed with the central idea before the speech. ___The speaker won me over completely to the central idea. ___The speaker moved me closer to his or her position. ___The speech moved me further away from his or her position.

What were the speaker's major strengths?

In what areas does he or she need improvement?

Other Comments:

SPEECH EVALUATION

Speaker's Name_____

Check the appropriate boxes. In some categories, you may want to check more than one item. For matters that require elaboration, use the Comments section at the end.

CONTENT

Introduction:
___Your opening was weak and uninteresting.
___Your opening was confusing (as to what you were going to talk about).
___Good, you got my interest.
___Your introduction needs to prepare me for the body of the speech.
___Your introduction helped me prepare mentally for the body of the speech.

Body:
___You need to get across a central idea.
___Your central ideas were made clear and understandable.
___You need to clearly state your main points.
___Your main points were clearly stated.
___You need to back-up your main points.
___Your main points were adequately supported.
___Your speech was poorly organized.
___Your speech was well-organized and easy to follow.
___You need to make smooth transitions between major ideas.
___You provided smooth transitions between ideas.
___You overwhelmed me with too many facts.

Conclusion:
___You stopped speaking abruptly.
___You gave me a clear sense that you were nearing the end.
___You need to reinforce your central idea in the conclusion.
___You reinforced your central idea.
___Your conclusion was clumsy.
___Your conclusion was graceful and effective.

Wording:
___Some of your words were unclear.
___Some of your words were inaccurate.
___Some of your words were inappropriate.
___Your words were clear.
___Your words were accurate.
___Your words were appropriate.

Impressions:
___Your speech was uninteresting.
___Your speech was moderately interesting.
___Your speech was very interesting.
___You seemed prepared.
___You seemed unprepared.

DELIVERY

Eye Contact:
___You needed to look at the audience more often.
___You should have looked at all parts of the audience.
___You shouldn't have looked so often at: ___walls ___ceiling ___floor ___notes ___other: _____
___Good, you looked at the audience throughout the speech.

Posture:
___You leaned on the lectern.
___You moved around too much.
___You played with: ___ears ___nose ___hair ___jewelry ___notes ___other: _____
___You looked comfortable, yet poised and alert.

Gestures:

___You needed more gestures.

___Your gestures were "hidden" behind the lectern.

___Your gestures were clumsy or inappropriate.

___You made good use of gestures.

Voice:

___Your voice sounded dull and unanimated.

___You spoke in a monotone.

___You failed to speak loud enough.

___You spoke too loud.

___You inserted too many fillers: ___*uh* ___*ah* ___*um* ___*er* ___*okay* ___*like* ___*ya know* ___ other:_____

___Your voice sounded animated and expressive.

___You mumbled.

Rate:

___You spoke too fast.

___You spoke too slow.

___Good, your rate was neither too fast nor too slow.

___You made good use of pauses.

Impressions:

___Your general attitude was unpleasant.

___Your general attitude was pleasant.

___You seemed unenthusiastic about your subject.

___You seemed enthusiastic about your subject.

___You seemed to be simply "making a speech"—going through the motions, not really caring about reaching your audience.

___You seemed to be speaking directly to me and the other listeners; you seemed genuinely interested in reaching us.

Strengths:

Weaknesses:

Other Comments:

EVALUATION OF A SPEECH

Speaker's Name_____

Write yes, no, or n/a (not applicable) in the spaces below:

Audience Analysis and Adaptation

_____Did the speaker show sensitivity to audience demographics (age, sex, educational level, racial and ethnic background, religious background, and economic and social status)?
_____Did the speaker attempt to make the speech interesting to this particular audience?
_____Did the speaker take into consideration the knowledge level of the audience?
_____Did the speaker take into consideration the attitudes of the audience?
_____Was the speech appropriate for the specific occasion?

Introduction

_____Did the speaker grab the listeners' attention at the beginning?
_____Did the speaker's opening remarks prepare the audience for the body of the speech (by stating the central idea and/or by previewing the main points)?

Body

_____Were the central idea and main points clear and understandable?
_____Did the speaker provide adequate support (such as examples, narratives, and statistics) to develop or prove the main points?
_____Did the speaker's sources appear to be authoritative, up-to-date, and trustworthy?
_____Was the speech well-organized and easy to follow?
_____Did the speaker provide smooth transitions from one part of the speech to another?
_____Did the speaker avoid overwhelming the audience with too many facts and figures?
_____Was the speaker's language clear, accurate, and appropriate?

Conclusion

_____Did the speaker signal (by words or tone of voice) that he or she was approaching the end of the speech?
_____Did the speaker end strongly and smoothly?
_____Did the speaker reinforce the central idea?

Delivery

_____Did the speaker avoid going too fast in the opening of the speech?
_____Did the speaker seem truly interested in communicating his or her ideas?
_____Did the speaker maintain good eye contact with the audience?
_____Did the speaker use notes effectively?
_____Did the speaker appear poised and confident?
_____Were gestures used effectively?
_____Did he or she speak at an ideal rate (neither too slow nor too fast)?
_____Was the speaker's voice animated, conversational, and easy to listen to?
_____Did he or she speak distinctly and loud enough for everyone to hear?
_____Did the speaker avoid distracting mannerisms (such as jingling coins)?
_____Did the speaker avoid too much movement (such as pacing)?

_____Did the speaker avoid verbal fillers (such as *uh, er, ah, okay, ya know*)?
_____Did the speaker use pauses effectively?
_____Were the speaker's visual aids simple, clear, and vivid?
_____Were the visual aids relevant and appropriate?
_____Were the visual aids explained adequately?

Overall Impressions

_____Was the speech worthwhile, interesting, and appropriate?
_____Did the speaker clearly and effectively convey the central idea of the speech?
_____Did the speaker seem to have a thorough knowledge of the subject matter?
_____Did the speaker seem well-prepared?
_____Did the speaker's general attitude seem pleasant?
_____Was the speaker enthusiastic about the subject?

What were the speaker's major strengths?

In what areas does he or she need improvement?

Other comments:

CENTRAL IDEA

Listen analytically for each speaker's central idea and write it down in the space provided.

1. Speaker:_____

Central Idea:

_____

2. Speaker:_____

Central Idea:

_____

3. Speaker_____

Central Idea:

_____

4. Speaker:_____

Central Idea:

_____

5. Speaker:_____

Central Idea:

Speaker's Name_____

ORAL READING

Key: 1=poor, 2=fair, 3=average, 4=good, 5=excellent

Was the selection appropriate for this audience? _____

Was the selection introduced properly? _____

Was the speaker's voice expressive? (Did it convey the idea, mood or emotion of the selection?) _____

Was the rate of reading appropriate for the material? _____

Did the speaker seem well-prepared? _____

Comments:

Grade:_____

EVALUATION OF SAMPLE OUTLINE

1. What is the title of the speech?

2. What is the speaker's specific purpose?

3. What is the speaker's central idea?

4. What technique does the speaker use to grab the audience's attention in the first part of the introduction?

5. In the second part of the introduction, what does the speaker plan to say to preview the body of the speech?

6. What is the speaker's transition between the introduction and the body?

7. List the speaker's main points:

8. Does each main point have adequate support? Yes No

9. Does the speaker have a transition between each main point? Yes No

10. What is the speaker's transition between the body and the conclusion?

11. In the conclusion, does the speaker reinforce the central idea of the speech? Yes No

12. How many sources are cited in the bibliography? _____

13. Are visual aids planned? Yes No

Chapter 1
Introduction to Public Speaking

Chapter Objectives and Resource Integrator

After studying this chapter, students should be able to:

Objectives	Resources

1. Explain at least three benefits of a public speaking course.	**In the Text:**
	• Pages 5-7
	
	On Speeches DVD and on connectpublicspeaking.com:
	• Full Speech #11: A sample speech that shows a speaker making a contribution to his classmates is Burch Wang's "How to Hide Valuables."
	• Full Speech #22: Amy Casanova ("Three Celebrity Heroes") demonstrates that preparing and giving a speech can be a rewarding personal experience and a delight to the listeners.
	
	On connectpublicspeaking.com:
	• Supplementary Readings:
	  o "How to Prepare a Speech Without Feeling Overwhelmed" – A good article for students to read early in the course.
	
	  o "Weekly Planner" – Students can print this sheet and use it to organize their time for speech preparation.
	
	  o "Tips for ESL Students" – This article provides friendly suggestions for students who speak English as a second language.
	
	  o "Career Opportunities" – A list of some of the professions in which public speaking plays a major role.
	
	In the Instructor's Manual (on Instructor's Resource DVD-ROM):
	• Form 1.1, Welcome sheet
	• Form 1.2, Self-Evaluation
	• Form 1.3, Instructor's Information Sheet
	• Form 1.4, Which Are the Most Important Skills?
	• Form 1.5, Most Important Skills for Job Applicants
	• Form 1.6, Careers Involving Communication Skills

2. Identify and explain the seven elements of the speech communication process.	**In the Text:** • Pages 7-12 • Key terms: channel, feedback, interference, listener, message, situation, speaker **On Speeches DVD and on connectpublicspeaking.com:** • Full Speech #14: Bicycle Helmets I, an Informative Speech that Needs Improvement, shows a speaker who creates interference by displaying a visual aid that is too small to be seen. **On connectpublicspeaking.com:** • Interactive Exercise ("What is Happening?") gives students practice in identifying the seven elements. **On Instructor's Resource DVD-ROM:** • "Lessons from the Movies" – An illustrated narrative based on the movie *A Beautiful Mind* demonstrates interference in the speech communication process.
3. Describe the main responsibilities that speakers have toward their listeners.	**In the Text:** • Pages 12-14 • Key terms: scapegoat, stereotypes
4. Prepare a speech introducing yourself or a classmate.	**In the Text:** • Pages 14-16 (including two sample speeches) • Appendix – sample speech (p. 000) **On Speeches DVD and on connectpublicspeaking.com:** • Full Speech #1: Christine Fowler, in a self-introduction speech, "Scars and Bruises," tells, with humor and grace, of her growing-up misadventures. This is a good model of a speech introducing oneself to the class. **In the Instructor's Manual (on Instructor's Resource DVD-ROM):** • Form 1.7, Memo – This memo can be used to alert students to delivery problems that you see in their self-introduction speech.

Resources For Entire Chapter:

At End of Chapter:

- Summary
- Key Terms
- Review Questions
- Building Critical-Thinking Skills
- Building Teamwork Skills

On connectpublicspeaking.com:

- Practice test for chapter
- Checklist (for Preparing and Delivering a Speech)
- Glossary of terms
- Key-term flashcards
- Interactive exercise for chapter
- Building Internet Skills (used to be in book, now online)
- Supplementary Readings:
    - "How to Prepare a Speech Without Feeling Overwhelmed" – A good article for students to read early in the course.

    - "Weekly Planner" – Students can print this sheet and use it to organize their time for speech preparation.

    - "Tips for ESL Students" – This article provides friendly suggestions for students who speak English as a second language.

    - "Job Interviews" – Tips for handling one of the most important oral communication events in a person's life.

    - "Frequently Asked Questions" – Some of the most popular questions asked during a job interview and suggestions on how to answer them.

    - "Letter of Application" – Guidelines and a sample letter.

    - "Résumé" – Guidelines and a sample résumé.

On Instructor's Resource DVD-ROM:

- PowerPoint: Chapter Highlights – A PowerPoint program gives highlights of each chapter and includes some video clips. **(NOTE: Many of the PowerPoint slides have no text and require the explanation given in the accompanying script.)**
- Tests – Ready-made chapter tests and a computerized test bank are provided.
- "Lessons from the Movies" – An illustrated narrative based on the movie *A Beautiful Mind* demonstrates interference in the speech communication process.

In the Instructor's Manual (on Instructor's Resource DVD-ROM):

- Form 1.1, Welcome sheet – This handout can be given to students as they walk into class on the first day and then taken up at the end of class. It is similar to sheet 1.2 (see comments below), but zeroes in on stage fright (so that the instructor can spot phobics early and discourage them from dropping the course).

- Form 1.2, Self-Evaluation – On the first day of class, you can have students fill in the sheet. This assignment not only gives you a picture of each student's strengths, weaknesses, and fears, but it also can be used as a before-and-after experience. You can save the papers and return them to the students at the end of the course, and then ask them to assess whether they have changed their opinions of themselves as speechmakers. Many students find this to be a satisfying way of contrasting their end-of-course confidence with their beginning-of-course negativity. You may even want to sit down with each student at the end of the course and discuss his or her progress, as measured against the initial self-evaluation. Note: If you use this sheet at the beginning of the course, you may want to encourage the students to be candid. You can reassure them, for example, that you will not be miffed if, on question #2, they hope only to get a passing grade.
- Form 1.3, Instructor's Information Sheet – During the student's self-introduction speech or during an interview, you can make notes, using one of these sheets for each student. You may want to keep the sheets in a folder or notebook to help you guide the students in choosing topics and developing materials. Space is provided at the bottom of the sheet for comments about possible speech topics and particular problems the student may be having.
- Form 1.4, Which Are the Most Important Skills? – Research shows the importance of oral communication skills in the job market. This sheet is designed as a class exercise (see instructions at top of sheet). Answers are given on sheet 1.5.
- Form 1.5, Most Important Skills for Job Applicants – This sheet is the same as 1.4 except that the missing numbers are supplied.
- Form 1.6, Careers Involving Communication Skills – A class discussion can be built around this sheet: Why are communication skills vital for nurses, military officers, attorneys, and so on? Have any students experienced communication foul-ups involving physicians, teachers, or supervisors?
- Form 1.7, Memo – This memo can be used to alert students to delivery problems that you see in their self-introduction speech.

Your Thoughts?

p. 7: Who is the most engaging public communicator (politician, teacher, minister, etc.) you have ever encountered? What are the reasons for his or her success?

(Answers will vary. Students should see the importance of credibility, message, and an engaging delivery style.)

p. 9: When nonverbal and verbal messages are contradictory, why do you think listeners tend to accept the nonverbal as the true message?

Most people assume that a nonverbal message reflects a person's real, unfiltered feelings.

p. 12: If you are crusading for a good cause, is it okay to falsify a few minor statistics to advance your argument? Defend your answer.

(Answers will vary.) No, it is always unethical to falsify – even for the sake of a good cause. Furthermore, a speaker's credibility can be destroyed if his or her dishonesty is discovered.

Key to questions on p. 21 in the textbook:

1. Why are communication skills important to your career?

   A person who speaks well and listens effectively is more likely to be hired and promoted than a person who lacks these skills.

2. Name five personal benefits of a public speaking course.

   (1) You learn how to speak to a public audience, (2) You learn skills that apply to one-on-one communication, (3) You develop the oral communication skills that are prized in the job market, (4) You practice and gain experience in an ideal laboratory, (5) You gain self-confidence

3. What are the seven elements of the speech communication process?

   Speaker, listener, message, channel, feedback, interference, and situation.

4. Why is speaking not necessarily the same thing as communicating?

   A speaker's message may not be received and interpreted accurately by the listener.

5. If there is a contradiction between the verbal and nonverbal components of a speaker's message, which component is a listener likely to accept as the true message?

   The nonverbal component.

6. If communication fails, who is to blame—the speaker or the listener?

   Depending on the situation, the blame could be placed on either, or both.

7. What two channels are most frequently used for classroom speeches?

   Auditory and visual.

8. What are the three types of interference?

   External, internal, and speaker-generated.

9. What are stereotypes? Give some examples.

   Stereotypes are oversimplified mental pictures. (Examples will vary.)

10. According to a survey, what is the number one mistake made by public speakers?

    Failing to tailor one's speech to the needs and interests of the audience.

Key to questions on p. 21 in the textbook:

1. Describe an instance of miscommunication between you and another person (friend, relative, salesperson, etc.). Discuss what caused the problem, and how the interchange could have been handled better.

   (Answers will vary.)

2. One of the elements of the speech communication process—feedback—is important for success in business. Imagine that you work in a travel agency, and you have to give presentations on crime prevention to clients who have purchased overseas tours. How would you seek and use feedback?

   Answers will vary. Students should be able to see the value of getting feedback (via interviews or surveys) from clients after they have returned from their trips. Which tips given beforehand actually worked to prevent crime? Which didn't work?

Activities

1. Assign skill builders at the end of the chapter in the text (Building Critical-Thinking Skills and Building Teamwork Skills).

2. Have students write an account of a speech transaction (such as an interview or a conversation) that they have experienced or observed. Ask them to label or identify the seven parts of the speech communication process as shown in their example, using Figure 1.1 in Chapter 1 of the text as their model.

Speeches

The assignments below are for "icebreaker" speeches—short, informal, loosening-up speeches at the beginning of the course. Since students have not yet studied much of the textbook, you may want to focus on the section in Chapter 1 entitled, "Quick Guide to Public Speaking," to give them some basic principles of speechmaking. It is recommended that these speeches be ungraded in order to hold down the anxiety level.

Speech of Self-Introduction: An excellent icebreaker, this speech gives students a chance to stand up and speak on a subject about which they are experts—themselves. Have the students briefly (2-4 minutes) introduce themselves, telling about their background, interests, and plans for the future. Give the students advance warning of this speech, so that they can prepare themselves psychologically. Tell them that a question-and-answer period is mandatory (for some reticent students, you will need the question-and-answer period to draw them out). The section in Chapter 1, "Introducing Yourself or a Classmate," can be assigned. Unless gently prodded, some reticent students will say very little about themselves, skipping over such items as "Tell one interesting or unusual thing about yourself." I suggest telling students in advance, "I want you to cover all the items on the checklist in the book. If you don't, I'm going to ask you about them during the question-and-answer period." This causes most students to comply; for the few who don't comply, you can follow through during the question-and-answer period and ask them to supply missing details.

A side benefit of this speech is that you learn information about your students that can help you guide them through such things as topic selection. You may want to set aside a notebook page or a file folder dedicated to each student. You can use Sheet 1.3 to take notes from this speech.

Since the self-introductions will provide valuable insights into the makeup of the audience for later classroom speeches, you may want to urge students to make notes on their classmates' backgrounds.

Speech Introducing a Classmate: An alternative to the self-introduction talk is a speech in which classmates pair off, interview each other, and then introduce each other to the class. The interviewing provides an excellent icebreaker, especially if the students do not already know each other. And in the speech itself, students are freer to mention accomplishments which the self-introducer might skip because of fear of being considered a braggart. On the negative side, however, the speakers do not know their subject matter (their peers) as well as they do in the self-introduction speech, and therefore, may have a higher anxiety level and a greater tendency to read their notes. (Suggestion: The student being introduced can stand near the lectern during the speech so that the audience will know the person being described.)

Pet Peeve Speech: Some instructors have their students give a brief (1-2 minute) speech on their pet peeve, sometimes without notes.

"I Believe" Speech: Some instructors ask their students to give a brief (1-2 minutes) speech on something they believe. This speech is sometimes given without notes.

Objective Tests

Four ready-to-print tests for Chapter 1 (Forms A, B, C, D) and answer keys for all tests are provided in this instructor's manual. The four forms cover the same material but are sufficiently different to permit one test to be used as the class test and the others as makeup tests for absentees. Form A features true-false questions, Forms B and C have multiple-choice questions, while Form D is more difficult, requiring students to fill in missing words or phrases. Instructors may want to combine Form D with some of the essay questions listed below.

The following can be used as essay questions for tests or as stimuli for class discussions.

1. Discuss the situations in which a person is likely to speak in public, regardless of the career he or she chooses.

2. What are the advantages of a classroom as an "ideal environment" for public speaking?

3. "Words are not things; they are symbols of things." Explain what this statement means.

4. How can a speaker use feedback to make adjustments in a speech?

5. Explain what is meant by "internal" interference.

6. Explain the seven elements of the speech communication process.

7. What are stereotypes, and what should be the speaker's attitude toward them?

8. Discuss a few of the ways in which some speakers show disrespect for their listeners.

Welcome to your public speaking class. In this course you will develop and enhance your ability to organize your thoughts and give a presentation with confidence, clarity, and power.

Many people who have taken this course said later that it helped them immensely in their careers. I hope that for you, too, this course will be a valuable experience.

To help me get to know you, please fill in the Self-Evaluation below. Thanks!

_____

(instructor)

Self-Evaluation

1. Your name_____

2. Have you had any experience in giving speeches?   Yes   No

   If yes, please describe:

3. Most people experience nervousness or stage fright when they speak to a group of strangers. How would you describe your level of anxiety?

   _____ No anxiety

   _____ Small amount of anxiety

   _____ Moderate amount of anxiety

   _____ Large amount of anxiety

   _____ Extreme, crippling level of anxiety

4. What do you hope to gain from this course? (Be honest! If you hope only to get a credit needed for graduation, say so.)

Self-Evaluation

Name_____

1. As you begin this course, how do you feel about yourself as a public speaker? (Mention your prior experience as a speaker, your strengths, your weaknesses, and any fears that you may have.)

2. What do you hope to gain from this course?

Instructor's Information Sheet

Student's name_____

Marital status and family background:

Work experience:

Background (high school, military, etc.):

Academic plans:

Post-Graduation plans:

Special interests (hobbies, sports, clubs, etc.)

Other:

_____

Possible Speech Topics:

Outlining/Organizational Problems:

Delivery Problems:

Which Are the Most Important Skills?

In a survey of 428 personnel directors in the U.S., these are the skills that were considered most important in hiring job applicants. Can you identify the top three in 1-2-3 order?

FACTORS/SKILLS

Oral communication skills

Listening ability

Enthusiasm

Written communication skills

Technical competence

Appearance

Poise

Work experience

Résumé

Specific degree held

Grade point average

Part-time or summer employment

Accreditation of program

Leadership in campus/community activities

Participation in campus/community activities

Recommendations

School attended

Most Important Skills for Job Applicants

In a survey of 428 personnel directors in the U.S., these are the skills that were considered most important in hiring job applicants—ranked from most important to least important.

RANK ORDER	FACTORS/SKILLS
1.	Oral communication skills
2.	Listening ability
3.	Enthusiasm
4.	Written communication skills
5.	Technical competence
6.	Appearance
7.	Poise
8.	Work experience
9.	Résumé
10.	Specific degree held
11.	Grade point average
12.	Part-time or summer employment
13.	Accreditation of program
14.	Leadership in campus/community activities
15.	Participation in campus/community activities
16.	Recommendations
17.	School attended

Careers Involving Communication Skills

Communication skills are important in any career, but they are vital in the following careers:

Engineer	Reporter	Physician or surgeon	Hotel manager
Military officer	Politician	Teacher or professor	Scientist
Union representative	Minister	Restaurant manager	Television newscaster
Therapist	Chef	Financial planner	Paramedic
Nurse	Writer	Actor	Public relations specialist
Air traffic controller	Restaurant server	Fund-raiser	Secretary
Psychiatrist	Pilot	Marriage counselor	Police officer
Travel agent	Counselor	Receptionist	Director of films or videos
Mediator	Insurance underwriter	Correctional officer	Salesperson
Bank teller	Medical Technician	Radio announcer	Graphics designer
Psychologist	Editor	Advertising copywriter	Real estate agent
Attorney	Scriptwriter	Business executive	Personnel director
Supervisor	Photographer	Flight attendant	Pharmacist

1.7

TO: _____

Your self-introduction speech was not graded, but the instructor noted that you had the
delivery problem(s) listed below. Try to make improvements during your next speech.

_____

_____

_____

TO: _____

Your self-introduction speech was not graded, but the instructor noted that you had the
delivery problem(s) listed below. Try to make improvements during your next speech.

_____

_____

_____

Chapter 2
Controlling Nervousness

Chapter Objectives and Resource Integrator

After studying this chapter, students should be able to:

Objectives	Resources
1. Describe the four kinds of fear that engender nervousness in speechmaking.	**In the Text:** • Page 25
2. Explain why controlled nervousness is beneficial for a public speaker.	**In the Text:** • Pages 25-26 • Key terms: adrenaline, positive nervousness
3. Apply techniques that can be used before and during a speech to control nervousness.	**In the Text:** • Pages 27-38 • Key terms: positive imagery **On Speeches DVD and connectpublicspeaking.com:** • Full Speeches #17: Ian Federgreen enters his speech, "Native American Crafts," with nervous tension, but he stays in control and is confident because he has prepared well and because he focuses his energies on reaching the audience. **On connectpublicspeaking.com:** • "Checklist for Preparing and Delivering a Speech"—Careful planning can minimize anxiety. This checklist can be used for both classroom and career speeches. **On Instructor's Resource DVD-ROM:** • "Lessons from the Movies" – An illustrated narrative based on the movie *Krippendorf's Tribe* shows a speaker whose lack of preparation fuels a crippling level of anxiety.

On connectpublicspeaking.com:

- Supplementary Readings:
  - "Speech Phobia" – This handout is designed for students who have an extreme degree of stage fright. For more information on the subject, see the section "Fear of Public Speaking" in the front part of this manual.

  - "The Curse of Perfectionism" – This essay is targeted at one of the most harmful notions that speakers can entertain: the idea that making a mistake is a terrible calamity.

  - Tips for Your Career: "As a Listener, Don't Be Afraid to Ask Questions" – This handout provides a helpful suggestion for the reticent listener.

  - Oral Interpretation of Literature – Reading literary passages dramatically can help students loosen up and break through their shell of self-consciousness. Some instructors use videotape for oral readings to give students a chance to analyze their voice and nonverbal behaviors.

- Interactive Exercise ("Is This Listener Sending You a Message?") deals with the problem of listeners who seem to have disapproving expressions.

Resources For Entire Chapter:

At End of Chapter:

- Summary
- Key Terms
- Review Questions
- Building Critical-Thinking Skills
- Building Teamwork Skills

On connectpublicspeaking.com:

- Practice test for chapter
- Glossary of terms
- Key-term flashcards
- Interactive exercise for chapter
- Building Internet Skills (used to be in book, now online)

Your Thoughts?

p. 26:   Many musicians make a distinction between "good nervousness" and "bad nervousness." What does this distinction mean? How does it apply to public speakers?

(Answers will vary). Good nervousness helps a musician to stay energetic and focused, while bad nervousness can cause errors. In public speaking, a moderate level of nervousness energizes a speaker, while an excessive level can interfere with effective delivery.

p. 31:   "It is folly for a speaker to focus on his or her personal appearance." Do you agree? Defend your answer.

(Answers will vary). Focusing on personal appearance is a distraction at a time when a speaker needs to focus on getting a message across to an audience.

Review Questions

Key to questions on p. 39 in the textbook:

1.   What are the four main reasons for speakers' nervousness?

     Fear of being stared at, fear of failure, fear of rejection, and fear of the unknown.

2.   Why are fear and nervousness beneficial to the public speaker?

     Fear and nervousness cause adrenaline to be released into the bloodstream, giving the speaker energy and vitality. This causes the speaker to be alert and dynamic rather than dull and listless.

3.   Why is delivering a speech from memory a bad method?

     A speaker who memorizes a speech usually sounds mechanical and dull, and he or she runs the risk of forgetting parts of the speech.

4.   Is shyness a liability for a speaker? Explain your answer.

     No. Many shy introverts succeed in show business and in the public speaking arena.

5.   How can a speaker reduce excessive tension before a speech?

     (1) Take a few deep breaths, inhaling and exhaling slowly; (2) do tension/release exercises; (3) mingle with listeners and chat with them to release tension from chest and larynx.

6. Does an audience detect most of a speaker's nervous symptoms? Explain your answer.

   No. Listeners are usually unaware of the physical symptoms that seem so severe to the speaker.

7. Why should you never call attention to your nervousness?

   If a speaker mentions some physical symptom of nervousness, such as trembling hands, the audience's attention is directed at the symptom instead of at the speech itself, and this can cause the symptom to worsen.

8. Explain the idea, "Think of communication, not performance."

   When speakers focus on getting their ideas across to the audience—rather than on performing well—their anxiety level comes down, and they become more conversational and effective.

9. Why should speakers not be upset when they see the solemn faces of their listeners?

   A peculiarity of human nature is that while most people have animated faces during a conversation, they wear blank masks when listening to a speech.

10. Why should a speaker act as if he or she is confident?

    Acting confident sometimes leads to actually being confident.

Building Critical-Thinking Skills

Key to questions on page 39 in the textbook:

1. In an experiment, psychologist Rowland Miller asked college students to do something embarrassing, such as singing *The Star Spangled Banner,* while classmates watched. Those students who reported a great degree of embarrassment thought that their classmates would consider them fools and like them less, but Miller found just the opposite: the classmates expressed greater regard for the easily embarrassed students after the performance than before. What lessons can a public speaker draw from this research?

   (Answers will vary.) When a speaker makes mistakes, the audience does not automatically lose respect for him or her. In fact, mistakes often cause an audience to have greater regard for the speaker. Therefore a speaker should not be obsessed with attaining perfection.

2. Imagine that while you are speaking to an audience, you notice that (a) everyone is very quiet, (b) a man in the front is rubbing his neck, and (c) a woman is looking in her purse. Using two columns on a piece of paper, give a negative interpretation of these events in the first column, and then give a positive interpretation in the adjacent column.

   (Answers will vary.) Some possible answers: (a) negative—everyone is bored and turned-off; positive—everyone is absorbed in the speech. (b) negative—the man is stiff and weary from a tedious speech, and is unconsciously signaling that the speaker is a "pain in the neck"; positive—the man is simply massaging a sore area. (c) negative— the woman has tuned the speaker out and is trying to find something to occupy her time;

positive—the woman is so excited about one of the speaker's ideas, she is looking for paper and pencil to make notes.

Activities

1. Assign skill builders at the end of the chapter in the text (Building Critical-Thinking Skills, and Building Teamwork Skills).

2. Have students conduct interviews—in person, on the telephone, or via e-mail—with persons who give speeches in their careers or in the community. Key questions to ask: Is nervousness a problem for you? How do you deal with it?

Objective Tests

Four ready-to-print tests for Chapter 2 (Forms A, B, C, D), and answer keys for all tests are provided in this instructor's manual. The four forms cover the same material, but are sufficiently different to permit one test to be used as the class test, and the others as makeup tests for absentees. Form A features true-false questions, Forms B and C have multiple-choice questions, while Form D is more difficult, requiring students to fill in missing words or phrases. Instructors may want to combine Form D with some of the essay questions listed below.

Essay & Discussion Questions

The following can be used as essay questions for tests or as stimuli for class discussions.

1. Discuss the four fears that accompany public speaking for most speakers.

2. Explain why a certain amount of nervousness is beneficial to a speaker.

3. "Public speakers usually look better than they feel." Explain what this means.

4. Why is it a good idea to pause a few moments before starting a speech?

George C. Scott's Fear and Trembling

Students find comfort in knowing of famous people who experience anxiety in public speaking. Here is an anecdote (that appeared in earlier editions of the text) that you might want to share with your students.

The late Hollywood actor George C. Scott, famous for his fierce, bulldog demeanor, played such gruff characters as General Patton, the dictator Mussolini, and Charles Dickens's Scrooge. Also known as a blunt, irascible person in real life, he admitted that his nose had been broken five times in brawls. When actress Maureen Stapleton once complained to her director, Mike Nichols, that she was afraid of her co-star Scott, Nichols replied: "Don't worry. The whole world's afraid of George Scott."

Yet, for all his intimidating ferocity, Scott confessed to a magazine reporter that "it's terrible when I have to make a speech. I really suffer. I'm a nervous wreck. When I get up, I shake all over like a dog shaking the water off." When Scott was asked why he was able to speak so effectively in films, he replied that while acting, he could "hide behind" whatever character he was playing, but in giving a speech "there's nothing to hide behind."

Chapter 3
Listening

Chapter Objectives and Resource Integrator

After studying this chapter, students should be able to:

Objectives	Resources
1. Explain the difference between hearing and listening.	**In the Text:** • Page 43 • Key terms: hearing, listening

2. Describe eight keys to effective listening.	**In the Text:**
	• Pages 43-49
	
	On Instructor's Resource DVD-ROM:
	• "Lessons from the Movies" – An illustrated narrative based on the movie *Kate and Leopold* shows a listener whose multi-tasking causes her to be embarrassed.
	
	• "Lessons from the Movies" – An illustrated narrative based on the movie *My Best Friend's Wedding* shows a listener whose cell phone conversation angers the rest of the audience.
	
	On connectpublicspeaking.com:
	• Supplementary Readings:
	
	  o "Listening Profile" – Students can analyze their own listening habits. The profile can be assigned either before or after the students read Chapter 3 in the text.
	
	  o "Notes" – This form, which corresponds with one of the notetaking systems suggested in Chapter 3 in the text, can be duplicated and distributed as merely a recommendation, or it can be assigned to be used with a particular speech.

3. Define three major responsibilities that listeners have toward speakers.	**In the Text:** • Pages 49-53 **On connectpublicspeaking.com:** • Supplementary Readings: "You Are a Rude Listener If …" – A takeoff on Comedian Jeff Foxworthy's "You Are a Redneck If…" is a good classroom discussion starter on rude behaviors among listeners. • Interactive Exercise ("How Should You React to a 'Weird' Speaker?") underscores the need to evaluate a speaker on his or her ideas – not on clothes or hairstyles.
4. Know how to give and receive evaluations of speeches.	**In the Text:** • Pages 53-55 **On connectpublicspeaking.com:** • Interactive Exercise ("How Should You React to a 'Weird' Speaker?") underscores the need to evaluate a speaker on his or her ideas – not on clothes and hairstyles. **In the Instructor's Manual (on Instructor's Resource DVD-ROM):** • **Evaluation Forms**—Ready-to-reproduce evaluation forms are located in the "Evaluation Forms" section of this manual.

Your Thoughts?

p. 45: Sometimes listening can be treated as passive receiving, while at other times it should be regarded as active participation. Give examples of when each approach is appropriate.

> *(Answers will vary). Listening to music while driving can be passive and appropriate, while listening to one's doctor explaining an illness requires active involvement.*

p. 49: Why do you think that the Chinese character for "listen" consists of pictures of the ear, the eye, and the heart?

> *(Answers will vary). Effective listening involves hearing sounds, seeing nonverbal clues, and responding with empathy and compassion.*

p. 50:   What do you think is the best way to solve the problem of electronic rudeness? Defend your answer.

(Answers will vary). Responses might include confronting rude behavior, asking listeners for cooperation, and requesting that obstinate individuals leave the room.

Review Questions

Key to questions on p. 56 in the textbook:

1. What is the difference between hearing and listening?

    Hearing occurs when the ears pick up sound waves being transmitted by a speaker, whereas listening involves making sense out of what is being transmitted.

2. Name at least four problems caused by ineffective listening in business.

    Answers may include: instructions misunderstood, equipment broken from improper use, productivity decreased, profits lowered, sales lost, feelings hurt, morale lowered, rumors started, and health harmed.

3. Why should a listener avoid faking attention?

    Fakery can cause a person to botch a personal or business encounter, and it can become a habit.

4. What is the difference between listening to easy material and listening to complex material?

    Listening to easy material is effortless, while listening to complex material requires concentration, alertness, and energy.

5. List at least two ways in which you can prepare yourself physically and intellectually to listen to a speech.

    Do research or background reading beforehand, get plenty of sleep the night before the speech, and exercise (such as taking a walk) right before going into the room.

6. The text lists four types of distractions—auditory, visual, physical, and mental. Give two examples of each type.

    (Answers will vary). Some possible answers: Auditory—a fly buzzing near one's ear, an air conditioner that creates a racket, people coughing or whispering; Visual—cryptic comments on the chalkboard, a nearby listener who is intriguing to look at, birds landing on a window sill; Physical—headaches or stuffy noses, seats that are too hard, and rooms that are too hot or cold; Mental—daydreams, worries, preoccupations.

7. What two speech elements should a listener examine analytically?

    Main ideas and support material.

8. List three advantages of taking notes during a speech.

    (1) Notetaking gives you a record of the speaker's most important points, (2) Notetaking sharpens and strengthens one's ability to listen analytically, and (3) Notetaking is a good way to keep attention on the speaker and not let one's mind wander.

9. When you are a listener, how can you encourage a speaker?

   Giving full attention, taking notes, leaning slightly forward instead of slouching back in a seat, looking directly at the speaker instead of at the floor, letting one's face show interest and animation, and nodding in agreement or smiling approval (when appropriate).

10. When you evaluate a speech, how should you handle both the positive and negative aspects that you observe?

   Give positive comments first so that the speaker is not deflated. When you give negative comments, couple them with positive alternatives.

Building Critical-Thinking Skills

Key to questions on p. 56 in the textbook:

1. Some psychologists characterize listening as "an act of love." To illustrate what this statement means, describe a real or imaginary conversation between two people (spouses, close friends, doctor/patient, etc.) who are truly listening to each other.

   (Answers will vary.)

2. Science writer Judith Stone wrote, "There are two ways to approach a subject that frightens you and makes you feel stupid: you can embrace it with humility and an open mind, or you can ridicule it mercilessly." Translate this idea into advice for listeners of speeches.

   When listeners encounter new or intimidating material, they should open their minds and examine it fairly, recognizing that it may contain valuable insights, rather than emotionally throwing up barriers and cutting off any chance of a fair appraisal.

Activities

1. Assign skill builders at the end of the chapter in the text (Building Critical-Thinking Skills, and Building Teamwork Skills).

2. Here is a listening game that can be played with the class at the beginning of a discussion on listening: Make up a brief story or a news item; write it down (so that you will have a record of exactly what you started off with); say it softly to one student; he or she then repeats it softly to the next student, and so on around the class. The rules of the game: (1) Each person should repeat the message in a low voice so that only the listener can hear. (2) No discussion is allowed; the listener should not ask the deliverer of the news to repeat any part of the message unless he or she failed to hear. When the story has been relayed to all students, ask the last student to write down what he or she heard. Then, for the benefit of the entire class, discuss what you started off with as contrasted with what the last student heard. The results are often amusing, and they underline a key point: most people do not listen well.

One year I used the following news item: "There was a head-on, two-car collision near Black Mountain this morning. Three people were killed and four were injured. The injured were taken to the emergency room at Memorial Mission Hospital." While a few classes ended up with a reasonable approximation of the original, some were wildly off the mark:

- "There was a car wreck in Black Mountain. Eight people died."

- "A drunk man was taken to the hospital."

- "There is some kind of accident somewhere and they are taking them to the hospital."

- "Wreck in Hickory. 3 people taken to Broughton."

- "There's an army on a mission on a hill. There were 4 injured and 2 killed and they had to take them to Mission Hospital."

The larger the class, the more distorted the message.

Only one class conveyed the message accurately; it was a class made up entirely of paramedics. This was reassuring, because it is their business to hear accident messages correctly.

Objective Tests

Four ready-to-print tests for Chapter 3 (Forms A, B, C, D), and answer keys for all tests are provided in this instructor's manual. The four forms cover the same material, but are sufficiently different to permit one test to be used as the class test, and the others as makeup tests for absentees. Form A features true-false questions, Forms B and C have multiple-choice questions, while Form D is more difficult, requiring students to fill in missing words or phrases. Instructors may want to combine Form D with some of the essay questions listed below.

Essay & Discussion Questions

The following can be used as essay questions for tests or as stimuli for class discussions.

1. Explain the difference between hearing and listening.

2. How can a person prepare physically and intellectually for listening?

3. Discuss the kinds of distractions that can hinder listening and how a listener can overcome them.

4. Discuss two reasons why it is a good idea for a listener to take notes during a speech.

5. Discuss the ways in which a listener can provide encouragement to a speaker during a speech.

6. How does a listener often profit from giving encouragement to a speaker?

7. How can a listener find value in a boring, seemingly worthless speech?

Chapter 4
Reaching the Audience

Chapter Objectives and Resource Integrator

After studying this chapter, students should be able to:

Objectives	Resources
1. Describe the difference between a speaker who is audience-centered and one who is not.	**In the Text:** • Pages 60-61 • Key term: audience-centered speaker **On Speeches DVD and on connectpublicspeaking.com:** • Full Speech #14 ("Bicycle Helmets I – Persuasive Speech That Needs Improvement") shows a speaker who is not audience-centered. He fails to connect with his listeners, and seems almost contemptuous of them. • Full Speech #15 ("Bicycle Helmets II – Improved Version") shows the same speaker as in Speech 14, but this time he is audience-centered. He wants his listeners to understand and accept his proposals.
2. Define audience analysis and audience adaptation and state why they are important.	**In the Text:** • Page 61 • Key terms: audience analysis, adaptation, customize **On Speeches DVD and on connectpublicspeaking.com:** • Video Clip 4.1 shows a speaker who does a good job of finding out in advance what his audience knows and doesn't know. • Video Clip 4.2 ("Helping Listeners Who Speak English as a Second Language") shows a speaker who uses a visual aid to make sure that all listeners understand a basic term. • Full Speech #5 ("Animal Helpers I – Informative Speech That Needs Improvement") shows a speaker who has not analyzed her audience. She fails to offer listeners new and interesting material.

	• Full Speech #6 ("Animal Helpers II – Improved Version") shows the same speaker as in Speech 5, but this time she has analyzed what her listeners know and don't know, and she has adapted her speech to their level of knowledge. She provides meaningful content.
	On Instructor's Resource DVD-ROM:
	• "Lessons from the Movies" – An illustrated narrative based on the movie *Mona Lisa Smile* shows a speaker who has a disastrous speaking experience because she failed to analyze her listeners.
	On connectpublicspeaking.com:
	• Supplementary Readings:
	○ "Checklist for Audience and Occasion" – This checklist not only provides a review of Chapter 4, but it also gives students a handy guide to use in future speeches in their careers. You may want to suggest that they keep a personal file on public speaking, into which they can put such items as this checklist.
	○ **Tips for Your Career:** "Know What Listeners Like and Dislike" — This handout can serve as a handy reminder of expectations that listeners have.
3. Use interviews and surveys to gain information about an audience in advance.	**In the Text:**
	• Pages 62-64
	On Speeches DVD and on connectpublicspeaking.com:
	• Full Speech #15 ("Bicycle Helmets II – Improved Version") shows a speaker who uses an audience questionnaire in preparing his speech and then refers to the results in the speech itself.
	In the Instructor's Manual (on Instructor's Resource DVD-ROM):
	• **Sheet 4.1, Audience Analysis Form**—This form will help students with their audience analyses. It can easily be used as an activity for the entire class: Pass out the sheets and tell the students not to write their names on them. Have them fill out the sheets; then you take them up and redistribute them at random. Go through each item, asking for a show of hands according to the answers marked on the paper in front of them. For example, "On number 7, how many have answer "a"—lower class—marked on the paper in front of you?" (Since the students are raising their hands on someone else's marks, their privacy and anonymity are

	not invaded.) As students raise their hands, you count and record the results on a master copy. After all the answers have been tabulated, you can announce the results to the class (for example, "We have 6 Democrats, 7 Republicans, and 12 independents"). As you announce the results, the students should write them down on their sheets. The virtue of this exercise is that the class gets a quick analysis of audience demographics and attitudes—and has fun in the process. **Suggestion:** Notice that page 2 of Sheet 4.1 has space for additional issues to be filled in. You can get input from students on this. If one student, say, is planning to talk on the 55-mile-per-hour speed limit, she can get some valuable advance information if you ask the class to fill in "The 55-mile-per-hour speed limit should be set for all interstate highways." • **Sheet 4.2, Sample Questionnaire**—This gives students a sample of the kind of questionnaire that they can write and distribute in order to get detailed information from their audience on the speaker's topic. • **Sheet 4.3, Commentary on Sample Questionnaire**—These remarks give an explanation of Sheet 4.2.
4. Explain how speakers can be responsive to diverse audiences.	**In the Text:** • Pages 65-71 • Key terms: taboo, ethnocentrism, sexist language **On Speeches DVD and on connectpublicspeaking.com:** • Video Clip 4.2 ("Helping Listeners Who Speak English as a Second Language") shows a speaker who uses a visual aid to make sure that all listeners understand a basic term. • Full Speech #8 ("Indian Weddings") is a speech by Preeti Vilkhu, who had recently married a man chosen by her parents. The speech demonstrates sensitivity to cultural differences (she shows respect for American views that are contrary to Indian customs). **On connectpublicspeaking.com:** • Supplementary Readings: "Tips for ESL Students" — Suggestions for students who speak English as a second language. • Interactive Exercise – "Which Nonverbal Signals Are Universal?"
5. Describe how speakers can adapt to varying	**In the Text:** • Pages 71-75

levels of audience knowledge, attitudes, interest, and needs and desires.	• Key term: attitude **On Speeches DVD and on connectpublicspeaking.com:** • Video Clip 4.2 ("Helping Listeners Who Speak English as a Second Language") shows a speaker who uses a visual aid to make sure that all listeners understand a basic term.
6. Explain how speakers should adapt to the occasion (time limit, purpose, and size of audience).	**In the Text:** • Pages 75-76 **On Speeches DVD and on connectpublicspeaking.com:** • Full Speech #2 – In "The Four-Day Work Week," Felipe Dieppa could have spoken at much greater length, but he stays within his time limits and ends up with an effective speech that would have been diminished by great length.
7. Describe how a speaker can adapt to the audience during a speech.	**In the Text:** • Pages 77-78

Resources For Entire Chapter:

At End of Chapter:

- Summary
- Key Terms
- Review Questions
- Building Critical-Thinking Skills
- Building Teamwork Skills

On Speeches DVD and on connectpublicspeaking.com:

- Video Clip 4.1 ("Analyzing the Audience") shows a speaker who does a good job of finding out in advance what his audience knows and doesn't know.
- Video Clip 4.2 ("Helping Listeners Who Speak English as a Second Language") shows a speaker who uses a visual aid to make sure that all listeners understand a basic term.

On connectpublicspeaking.com:

- Interactive exercise for chapter
- Practice test for chapter
- Checklist (for Preparing and Delivering a Speech)
- Glossary of terms
- Key-term flashcards
- Building Internet Skills (used to be in book, now online)

On Instructor's Resource DVD-ROM:

- PowerPoint: Chapter Highlights – A PowerPoint program gives highlights of each chapter and includes some video clips. **(NOTE: Many of the PowerPoint slides have no text and require the explanation given in the accompanying script.)**

- Tests – Ready-made chapter tests and a computerized test bank are provided.

- "Lessons from the Movies" – An illustrated narrative based on the movie *Mona Lisa Smile* shows a speaker who has a disastrous speaking experience because she failed to analyze her listeners.

Your Thoughts?

p. 61:   For a speech on your favorite musician, what would you do to analyze your audience in advance?

> *(Answers will vary). Conduct interviews with listeners or distribute a questionnaire. Do listeners know who the musician is? Do they like his or her music? Do they already know his or her life story and musical techniques?*

p. 65:   A 65-year-old man is preparing a speech to high school students on the need to save money throughout one's life. What advice would you give him to enhance his chances of persuading his youthful audience?

(Answers will vary). Give tips that relate to listeners' everyday lives. Use your own experience whenever it illustrates an important point. Don't talk down to the listeners as if they were a bunch of children.

p. 76:   While you are waiting to give a speech, you discover that the person speaking just before you is covering the same topic. When you stand up, what would you do and say?

(Answers will vary). Acknowledge the situation to the audience. Use a light touch – try not to become angry or defensive. If your approach differs from that of the preceding speaker, tell the audience that you will discuss points of agreement and disagreement. If your speech is more or less the same as the preceding one, you could explain the situation to the audience and (1) conduct a question-and-answer period, or (2) announce that you will be happy to return on another date to speak on another topic.

Review Questions

Key to questions on p. 79 in the textbook:

1.   What is an audience-centered speaker?

An audience-centered speaker strives to understand the listeners so that he or she can meet their needs and interests.

2.   What is meant by audience analysis and adaptation?

Analysis means finding out exactly who the listeners are and what they know. Adaptation means shaping a speech to satisfy the listeners' particular needs and interests.

3.   How can a speaker get advance information about an audience?

Interview the program director, talk to a few prospective listeners, or send a questionnaire to the future audience.

4.   What are taboos, and why are they an important concern for a speaker?

Taboos are prohibitions in a culture; violating them can offend an audience.

5.   Do international audiences usually prefer a presentation that is humorous and informal, or one that is serious and formal? Explain your answer.

International audiences usually prefer a serious, formal tone. An informal approach is often viewed as frivolous and disrespectful.

6.   What is ethnocentrism?

The belief that one's own cultural group is superior to other groups.

7. Who is the best source of information about the needs of listeners with disabilities, and why?

   The disabled listener—because he or she knows best what accommodations need to be made.

8. What are the three elements of audience psychology that should be analyzed?

   Interest level, attitudes, and needs and desires.

9. What guidelines should be followed for a speech to an audience that knows little or nothing about your topic?

   (1) Limit the number of new ideas, (2) If possible, use visual aids, (3) Use down-to-earth language, (4) Repeat key ideas, and (5) Give vivid examples.

10. What aspects of the speech occasion should you examine before giving your talk?

    Time limit, purpose of the occasion, other events on the program, and number of people in the audience.

Building Critical-Thinking Skills

Key to questions on p. 79 in the textbook:

1. Several books provide ready-made speeches that readers are welcome to use as their own. Aside from the dishonesty involved, why would using such speeches be a mistake?

   A speech should be customized for each audience. Giving all audiences the same speech would be like a physician giving all patients the same medication.

2. At what time of day are you normally least alert? What conditions in a room (such as temperature and noise) cause you to be inattentive? Now imagine that you are a listener in these circumstances. What would a speaker need to do to keep you awake and engaged?

   (Answers will vary.)

Activities

1. Assign skill builders at the end of the chapter in the text (Building Critical-Thinking Skills, and Building Teamwork Skills).

2. Have students bring magazine or newspaper advertisements to class. Divide the class into groups to discuss the ads, using questions such as these: What audiences are being targeted? What appeals are being used? Are the appeals effective? What ideas or responses are the advertisers trying to elicit?

3. Assign students to write a paper or give an oral report analyzing a speaker (such as a teacher or minister) on audience adaptation. Does the speaker show an awareness of the audience's needs and interests? How does the speaker adapt his or her remarks to meet those needs and interests?

Objective Tests

Four ready-to-print tests for Chapter 4 (Forms A, B, C, D), and answer keys for all tests are provided in this instructor's manual. The four forms cover the same material, but are sufficiently different to permit one test to be used as the class test, and the others as makeup tests for absentees. Form A features true-false questions, Forms B and C have multiple-choice questions, while Form D is more difficult, requiring students to fill in missing words or phrases. Instructors may want to combine Form D with some of the essay questions listed below.

Essay & Discussion Questions

The following can be used as essay questions for tests or as stimuli for class discussions.

1. What is meant by audience analysis and adaptation?

2. Discuss diversity variables in audience analysis and why they are important for the speaker to know and act upon.

3. Why is it important for speakers to stay within their time limits?

4. What does the speaker need to know about the occasion for the speech?

5. How can the speaker get information about the audience in advance?

6. How can a speaker find out what accommodations need to be made for listeners with disabilities?

7. How should a speaker relate to listeners with mobility impairments? with visual disabilities? with hearing disabilities?

Audience Analysis Form

Directions: Circle the appropriate answers.

Part I. Personal Inventory

1. My age:
    a. under 18
    b. 18-25
    c. 26-35
    d. over 35

2. Sex:
    a. male
    b. female

3. Marital status:
    a. single
    b. married
    c. separated
    d. divorced
    e. widowed

4. I have:
    a. no children
    b. one child
    c. more than one child

5. Religious preference:
    a. Roman Catholic
    b. Eastern Orthodox
    c. Protestant
    d. Jewish
    e. Muslim
    f. Buddhist
    g. a religious group not recognized by the major faiths
    h. agnostic ("There may be a God but we can't know for sure")
    i. atheist ("There is no God")
    j. other

6. I identify myself as:
    a. Democrat
    b. Republican
    c. independent
    d. supporter of a third party
    e. non-political

7. When I was growing up, my family's income was in the following category:
    a. lower class
    b. lower middle class
    c. middle class
    d. upper middle class
    e. upper class

8. My financial support mainly comes from:
    a. parents
    b. spouse
    c. full-time job
    d. part-time job
    e. summer work
    f. savings
    g. scholarship
    h. loans
    i. veterans' benefits

Part II. Attitude Survey

Circle "A" if you tend to agree with the statement, "D" if you tend to disagree, and "U" if you're undecided or unsure.

A D U   1. Cloning of human beings should be permitted.

A D U   2. The death penalty should be mandatory for convicted murderers.

A D U   3. Sending astronauts to explore Mars should be a top priority of our nation.

A D U   4. Surgeons should be required to warn their patients of possible side effects, including death, before cosmetic surgery is performed.

A D U   5. The age for legally purchasing alcohol should be 18 in all states.

A D U   6. The sale of marijuana should be legalized.

A D U   7. A national, universal health-insurance program should be instituted so that all Americans will be guaranteed health care whenever they need it.

A D U   8. Automatic weapons such as machine guns should be outlawed.

A D U   9. We should require registration of all firearms.

A D U   10. Pornography in books and films should be censored.

Additional issues (to be filled in):

A D U   11. _____

A D U   12. _____

A D U   13. _____

A D U   14. _____

A D U   15. _____

Sample Questionnaire

If you wish to determine the listeners' views and attitudes about a particular subject, you can prepare a questionnaire and distribute it to them in advance. Below is a sample of a questionnaire that could be used in preparation for a speech that argues against the death penalty in the United States:

1.   Do you favor the death penalty for convicted murderers?
      a. yes
      b. no
      c. undecided

2.   Do you favor the death penalty for crimes other than murder?
      a. no
      b. yes
      c. undecided

3.   If you answered yes for #2, what crimes would warrant the death penalty? (You may circle more than one.)
      a. rape
      b. kidnapping
      c. attempted assassination of a President
      d. skyjacking
      e. other: _____

4.   What is your religious preference:
      a. Roman Catholic
      b. Eastern Orthodox
      c. Protestant
      d. Jewish
      e. Muslim
      f. Buddhist
      g. a religious group not recognized by the major faiths
      h. agnostic ("There may be a God but we can't know for sure")
      i. atheist ("There is no God")
      j. other: _____

5.   Do you agree or disagree with the following statement: "If the death penalty were carried out frequently throughout the United States, the murder rate in this country would go down."
      ___Strongly Agree
      ___Mildly Agree
      ___Undecided
      ___Mildly Disagree
      ___Strongly Disagree

6.   If the death penalty is not used in a particular state, what would be the best alternative punishment?

Commentary on Sample Questionnaire (Handout 4.2)

Question #1: By knowing in advance where the audience stands, you can plan your strategy accordingly.

Question #2: If none of the listeners want the death penalty for crimes other than murder, there is no reason for you to discuss other crimes.

Question #3: If some listeners want the death penalty for rape, you can try to convince them that this would be a mistake, since a rapist would be tempted to commit murder to eliminate a "witness" to a capital crime.

Question #4: If most of the listeners are members of religious groups, you might want to use quotations from religious writings or authorities to bolster your arguments.

Question #5: One of the strongest arguments for the death penalty is that it would reduce the number of murders. If the audience strongly supports this view, you must try to refute it if you hope to change your listeners' minds.

Question #6: In this open-ended question, you are probing to see how receptive the listeners will be to suggestions about alternatives to the death penalty.

Chapter 5
Selecting Topic, Purpose & Central Idea

Chapter Objectives and Resource Integrator

After studying this chapter, students should be able to:

Objectives	Resources

1. Select appropriate and interesting speech topics.	**In the Text:**
	• Pages 83-88
	• Key term: brainstorming
	
	On Speeches DVD and on connectpublicspeaking.com:
	• Video Clip 5.1 shows a speaker who chooses a topic that he had always wanted to investigate.
	
	• Full Speech #8: Preeti Vilkhu ("Indian Weddings") illustrates a speaker who chooses a topic from her own experience.
	
	• Full Speech #7 ("Humanoid Robots") demonstrates that a speaker can choose a topic from current events and then fully research it.
	
	On connectpublicspeaking.com:
	• Interactive Exercises:
	  o Personal Inventory—This worksheet is the same as the one illustrated and explained in Chapter 5 of the text. It can be assigned as an out-of-class assignment and then you can go over it, writing comments in the margins on which items look like promising speech topics. I like to keep the inventories to use with those students who can't think of speech topics. One student told me there was nothing interesting in his life, but when I looked at his Inventory, I discovered that he had once been trapped outdoors in a blizzard. I suggested that this could lead to several good topics; he ended up giving a speech on winter survival skills—one of the best student speeches of the year.
	
	  o Brainstorming Guide—This worksheet is the same as the one illustrated and explained in Chapter 5 of the text. It can be used in class or assigned as out-of-class work.

	o Possible Topics—Students can print this page out, and keep it in their notebooks and jot down possible topics as they occur to them while reading the text and listening to class lectures or discussions.
	• Topic Helper—Students can browse through hundreds of sample topics for demonstration, informative, and persuasive speeches.
	• Outline Tutor—Students can fill in the planning stages of an outline: General Purpose, Specific Purpose, and Central Idea.
2. Specify the general purpose of a speech.	**In the Text:** • Pages 88-89 • Key term: general purpose **On Speeches DVD and on connectpublicspeaking.com:** • Full Speech videos include several informative speeches and several persuasive speeches. **On connectpublicspeaking.com:** • **Checklist for Preparing and Delivering a Speech**—This checklist can be used for both classroom and career speeches.

3. Develop a clear, concise specific purpose statement for every speech he or she prepares.	**In the Text:**
	
	• Pages 89-91
	• Key terms: specific purpose, infinitive
	
	On connectpublicspeaking.com:
	
	• Interactive Exercises:
	  o "What's Wrong With These Statements?" – This exercise gives students practice in spotting incorrectly worded specific purpose statements.
	
	  o Developing Topics for Informative Speeches—This worksheet will help students learn how to formulate purpose statements and central ideas for informative speeches.
	
	  o Developing Topics for Persuasive Speeches—This worksheet will help students learn how to formulate purpose statements and central ideas for persuasive speeches.
	
	  o Specific Purpose Statements—This worksheet gives practice in spotting mistakes in specific purpose statements.

4. Develop a clear, coherent central idea for every speech he or she prepares.	**In the Text:**
	
	• Pages 91-95
	• Key term: central idea
	
	On Speeches DVD and on connectpublicspeaking.com:
	
	• Video Clip 5.2 shows a speaker who conveys the central idea of a speech clearly and effectively.
	
	• Full Speech #5 ("Animal Helpers I – Informative Speech That Needs Improvement") shows a speech that lacks focus.
	
	• Full Speech #6 ("Animal Helpers II – Improved Version") shows the same speaker as in Speech 5, but this time she has brought her material into focus by devising an effective central idea.
	
	On connectpublicspeaking.com:
	
	• Interactive Exercises:
	  o Exercise on Topic, Purposes, and Central Idea – This worksheet can be used to help students distinguish between topic, purposes, and central idea.
	
	  o Desired Responses—Some instructors go one step beyond the specific purpose statement and the central idea by requiring students to formulate the responses they desire from their audience.

5. Understand how the specific purpose and the central idea fit into the overall design of a speech.	**In the Text:** • Pages 95-96

At End of Chapter:

- Summary
- Key Terms
- Review Questions
- Building Critical-Thinking Skills
- Building Teamwork Skills

On Speeches DVD and on connectpublicspeaking.com:

- Video Clip 5.1 shows a speaker who chooses a topic that he had always wanted to investigate.
- Video Clip 5.2 shows a speaker who conveys the central idea of a speech clearly and effectively.

On connectpublicspeaking.com:

- Interactive exercise for chapter
- Practice test for chapter
- Checklist (for Preparing and Delivering a Speech)
- Glossary of terms
- Key-term flashcards
- Building Internet Skills (used to be in book, now online)

On Instructor's Resource DVD-ROM:

- PowerPoint: Chapter Highlights – A PowerPoint program gives highlights of each chapter and includes some video clips. **(NOTE: Many of the PowerPoint slides have no text and require the explanation given in the accompanying script.)**
- Tests – Ready-made chapter tests and a computerized test bank are provided.

Your Thoughts?

p. 87:   Regarding the topic "investing in the stock market," how could you make it interesting to an audience of college students? How could you make it boring?

(Answers will vary). To make the topic interesting, show listeners how they can make money. To make the topic boring, use technical terms to describe arcane aspects of investments.

p. 89:   The best way to write a love letter, the Swiss-French philosopher Jean Jacques Rousseau said, is to begin without knowing what you are going to say. This may be a good formula for a love letter, but would it be wise for speechmaking? Explain your answer.

(Answers will vary). The approach would be wrong for speechmaking. It would cause the speaker to stumble, ramble, repeat information, confuse the audience, and exceed the time limit.

p. 90:   "Telling about my first cruise vacation." How could you improve this statement of a specific purpose?

The statement needs a general purpose, an infinitive, and a more precise target. For example: To inform my listeners of the pros and cons of a cruise vacation.

Review Questions

Key to questions on p. 97 in the textbook:

1. When a speaker is enthusiastic about his or her ideas, how do listeners usually react?

    They often become enthusiastic because enthusiasm is contagious.

2. How does brainstorming work?

    You write down words as they flow in your mind, without making any effort to censor, edit, or evaluate them. Then you go back and analyze the list for possible topics.

3. What are the characteristics of speeches that listeners find boring?

    Possible answers: They cover material the audience already knows; they belabor the obvious; they promote beliefs that listeners already possess; they offer nothing new and worthwhile.

4. List three general purposes for speeches.

    Answers might include any of the following: to inform, to persuade, to entertain, to inspire, to stimulate, to introduce, to create goodwill.

5. Are jokes required for an entertaining speech? Explain your answer.

    No. An entertaining speech can amuse or divert listeners with anecdotes, quotations, examples, and descriptions.

6. List the six criteria discussed in this chapter for writing a specific purpose statement.

    (1) Begin the statement with an infinitive, (2) Include a reference to your audience, (3) Limit the statement to one major idea, (4) Make your statement as precise as possible, (5) Make sure you can achieve your objective in the time allotted, and (6) Don't be too technical.

7. What is the central idea of a speech?

    The central idea is the basic message of a speech expressed in one sentence.

8. What is the difference between the specific purpose and the central idea?

    The specific purpose is written from the speaker's point of view—it's what he or she sets out to accomplish. The central idea is written from the listeners' point of view—it's the message they should go away with.

9. Give an example of an infinitive.

    (Answers will vary.) Examples: To hope, to jump, to sympathize.

10. What are hidden purposes, and how should you handle them?

    Hidden purposes are unstated objectives that a speaker must be aware of so that he or she does not let them undermine the stated purpose of a speech.

Key to questions on p. 97 in the textbook:

1. Narrow down the following broad subjects to specific, manageable topics:
    a. Outdoor recreation
    b. Musical groups
    c. Illegal drugs
    d. Saving money
    e. Cloning

    (Answers will vary.)

2. All but one of these specific purpose statements are either inappropriate for a brief classroom speech or they are incorrectly written. Name the good one, and rewrite the bad ones so that they conform to the guidelines in this chapter
    a. To inform my audience of the basics of quantum inelastic scattering and photodissociation code
    b. To inform my listeners about creativity on the job, getting raises, and being an effective manager
    c. To explain to my audience how to perform basic yoga exercises
    d. How persons with disabilities can fight back against job discrimination
    e. Immigration since 1800
    f. To persuade my audience to be careful

    a. *too technical—a less arcane objective should be chosen*
    b. *too many topics for a brief speech*
    c. *appropriate—no change needed*
    d. *lacks an infinitive and a reference to the audience*
    e. *a topic that is too broad—lacks a focus, an infinitive, and a reference to the audience*
    f. *too vague—needs a clear, precise target*

Activities

1. Assign skill builders at the end of the chapter in the text (Building Critical-Thinking Skills, and Building Teamwork Skills).

2. Have students write down five topics drawn from their own background. Each student's paper is then circulated among classmates, who check off items in which they are most interested. (A numbering system indicating degree of interest—1 for low and 5 for high—could be used as an alternative to checks.) When students get their papers back, they get an idea of what topics are interesting to the classroom audience and what topics are not interesting.

3. Have students analyze a speech reprinted on the Internet. They should write down the speaker's general purpose, specific purpose, and central idea. (Students will need to be reminded that these items are not always stated explicitly; in other words, in some cases students will need to formulate statements that reflect what the speaker seemed to be saying.)

Objective Tests

Four ready-to-print tests for Chapter 5 (Forms A, B, C, D), and answer keys for all tests are provided in this instructor's manual. The four forms cover the same material, but are sufficiently different to permit one test to be used as the class test, and the others as makeup tests for absentees. Form A features true-false questions, Forms B and C have multiple-choice questions, while Form D is more difficult, requiring students to fill in missing words or phrases. Instructors may want to combine Form D with some of the essay questions listed below.

Essay & Discussion Questions

The following can be used as essay questions for tests or as stimuli for class discussions.

1. Discuss three ways in which a speaker can go about finding a speech topic.

2. What is brainstorming? Give a brief example.

3. What is the goal of the informative speech? Give an example of a topic for an informative speech.

4. What is the goal of the persuasive speech? Give an example of a topic for a persuasive speech.

5. What is the difference between the specific purpose statement and the central idea? Illustrate your answer by writing a specific purpose statement and a central idea for a speech.

Chapter 6
Finding Information

Chapter Objectives and Resource Integrator

After studying this chapter, students should be able to:

Objectives	Resources
1. Develop research strategies for finding materials quickly and efficiently.	**In the Text:** • Pages 100-102 **On connectpublicspeaking.com:** • Interactive Exercise o "What Are the Best Strategies for Finding Information?" – A critical-thinking exercise demonstrating how different situations require different research strategies.

2. Understand why the Internet is sometimes a less desirable source than traditional library materials.	**In the Text:**
	
	• Pages 102-103
	
	On connectpublicspeaking.com:
	
	Interactive Exercise
	   o Finding Information on the Internet – Provides Internet search practice.
	
	   o "What Are the Best Strategies for Finding Information?" – A critical-thinking exercise demonstrating how different situations require different research strategies.

3. Use electronic search techniques for finding books, articles, and Web sites.	**In the Text:** • Pages 103-104; 119-121 • Key terms: keyword

4. Take advantage of the services and materials offered by librarians and libraries.	**In the Text:**
	
	• Pages 104-105; 118-121
	• Key terms: citation, abstract, full text, reference librarian
	
	On Speeches DVD and on connectpublicspeaking.com:
	
	• Video Clip 6.1 shows a speaker who uses books as a source for his speech.
	
	On connectpublicspeaking.com:
	
	• Supplementary Readings
	  o Library Classification Systems—This handout can help students learn the classification scheme of any library they visit. (You might mention that most college libraries use the Library of Congress system, while many public libraries use the Dewey system.)
	
	• Interactive Exercises
	  o Library Assignment—This exercise gives students practice in using the library catalog, periodicals indexes, and the Internet.
	
	  o Finding Articles—This exercise gives students practice in using indexes to periodicals.
	
	  o Library Investigation—This assignment compels students to investigate the campus library and learn what is has to offer.
	
	In the Instructor's Manual (on Instructor's Resource DVD-ROM):
	
	• Sheet 6.1, Research Assignment—If students are permitted to research and speak on a topic that is beyond the instructor's realm of expertise, it is difficult for the instructor to evaluate the student's research and speech. The project outlined in Sheet 6.4 points students toward research in an area that many speech instructors are competent to evaluate. Each instructor can decide how many sources to require, the time limit for the speech, and other rules.

5. Locate useful materials on the Internet.	**In the Text:** • Pages 105-198; 118-121 • Key terms: search engine, keyword, expert site, discussion forum, subject directory **On connectpublicspeaking.com:** Interactive Exercise o Finding Information on the Internet – Provides Internet search practice.

	○ "What Are the Best Strategies for Finding Information?" – A critical-thinking exercise to demonstrate how different situations require different research strategies.
6. Recognize the value of deriving material from experiences and investigations.	**In the Text:** • Page 108 **On Speeches DVD and on connectpublicspeaking.com:** • Full Speech #8 ("Indian Weddings") shows a speaker who draws on her personal experiences (she had recently married a man chosen by her parents).
7. Conduct effective interviews with experts.	**In the Text:** • Pages 108-112 • Key terms: closed question, open question, clarifying question, follow-up question, field research **On Speeches DVD and on connectpublicspeaking.com:** • Video Clip 6.2 shows a speaker who conducts an e-mail survey to gather key information for his speech. • Full Speech #15 ("Bicycle Helmets II") shows a speaker who based some of his information on a personal interview with the director of the emergency department at a hospital.
8. Take notes with precision, care, and thoroughness.	**In the Text:** • Pages 112-115 **On connectpublicspeaking.com:** • Bibliography Formats—For the sake of convenience, the same illustrations of MLA and APA style formats that are printed in the chapter are also included on the Web site.

Resources For Entire Chapter:

At End of Chapter:

- Summary
- Key Terms
- Review Questions
- Building Critical-Thinking Skills
- Building Teamwork Skills

On Speeches DVD and on connectpublicspeaking.com:

- Video Clip 6.1 shows a speaker who uses books as a source for his speech.
- Video Clip 6.2 shows a speaker who conducts an e-mail survey to gather key information for his speech.
- Full Speech #5 ("Animal Helpers I – Informative Speech That Needs Improvement") illustrates the lamentable results of failing to do adequate research.
- Full Speech #6 ("Animal Helpers II – Improved Version") shows the value of using solid research to make a speech credible and interesting.
- Full Speech #16 ("The Deadliest Natural Disaster") shows a speaker who has made good use of research in preparing a speech.

On connectpublicspeaking.com:

- Bibliography Formats—For the sake of convenience, the same illustrations of MLA and APA style formats that are printed in the chapter are also included on connectpublicspeaking.com.
- Interactive exercise for chapter
- Practice test for chapter
- Checklist (for Preparing and Delivering a Speech)
- Glossary of terms
- Key-term flashcards
- Building Internet Skills (used to be in book, now online)

On Instructor's Resource DVD-ROM:

- PowerPoint: Chapter Highlights – A PowerPoint program gives highlights of each chapter and includes some video clips. (NOTE: Many of the PowerPoint slides have no text and require the explanation given in the accompanying script.)
- Tests – Ready-made chapter tests and a computerized test bank are provided.

Your Thoughts?

p. 101:   Some speakers spend a large portion of their speech on fascinating material they found in their research, but unfortunately the material does not relate directly to their key ideas. Why do they make this mistake, and how can they avoid it?

(Answers will vary). Such speakers fail to stay focused on their specific purpose. They are easily dazzled and distracted by interesting, but irrelevant information. They can avoid this

mistake by keeping their specific purpose statement in front of them during research and making sure they don't wander from it.

p. 108:   Imagine a speech on investing in the stock market, given by a speaker who has been successful with her own investments. Should she speak only from her own experience? Defend your answer.

(Answers will vary). She can spend much of her speech talking of her own experiences, but she would need to show how her situation fits into the overall picture of investing. Is she typical? Would listeners profit by following her example?

p. 112:   How do you save key information? What are the pros and cons of your method?

(Answers will vary – students should see the value of a system that permits easy retrieval).

Review Questions

Key to questions on p. 117 in the textbook:

1. What role should your specific purpose statement play in the research stage of preparation?

    It should be written before research is begun, and it should help you stay focused on precisely what you are searching for.

2. What is interlibrary loan and how can it help you?

    Interlibrary loan permits a library to order books and photocopies of magazine articles from other libraries. If you can't get a book or magazine article in your own library, you might be able to order it through interlibrary loan.

3. In what ways are traditional library resources superior to the Internet?

    Relatively few reference works, books, and specialized magazines are on the Internet; these resources give greater depth and elaboration than one can usually find on the Internet.

4. Which Internet search option returns results in order of relevance, with the most relevant at the top?

    Search engine

5. Which Internet search option begins with broad subject areas that are subdivided into smaller categories?

    Subject directory

6. Which kinds of blogs are most useful to a researcher?

    The most useful blogs are those that give the latest news in a particular field and provide links to other sources.

7. Why should most of your research be done *before* you call someone for an interview?

Doing research in advance will enable you to ask intelligent questions during the interview, get clarification of confusing issues, and find information that you couldn't find in library research.

8. What are the advantages and disadvantages of using a video- or audio-tape recorder in an interview?

   Advantages: You get a permanent record of what the person actually said—you need not worry about forgetting key points or misquoting the source.

   Disadvantages: There is the danger of mechanical malfunction, and you have to spend a lot of time afterwards analyzing and transcribing information from the tape.

9. What steps should you take after an interview is completed?

   Expand your notes while the interview is fresh in your mind and then evaluate them to see if you need additional help.

10. In your research, why should you take more notes than you probably will need?

    It is better to have too much raw material than not enough. You can disregard what is not needed.

Building Critical-Thinking Skills

Key to questions on p. 118 in the textbook:

1. Any person of any age can host a Web site on any subject and include anything he or she desires. From the viewpoint of a researcher, what are the advantages and disadvantages of this wide-open system?

   Advantages: The open, democratic nature of the web permits publication of a wide range of diverse viewpoints; a person or organization does not require great wealth to disseminate a message.

   Disadvantages: On some subjects, a researcher is faced with a mountain of material— too much to sort through; he or she sometimes has difficulty distinguishing the good from the bad, the honest from the dishonest, and the reliable from the unreliable.

2. If you use a search engine to find information on the Internet about a breed of dogs and you enter the keyword *bulldogs*, what kind of irrelevant Web sites are you likely to find in your list of results?

   Schools with bulldogs as mascots (for example, the University of Georgia Bulldogs); companies that include bulldogs as part of their name (Bulldog Plumbing Company); articles that speak of bulldogs in a metaphorical sense ("The British soldiers were bulldogs in the stubborn defense of their homeland").

Activities

1. Assign skill builders at the end of the chapter in the text (Building Critical-Thinking Skills, and Building Teamwork Skills).

2. Have students interview someone who does research as part of his or her profession (such as scholar, lawyer, minister, or scientist). Students should gather information on what research techniques the person has found to be most effective.

3. If your school's library provides guided tours or audiovisual shows on what materials are available and how to find them, you can assign students to sign up for the service individually or you can arrange to take the entire class during a class period.

Objective Tests

Four ready-to-print tests for Chapter 6 (Forms A, B, C, D), and answer keys for all tests are provided in this instructor's manual. The four forms cover the same material, but are sufficiently different to permit one test to be used as the class test, and the others as makeup tests for absentees. Form A features true-false questions, Forms B and C have multiple-choice questions, while Form D is more difficult, requiring students to fill in missing words or phrases. Instructors may want to combine Form D with some of the essay questions listed below.

Essay & Discussion Questions

The following can be used as essay questions for tests or as stimuli for class discussions.

1. What is interlibrary loan and how can it help the researcher?

2. Why are books sometimes better sources of information than the Internet?

3. What are the advantages and disadvantages of using the Internet for research?

4. Why is it a good idea to take notes during an interview, even if you are using a video- or audiotape recorder?

5. What are the advantages of conducting field research?

Research Assignment

Choose a topic from the list below (or another related to oral communication—check with your instructor). Research it. Be prepared to present your findings in a talk.

1. Linguistics (science of language—including phonetics, morphology, syntax)
2. Semantics (word meaning)
3. Euphemisms (saying "revenue enhancement" instead of "raising taxes")
4. Dialect (regional variety of language)

Personality

5. Self-concept
6. Self-esteem
7. Self-disclosure
8. Gestures or posture use in public speaking
9. Jargon (technical terminology)

Body language, also called "kinesics"

10. Eye contact
11. Facial expression
12. Body movements
13. Territorial space (proxemics)
14. Cultural differences in use of body language

Voice

15. How voice is produced
16. Steps to improving voice
17. What your voice tells about you
18. Deceptions in advertising
19. Language development in children (0-6 years)

Speech Defects

20. Stuttering (definition, causes, symptoms, treatment)
21. Speech of people with cerebral palsy (breathing, voice, language, hearing, articulation, etc.)
22. Aphasia (language problems resulting from head injury or stroke)
23. Cleft palate speech problems
24. Autism (severe condition wherein child withdraws from communication)

Deafness

25. Types of deafness

26. Ways deaf people communicate

27. Ways to recognize hearing loss in children

Miscellaneous

28. Language delay in children (mental retardation, environmental deprivation, brain damage, deafness, illness)

29. Laryngectomee (speaking without a voice box)

30. Speech/Stage fright (tell something new!)

31. Persuasion in sales

32. Credibility of public speakers (Ethos — subject knowledge, reputation, dynamism, sincerity)

33. Communication for leadership in business

34. Sex differences in communication (how men and women communicate differently, both verbally and nonverbally)

35. Audience analysis (psychology of the audience)

36. Shyness

37. Humor in speeches

38. Grooming and communication

39. Phonetics (study of the sounds of spoken language)

40. Your choice — if approved by the instructor

SOURCES OF INFORMATION

- General speech book (use index and table of contents)
- Books on interpersonal communication
- Pamphlets
- Magazines
- Journals
- Popular paperbacks
- Videos
- Web sites
- Personal interviews

[These instructions are adapted and reprinted, by permission, from a handout provided by Bob Sampson of Central Piedmont Community College.]

Chapter 7
Evaluating Information & Avoiding Plagiarism

Chapter Objectives and Resource Integrator

After studying this chapter, students should be able to:

Objectives	Resources
1. Explain the criteria for high-quality information.	**In the Text:** • Page 125 **On Speeches DVD and on connectpublicspeaking.com:** • Full Speech #19 ("Are You Being Overcharged?") exemplifies the use of information that is timely, reliable, and responsible.
2. Reject claims based solely on anecdotes, testimonials, and opinions.	**In the Text:** • Pages 126-128 • Key terms: anecdote, testimonial, opinion **On Speeches DVD and on connectpublicspeaking.com:** • Full Speech #12 (Detox I – Needs Improvement) shows a gullible, careless researcher who accepts dubious claims on the Internet. • Full Speech #13 (Detox II – Improved Version) shows the speaker in Speech 12 as he does a good job of analyzing material and using only credible sources. **On connectpublicspeaking.com:** • Interactive Exercise – "Can You Identify the Different Types of Dubious Evidence?" – gives students practice in labeling three kinds of problematic evidence.
3. Recognize the fallibility of polls and experts.	**In the Text:** • Pages 128-129
4. Investigate impressive-sounding names of organizations.	**In the Text:** • Pages 129-130
5. Know how to scrutinize Internet sites for signs of bias and deception.	**In the Text:** • Pages 130-135

	On Speeches DVD and on connectpublicspeaking.com:
	• Full Speech #6 ("Animal Helpers II") – Note that the speaker uses solid information from reliable sources. She avoids far-out, dubious claims of animal feats that are frequently reported on the Internet.
6. Avoid plagiarism	**In the Text:** • Pages 135-137 • Key term: plagiarism
7. Give proper credit to sources.	**In the Text:** • Pages 137-139 • Key term: oral footnote **On Speeches DVD and on connectpublicspeaking.com:** • Clip 7.1 shows a speaker who gives proper credit to sources. **On connectpublicspeaking.com:** • Bibliography Formats—For the sake of convenience, the same illustrations of MLA and APA style formats that are printed in the chapter are also included on connectpublicspeaking.com.
8. Avoid improper use of copyrighted materials.	**In the Text:** • Pages 139-141 • Key terms: copyright infringement, public domain, fair use, royalty-free

Resources For Entire Chapter:

At End of Chapter:

- Summary
- Key Terms
- Review Questions
- Building Critical-Thinking Skills
- Building Teamwork Skills

On Speeches DVD and on connectpublicspeaking.com:

- Full Speech #12 (Detox I – Needs Improvement) shows a gullible, careless researcher who accepts dubious claims on the Internet.
- Full Speech #13 (Detox II – Improved Version) shows the speaker in Speech 12 as he does a good job of analyzing material and using only credible sources.
- Clip 7.1 shows a speaker who gives proper credit to sources.

On connectpublicspeaking.com:

- Bibliography Formats—For the sake of convenience, the same illustrations of MLA and APA style formats that are printed in the chapter are also included on connectpublicspeaking.com.
- Interactive exercise for chapter
- Practice test for chapter
- Glossary of terms
- Key-term flashcards
- Building Internet Skills (used to be in book, now online)

On Instructor's Resource DVD-ROM:

- PowerPoint: Chapter Highlights – A PowerPoint program gives highlights of each chapter and includes some video clips. **(NOTE: Many of the PowerPoint slides have no text and require the explanation given in the accompanying script.)**
- Tests – Ready-made chapter tests and a computerized test bank are provided.

Your Thoughts?

p. 127: In a TV commercial, a tennis star claims that a certain herbal supplement increases one's stamina. Should consumers be skeptical? Defend your answer.

(Answers will vary). Skepticism is called for. The tennis star is being paid to give comments.

p. 129: Imagine pollsters who want to survey public opinion on whether corporal punishment (spanking) should be permitted in elementary schools. If they wanted to make it appear that most people support spanking, what question could they ask?

(Answers will vary). "Do you agree that corporal punishment is necessary to instill self-discipline into young people?" Or: "If we are going to teach children right from wrong, shouldn't we spank them when they misbehave?"

p. 136: Some people think that plagiarism involves written work, but not spoken. Should the two be treated differently? Defend your answer.

(Answers will vary). Using someone else's ideas and words is theft, whether it involves speech or print.

Review Questions

Key to questions on p. 142 in the textbook:

1. What are the characteristics of high-quality information?

    Factual, reliable, well supported, current, verifiable, fair, comprehensive.

2. What is anecdotal evidence, and why does it fail to constitute proof of an assertion?

    Anecdotes, short accounts of an incident, do not by themselves constitute evidence because they are mere fragments of the "big picture." Corroborating evidence is needed.

3. How do opinions differ from facts?

    Facts are pieces of information that are generally accepted as objective reality. Opinions are conclusions or judgments that remain open to dispute. They are not universally accepted as accurate reflections of reality.

4. Why should more than one source be consulted?

    The first source may say one thing (which turns out to be wrong), while the next five or ten say the opposite.

5. Why are polls often unreliable?

    Some people do not respond honestly, and results often depend upon how a question is asked.

6. What are the domain names for commercial, nonprofit, and educational Web sites?

    .com (and .biz), .org, and .edu

7. What is the meaning of the term *cut and paste plagiarism*?

    "Cut and paste" is stitching together bits and pieces from a variety of sources without paraphrasing and without giving proper credit.

8. What is an *inappropriate paraphrase*?

    Inappropriate paraphrase occurs when a researcher sticks too closely to the original, making only a few changes in material.

9. What is an *oral footnote*?

    An oral footnote is a speaker's spoken citation of the source of his or her material.

10. Define *fair use*.

Fair use is a legal exception that permits writers, speakers, and researchers to use small amounts of copyrighted material for non-commercial, educational purposes.

Building Critical-Thinking Skills

Key to questions on pp. 142 in the textbook:

1. Imagine a Web site called www.clearskin.com that touts a miracle drug that banishes facial blemishes. The drug is praised on the Web site by a man identified as Roger Taschereau, M.D. You are trying to decide whether to recommend the medicine in a speech you are preparing. What is your evaluation of the Web site up to this point? What additional steps should you take before recommending the drug?

   Even though an M.D. is cited, a researcher should beware of Web sites that tout miracle substances. Further investigation should be carried out to find whether reliable, prestigious medical sources give positive evaluations of the drug.

2. Project Gutenberg (promo.net/pg) is a Web site with links to hundreds of books, poems, and plays that are in the public domain. If you want to copy a poem or book chapter for distribution to listeners at a business presentation, must you get permission? Explain your answer.

   No permission is needed because documents in the public domain are no longer protected by copyright and may be used freely and legally by anyone.

Activities

1. Assign skill builders at the end of the chapter in the text (Building Critical-Thinking Skills, and Building Teamwork Skills).

2. Lead the class in a discussion of how rapidly rumors and falsehoods can be spread on the Internet. Using a calculator, analyze how many people would be contacted if everyone in the class received an e-mail and then relayed it to five friends, who in turn relayed it to five of *their* friends, and so on . . . until a huge number is quickly reached.

Objective Tests

Four ready-to-print tests for Chapter 7 (Forms A, B, C, D), and answer keys for all tests are provided in this instructor's manual. The four forms cover the same material, but are sufficiently different to permit one test to be used as the class test, and the others as makeup tests for absentees. Form A features true-false questions, Forms B and C have multiple-choice questions, while Form D is more difficult, requiring students to fill in missing words or phrases. Instructors may want to combine Form D with some of the essay questions listed below.

Essay & Discussion Questions

The following can be used as essay questions for tests or as stimuli for class discussions.

1. What is meant by the term *healthy skepticism*?

2. Why are public opinion polls often unreliable sources of information?

3. What is *web manipulation* and how can you avoid it?

4. What is the meaning of the term *public domain*?

5. Explain the legal concept known as *fair use*.

Chapter 8
Supporting Your Ideas

Chapter Objectives and Resource Integrator

After studying this chapter, students should be able to:

Objectives	Resources
1. Explain why support materials are needed in a speech.	**In the Text:** • Pages 147-148

2. Describe nine types of support materials: definitions, vivid images, examples, narratives, comparison, contrast, analogies, testimony, and statistics.	**In the Text:**
	• Pages 148-158
	• Key terms: definition, vivid image, example, narrative, hypothetical narrative, comparison, contrast, analogy, testimony, quote verbatim, summarize, paraphrase, statistics
	
	On Speeches DVD and on connectpublicspeaking.com:
	• Video Clips can be used to reinforce some of the key types of support materials:
	  o 8.1 – Using a Vivid Image
	  o 8.2 – Using an Example
	  o 8.3 – Making a Contrast
	  o 8.4 – Using an Analogy
	  o 8.5 – Using Testimony
	  o 8.6 – Using Statistics
	• Full Speech #3 ("One Slip – and You're Dead") demonstrates effective use of narratives.
	• These videos show good use of a variety of support materials:
	  o Full Speech #18 ("Inmates and Tomatoes")
	  o Full Speech #19 ("Are You Being Overcharged?")
	  o Full Speech #21 ("Too Much of a Good Thing")
	
	On connectpublicspeaking.com:
	• Interactive Exercises:
	  o "Can You Identify the Types of Support Materials?"

	o Support Materials—This exercise can be used to review seven of the types of support materials covered in Chapter 8. o Exercise on Support Materials – Another review sheet. **In the Instructor's Manual (on Instructor's Resource DVD-ROM):** • Sheet 8.1, Worksheet—This sheet can be used by students who have been assigned to analyze a speech and make note of all support materials.
3. Discuss the use and abuse of statistics in speeches.	**In the Text:** • Pages 153-158 • Key terms: average, mean, median, mode, percentage, correlation

Resources For Entire Chapter:

At End of Chapter:

- Summary
- Key Terms
- Review Questions
- Building Critical-Thinking Skills
- Building Teamwork Skills
- Building Internet Skills

On connectpublicspeaking.com:

- Practice test for chapter
- Checklist (for Preparing and Delivering a Speech)
- Glossary of terms
- Key-term flashcards
- Interactive exercise for chapter
- Building Internet Skills (used to be in book, now online)

On Instructor's Resource DVD-ROM:

- PowerPoint: Chapter Highlights – A PowerPoint program gives highlights of each chapter and includes some video clips. **(NOTE: Many of the PowerPoint slides have no text and require the explanation given in the accompanying script.)**
- Tests – Ready-made chapter tests and a computerized test bank are provided.

Your Thoughts?

p. 150:   Narratives are the most frequent device used in television commercials. Why are they so effective in selling products?

(Answers will vary). A narrative, or story, catches our attention, whets our curiosity, and makes us want to listen to the end.

p. 152:   A scientist gives an opinion on global warming and then four years later recants those views. For a speech, would it be acceptable to cite only the original opinion? Defend your answer.

(Answers will vary). No. This would mislead the audience. The best approach is to mention both the original and the revised view.

p. 156:   When ice cream sales increase, the number of shark attacks on swimmers increases. Does this correlation prove that one causes the other? How can the correlation be explained?

(Answers will vary). Just because two events are correlated, this does not mean that one caused the other. Ice cream sales and shark attacks increase in the summer when people crave a frozen treat and are more likely to swim in the ocean.

Review Questions

Key to questions on p. 163 in the textbook:

1.   List five reasons why support materials are important in a speech.

   Support materials can develop and illustrate ideas, clarify ideas, make a speech more interesting, help listeners remember key ideas, and help prove an assertion.

2.   Why are informal definitions usually superior to dictionary definitions in a speech?

   Informal definitions can be easily understood by the audience, while dictionary definitions tend to be tedious and hard to grasp.

3.   What must speakers use in order to make vivid images successful?

   Specific details

4.   What is the main advantage of using testimony in a speech?

   The main advantage of using testimony is that it gives you instant credibility; quoting an expert is a way of saying, "I'm not the only one who has this idea; it has the backing of a leading authority on the subject."

5.   The boss of a small firm has an annual salary of $100,000. Each of his 13 employees makes $12,000 a year. Give the average salary of the firm in terms of *mean, median,* and *mode.*

   Mean—$18,286

   Median—$12,000

   Mode—$12,000

6. How many examples are needed to develop a point?

    Only as many as are necessary for listeners to understand, remember, or be convinced.

7. What term is used to refer to a story about an imaginary situation?

    Hypothetical narrative

8. What is the difference between a comparison and a contrast?

    A comparison shows how two or more items are alike; a contrast shows how they are different.

9. A speaker who likens worrying to rocking in a rocking chair is using which kind of support material?

    Analogy

10. If we say that there is a positive relationship between height and landing a spot on a basketball team, we are using which type of statistics?

    Correlation

Building Critical-Thinking Skills

Key to questions on p. 163 in the textbook:

1. Whenever tar on asphalt roads gets hot enough to bubble on a summer day, the incidence of heat exhaustion among citizens goes up. In other words, there is a strong correlation between bubbling tar and heat exhaustion. Does the correlation prove that tar fumes cause people to pass out? Explain your answer.

    No. Just because two events are correlated does not mean that one causes the other.

2. In three or four sentences, give an informal definition (not a dictionary definition) of one of these terms:

    a. friendship

    b. pizzazz

    c. ideal pet

    (Answers will vary.)

Activities

1. Assign skill builders at the end of the chapter in the text (Building Critical-Thinking Skills, and Building Teamwork Skills).

2. Assign students to analyze a speech reprinted on the Internet, identifying the various forms of support that are used.

3. Have students collect newspaper, magazine, or Web articles containing examples of the types of supports discussed in Chapter 8.

Objective Tests

Four ready-to-print tests for Chapter 8 (Forms A, B, C, D), and answer keys for all tests are provided in this instructor's manual. The four forms cover the same material, but are sufficiently different to permit one test to be used as the class test, and the others as makeup tests for absentees. Form A features true-false questions, Forms B and C have multiple-choice questions, while Form D is more difficult, requiring students to fill in missing words or phrases. Instructors may want to combine Form D with some of the essay questions listed below.

Essay & Discussion Questions

The following can be used as essay questions for tests or as stimuli for class discussions.

1. Give three reasons why support materials are important in a speech.
2. What is a hypothetical narrative and when should it be used?
3. What criteria should be met before testimony is used in a speech?
4. What criteria should be met before statistics are used in a speech?
5. Describe the three types of averages.
6. What is the danger to be avoided in using correlations?

Name_____

Worksheet

Speech: _____

Support Materials:

Definitions:

Vivid Images:

Examples:

Narratives:

Comparison:

Contrast:

Analogies:

Testimony:

Statistics:

Other:

Support Materials

Match the type of support materials listed below with the corresponding excerpt. Each type is used only once.

a.   Testimony

b.   Examples

c.   Narrative

d.   Comparison

e.   Contrast

f.   Definition

g.   Vivid images (description)

h.   Analogies

____   1.   The "working poor" are those who work full time but still live below the poverty line of $15,141 for a family of four.

____   2.   Among the working poor are schoolteachers, chefs, computer-maintenance workers, and airline flight attendants.

____   3.   Near Disney World in Florida is the community of Kissimmee. Behind the souvenir shops and motels live America's working poor. The lawns are mowed, and the kids can play safely in the street. The neighborhood looks like a solid, secure all-American neighborhood, but if you look closely at the employed adults, you will see weariness in their eyes, for most of them work at 2 or 3 jobs and even then, they are barely able to pay the bills.

____   4.   Linda Hargroves came home at 10:30 one night last week after finishing the second of her two jobs. Her 14-year-old son greeted her with news that he had been selected to compete in a statewide gymnastics event and needed $75 to pay for the trip. Hargroves had to tell him that he couldn't go—she had no dollars to spare.

____   5.   The working poor and the unemployed poor are alike in one respect: they fear a serious medical problem will ruin their chances of ever achieving financial security.

____   6.   "It doesn't take much in the way of an unforeseen circumstance to spin these people right out of control," says Anita Beaty, director of Atlanta's Task Force for the Homeless. "You cannot pay rent and child care on minimum wage."

____   7.   If you are a college graduate, your chances of living in poverty are less than 2%, but if you are a high-school dropout, the chances are 20%.

____   8.   The working poor are like trapeze artists struggling to maintain their balance on a high wire.

Source: Nancy Gibbs, "Working Harder, Getting Nowhere," *Time*, July 3, 1995, pp. 17-20.

Support Materials

Match the type of support materials listed below with the corresponding excerpt. Each type is used only once.

Testimony

Examples

Narrative

Comparison

Contrast

Definition

Vivid images (description)

Analogies

__f__   1.   The "working poor" are those who work full time but still live below the poverty line of $15,141 for a family of four.

__b__   2.   Among the working poor are schoolteachers, chefs, computer-maintenance workers, and airline flight attendants.

__g__   3.   Near Disney World in Florida is the community of Kissimmee. Behind the souvenir shops and motels live America's working poor. The lawns are mowed, and the kids can play safely in the street. The neighborhood looks like a solid, secure all-American neighborhood, but if you look closely at the employed adults, you will see weariness in their eyes, for most of them work at 2 or 3 jobs and even then, they are barely able to pay the bills.

__c__   4.   Linda Hargroves came home at 10:30 one night last week after finishing the second of her two jobs. Her 14-year-old son greeted her with news that he had been selected to compete in a statewide gymnastics event and needed $75 to pay for the trip. Hargroves had to tell him that he couldn't go—she had no dollars to spare.

__d__   5.   The working poor and the unemployed poor are alike in one respect: they fear a serious medical problem will ruin their chances of ever achieving financial security.

__a__   6.   "It doesn't take much in the way of an unforeseen circumstance to spin these people right out of control," says Anita Beaty, director of Atlanta's Task Force for the Homeless. "You cannot pay rent and child care on minimum wage."

__e__   7.   If you are a college graduate, your chances of living in poverty are less than 2%, but if you are a high-school dropout, the chances are 20%.

__h__   8.   The working poor are like trapeze artists struggling to maintain their balance on a high wire.

Source: Nancy Gibbs, "Working Harder, Getting Nowhere," *Time*, July 3, 1995, pp. 17-20.

Chapter 9
Presentation Aids

Chapter Objectives and Resource Integrator

After studying this chapter, students should be able to:

Objectives	Resources
1. Explain at least seven advantages of using visual aids in a speech.	**In the Text:** • Page 167

2. Describe the types of visual aids.	**In the Text:**
	• Pages 167-176
	• Key terms: line graph, bar graph, pie graph, pictorial graph, table, low resolution, high resolution, thumbnail
	
	On Speeches DVD and on connectpublicspeaking.com:
	• Video Clips:
	  o 9.1 – Using Internet Graphics
	  o 9.2 – Using a Poster
	  o 9.3 – Using a Photograph
	• Videos:
	  o Full Speech #3 ("One Slip – and You're Dead") demonstrates effective us of photos on PowerPoint slides.
	  o Full Speech #10 ("How to Make Avocado Salsa") demonstrates the use of objects (food).
	  o Full Speech #11 ("How to Hide Valuables") shows effective use of photos.
	  o Full Speech #20 ("Would You Vote for Aardvark?") illustrates the use of a pie graph.

3. Describe the media for visual aids.	**In the Text:** • Pages 176-180 (and Appendix on PowerPoint, 189-195) • Key terms: flip chart, handout, visual presenter, transparency

	On Speeches DVD and on connectpublicspeaking.com: • Full Speech #11 ("How to Hide Valuables") shows effective use of PowerPoint slides. • Full Speech #16 ("The Deadliest Natural Disaster") illustrates the use of large, vivid posters. • Full Speech #21 ("Too Much of a Good Thing") demonstrates the use of posters.

4. Prepare appropriate visual aids.	**In the Text:**
	
	 • Pages 180-183 (and Appendix on PowerPoint, 189-195)
	
	 On Speeches DVD and on connectpublicspeaking.com:
	
	 • Videos:
	   o Video Clip 9.4 – Presenting a PowerPoint "Build"
	
	   o Full Speech #14 ("Bicycle Helmets I – Persuasive Speech That Needs Improvement") spotlights hard-to-read PowerPoint slides and the wrong way to present them.
	
	   o Full Speech #11 ("How to Hide Valuables") shows effective use of photos on PowerPoint slides.
	
	   o Full Speech #7 ("Humanoid Robots") illustrates the use of photos on PowerPoint slides.
	
	 On connectpublicspeaking.com:
	
	 • PowerPoint Tutorial—Basic steps in creating and using PowerPoint in presentations are explained in this tutorial.
	 • PowerPoint Design Tips—Guidelines on making slides look attractive and uncluttered.
	 • Interactive Exercise:
	   o "Which PowerPoint Slide is Most Effective?"

5. Present visual aids effectively.	**In the Text:** • Pages 183-186 (and Appendix on PowerPoint, 189-195) • Key terms: progressive revelation **On Instructor's Resource DVD-ROM:** • "Lessons from the Movies" – An illustrated narrative called "Murphy's Law" – based on the movie *The Business of Strangers* – shows the need to have a backup plan in case equipment malfunctions or is unavailable.

	On Speeches DVD and on connectpublicspeaking.com:
	• Videos – Effective use of visual aids is shown in: o Clip 9.1 ("Using Internet Graphics") o Full Speech #3 ("One Slip – and You're Dead") demonstrates effective us of photos on PowerPoint slides.
6. Appeal to channels other than visual.	**In the Text:** • Pages 186-187

Resources For Entire Chapter:

At End of Chapter:

- Summary
- Key Terms
- Review Questions
- Building Critical-Thinking Skills
- Building Teamwork Skills

On connectpublicspeaking.com:

- Interactive exercise for chapter
- Building Internet Skills (used to be in book, now online)
- Practice test for chapter
- Checklist (for Preparing and Delivering a Speech)
- Glossary of terms
- Key-term flashcards

On Instructor's Resource DVD-ROM:

- PowerPoint: Chapter Highlights – A PowerPoint program gives highlights of each chapter and includes some video clips. **(NOTE: Many of the PowerPoint slides have no text and require the explanation given in the accompanying script.)**
- Tests – Ready-made chapter tests and a computerized test bank are provided.
- "Lessons from the Movies" – An illustrated narrative called "Murphy's Law" – based on the movie *The Business of Strangers* – shows the need to have a backup plan in case equipment malfunctions or is unavailable.

Your Thoughts?

p. 167:   Using a good visual bolsters a speaker's credibility. Why do you think that listeners react in this way?

(Answers will vary). Listeners are impressed that the speaker spent time and energy to create a good visual. Listeners may make these assumptions: (1) The speaker cares about the listeners and wants them to understand key points. (2) The speaker must have done a lot of research and is quite knowledgeable about the topic.

p. 175:   What are the advantages and disadvantages of using a video clip from YouTube (the popular video sharing Web site)?

(Answers will vary). Advantages: up-to-date, interesting, short. Disadvantages: video quality is sometimes poor; parts of the clip might not really relate to the speech.

p. 180:   Regarding visual aids, trial attorney Joe Jamail says, "If you use too many pictures and make it like a circus or going to a matinee, jurors will think you think they're stupid." What advice would you give attorneys for using visual aids in the courtroom?

(Answers will vary). Don't overwhelm the audience with visuals – use just enough to make your points. Make visuals simple, but don't treat jurors as if they are ignorant children.

Review Questions

Key to questions on p. 188 in the textbook:

1.   List at least six types of visual aids.

   Answers may include any of the following: graphs, charts, drawings, photographs, computer graphics, objects, models, yourself.

2.   List at least five media for presenting visual aids.

   Answers may include any of the following: chalkboards, posters, flip charts, handouts, overhead transparencies, slides, films and videotapes.

3.   What is progressive revelation?

   Progressive revelation means revealing only one part or item at a time, thereby building suspense and keeping listeners from reading or studying ahead of the speaker.

4.   *A list of key ideas* is another name for which kind of chart?

   Information chart

5.   Is it legal to use graphics from the Internet in a student speech in the classroom? Explain your answer.

   Yes. Copyright restrictions do not apply because you are engaged in noncommercial, educational, one-time use of material.

6.   The text recommends that you "aim for back-row comprehension." What does this mean and why is the advice necessary?

   Letters, numbers, and graphics should be large enough so that a person on the back row can see them clearly and easily. This advice is necessary because many presenters in the business world make the mistake of having a too-small visual.

7. How can speakers test the visibility of their visuals?

Before the day of a speech, sit on the back row and examine the clarity and legibility of the visual. Better yet, have a friend sit on the back row to give a candid assessment.

8. Is it always a mistake for a speaker to wait until the conclusion of a presentation to show a visual or perform a demonstration? Explain your answer.

No, sometimes a speaker can build suspense by withholding a visual or a demonstration until the end.

9. Why would it be a mistake to circulate a small photograph during your speech?

The listeners might scrutinize the visual aid instead of paying attention to the speech.

10. Explain three options that a speaker can take to magnify a too-small visual.

Possibilities include (1) Use a camcorder with a zoom lens to enlarge the visual on videotape; (2) Use a visual presenter (or ELMO); (3) Make an enlargement of an illustration onto an overhead transparency; (4) Scan a photo or drawing for use in an electronic presentation.

Building Critical-Thinking Skills

Key to questions on p. 188 in the textbook:

1. "Some pictures may be worth a thousand words, but a picture of a thousand words isn't worth much," says corporate executive Don Keough. Explain what this means in terms of oral presentations.

A picture can save words and be more interesting than words, but "a picture of a thousand words" (that is, a visual heavy with text) is tedious and boring.

2. At one Web site devoted to communication, public speakers are advised to distribute thought-provoking handouts at the beginning of a speech so that "if members of the audience get bored during the speech, they will have something interesting to read." Do you agree with this advice? Defend your position.

(Answers will vary.) A speaker should never give material that might compete with the speech itself.

Activities

1. Assign skill builders at the end of the chapter in the text (Building Critical-Thinking Skills and Building Teamwork Skills).

2. An effective way to demonstrate the use of visual aids is to display various good and bad ones and let the class discuss the positive and negative features. You can make both good and bad visual aids yourself, or you can collect them from students in previous classes (most students are willing to let you keep inexpensive aids such as posters).

3. You may want to require students to use visual aids with most or all of their classroom speeches. If visuals are merely optional, most students will omit them.

Objective Tests

Four ready-to-print tests for Chapter 9 (Forms A, B, C, D), and answer keys for all tests are provided in this instructor's manual. The four forms cover the same material, but are sufficiently different to permit one test to be used as the class test, and the others as makeup tests for absentees. Form A features true-false questions, Forms B and C have multiple-choice questions, while Form D is more difficult, requiring students to fill in missing words or phrases. Instructors may want to combine Form D with some of the essay questions listed below.

Essay & Discussion Questions

The following can be used as essay questions for tests or as stimuli for class discussions.

1. Discuss the advantages of using visual aids in a speech.

2. When may handouts be used in a speech and when should they not be used?

3. Why should a speaker not pass around materials during a speech?

4. If you want to show a small visual aid such as a piece of jewelry, what options do you have for making sure that everyone sees it clearly?

5. What is progressive revelation?

6. Why should a graphic in a speech be less complex than a graphic in a book?

7. What are the disadvantages of using a board for visual aids?

Chapter 10
The Body of the Speech

Chapter Objectives and Resource Integrator

After studying this chapter, students should be able to:

Objectives	Resources
1. Explain the importance of skillfully organizing the body of the speech.	**In the Text:** • Page 199 **On connectpublicspeaking.com:** • Supplementary Readings o Using Your Subconscious Mind—This article shows part of the creative process that one goes through in devising material.

2. Create the body of a speech by using a central idea to develop main points.	**In the Text:**
	• Pages 199-203
	• Key term: main points, parallel language
	
	On Speeches DVD and on connectpublicspeaking.com:
	• Full Speech #21 ("Too Much of a Good Thing") illustrates well-developed main points, supporting points, and transitions.
	
	On connectpublicspeaking.com:
	• Outlines: Most of the full speeches are accompanied by:
	  o Complete Outlines: These outlines can be viewed and printed out.
	
	  o Outline Exercises: By dragging and dropping parts of a scrambled outline into a properly sequenced outline, students can practice outlining with actual content, and become skilled at outlining five types of speeches: informative, persuasive, demonstration, speech of tribute, and self-introduction.
	
	• Outline Tutor – Students can use this software program to fill in the body of the speech (and later they can add the other components of an outline). This interactive program shows the various parts of an outline and makes it easy to insert content into the appropriate sections of the outline.
	
	• Supplementary Readings
	  o Tips for Your Career: Give Your Audience a Pretest on Your

	Main Points—This article provides a real-life extension of Chapter 10. • Interactive Exercise: o Desired Responses—Some instructors require students to formulate the responses they desire from their audience. **Instructor's Resource DVD-ROM:** • Building an Outline – This PowerPoint program demonstrates the step-by-step creation of an outline. It is also available on the Instructor's section of connectpublicspeaking.com.
3. Identify and use five patterns of organization: chronological, spatial, cause-effect, problem-solution, and topical.	**In the Text:** • Pages 204-208 • Key terms: chronological pattern, spatial pattern, cause-effect pattern, problem-solution pattern, topical pattern, statement-of-reasons pattern **On Speeches DVD and on connectpublicspeaking.com:** • Full Speech #10 ("How to Make Avocado Salsa") illustrates the chronological pattern. • Full Speech #20 ("Would You Vote for Aardvark?") illustrates the problem-solution pattern. **On connectpublicspeaking.com:** • Interactive Exercise o "Can You Identify the Organizational Patterns?"
4. Identify and use four types of transitional devices: bridges, internal summaries, signposts, and spotlights.	**In the Text:** • Pages 210-213 • Key terms: transition, bridge, internal summary, signpost, spotlight **On Speeches DVD and on connectpublicspeaking.com:** • Video Clip 10.1 ("Providing Transitions") shows the smooth use of transitions. • Full Speech #22 ("Three Celebrity Heroes") shows how transitions can be inserted effectively.
5. Simplify the process of organizing speech material.	**In the Text:** • Pages 213-214

Resources For Entire Chapter:

At End of Chapter:

- Summary
- Key Terms
- Review Questions
- Building Critical-Thinking Skills
- Building Teamwork Skills

On connectpublicspeaking.com:

- Practice test for chapter
- Checklist (for Preparing and Delivering a Speech)
- Glossary of terms
- Key-term flashcards
- Interactive exercise for chapter
- Building Internet Skills (used to be in book, now online)

On Instructor's Resource DVD-ROM:

- PowerPoint: Chapter Highlights – A PowerPoint program gives highlights of each chapter and includes some video clips. (**NOTE: Many of the PowerPoint slides have no text and require the explanation given in the accompanying script.**)
- Tests – Ready-made chapter tests and a computerized test bank are provided.

Your Thoughts?

p. 202: Most public speaking experts recommend that you use complete sentences to create your central idea and main points. Why do you think this advice is given?

(Answers will vary). Having a complete sentence increases the chances of having coherent, fully-thought-out idea.

p. 208: Which pattern would a speaker probably choose for a speech on how society's obsession with thinness has led to unhealthy weight-loss methods and eating disorders?

Cause-effect. The obsession is the cause, the unhealthy methods and disorders are the result.

p. 211: In a speech, transitions must be more prominent than they are in a book. Why?

(Answers will vary). In a book, to signal transition, one can put space between sections and set headings in larger type. In a speech, a speaker must signal transitions with phrases or sentences.

Review Questions

Key to questions on p. 215 in the textbook:

1. How many main points should you have in a speech?

   Most speeches should have no more than two or three (or occasionally four) main points.

2. How many ideas should be represented in each main point?

   Only one idea should be expressed in each main point.

3. What is meant by the advice to "customize points for each audience"?

   Tailor a speech to the needs and interests of each audience. Main points that work with one audience might not work with another.

4. Which pattern of organization would be best suited for a speech on the solar system?

   The spatial pattern would be ideal, such as Sun, Mercury, Venus, Earth, etc.

5. Which pattern of organization would be ideal for a speech on food contamination and how the problem can be corrected?

   Problem-solution pattern

6. Which pattern of organization would be best suited for a speech on the three major reasons why businesses declare bankruptcy?

   Topical

7. Why are transitions important in a speech?

   Transitions help the listeners stay with you as you move from one part of your speech to another.

8. In terms of speech organization, what is an internal summary?

   An internal summary—given during a speech—reviews material that has been covered up to that point.

9. Describe the transitional device called *bridge*.

   A bridge links what went before with what will now come in the speech.

10. Describe the transitional device called *spotlight*.

    A spotlight alerts listeners to important points.

Building Critical-Thinking Skills

Key to questions on p. 215 in the textbook:

1. Which organizational pattern is used [in the example in the book]?

   Spatial

2. Which organizational pattern is used [in the example in the book]?

Chronological

Activities

1. Assign skill builders at the end of the chapter in the text (Building Critical-Thinking Skills and Building Teamwork Skills).

2. To help students understand how to formulate main points, you can require, for every speech, that main points be submitted (along with the specific purpose statement and the central idea) before the entire outline is due. Once the main points are organized properly, the students can work on developing their support materials for each main point.

Objective Tests

Four ready-to-print tests for Chapter 10 (Forms A, B, C, D), and answer keys for all tests are provided in this instructor's manual. The four forms cover the same material, but are sufficiently different to permit one test to be used as the class test, and the others as makeup tests for absentees. Form A features true-false questions, Forms B and C have multiple-choice questions, while Form D is more difficult, requiring students to fill in missing words or phrases. Instructors may want to combine Form D with some of the essay questions listed below.

Essay & Discussion Questions

The following can be used as essay questions for tests or as stimuli for class discussions.

1. What are the advantages of a well-organized speech over a poorly organized one?

2. Define and give an example of three of the following organizational patterns: chronological, spatial, cause-effect, problem-solution, and topical.

3. What are transitions and why are they important?

4. Define and give an example of three of the following transitional devices: bridges, internal summaries, signposts, and spotlights.

5. Why should every speech have more than one main point?

6. Why should you customize main points for each different audience?

Chapter 11
Introductions and Conclusions

Chapter Objectives and Resource Integrator

After studying this chapter, students should be able to:

Objectives	Resources

1. Formulate effective attention material for the introductions of their own speeches.	**In the Text:**
	• Pages 219-223
	• Key terms: attention material, hypothetical illustration, rhetorical question, overt-response question
	
	On Speeches DVD and on connectpublicspeaking.com:
	• Video Clips – Three clips illustrate effective introductions:
	  o 11.1 – Introductions: Relating a Story
	  o 11.2 – Introductions: Citing a Quotation
	  o 11.3 – Introductions: Arousing Curiosity
	
	• Full Speech Videos – Several speeches provide good models for openers:
	  o Full Speech #3 ("One Slip – and You're Dead") illustrates an intriguing opener.
	  o Full Speech #6 ("Animal Helpers II") uses an engaging photo and story.
	  o Full Speech #11 ("How to Hide Valuables") shows how to capture attention by involving the listeners and their lives.
	  o Full Speech #16 ("The Deadliest Natural Disaster") uses provocative questions.
	  o Full Speech #20 ("Would You Vote for Aardvark?") has a hypothetical narrative.
	
	On connectpublicspeaking.com:
	• Outlines: Most of the full speeches are accompanied by:
	  o Complete Outlines: These outlines can be viewed and printed out.
	  o Outline Exercises: By dragging and dropping parts of a scrambled outline into a properly sequenced outline, students can practice outlining with actual content, and become skilled

	at outlining five types of speeches: informative, persuasive, demonstration, speech of tribute, and self-introduction.
	• Outline Tutor – Students can insert their introduction into an outline. This interactive program shows the various parts of an outline and makes it easy to insert content into the appropriate sections of the outline. Alternatively, an outline template in Microsoft Word format is provided for those students who prefer to do their work in Word. • Interactive Exercise ○ "Which is the Best Introduction?"
2. Formulate effective orienting material for the introductions of their own speeches.	**In the Text:** • Pages 223-226 • Key terms: orienting material, credibility, preview **Instructor's Resource DVD-ROM:** Building an Outline – This PowerPoint program demonstrates the step-by-step creation of an outline. It is also available on the Instructor's section of connectpublicspeaking.com.

3. Create effective conclusions for their own speeches.	**In the Text:**
	
	• Pages 227-230
	• Key terms: clincher
	
	On Instructor's Resource DVD-ROM:
	
	"Lessons from the Movies" – An illustrated narrative based on the movie *Four Weddings and a Funeral* demonstrates the effective use of a quotation in the conclusion of a speech.
	
	On Speeches DVD and on connectpublicspeaking.com:
	
	• Video Clips – These clips illustrate effective conclusions:
	   ○ 11.4 – Conclusions: Citing a Quotation
	   ○ 11.5 – Conclusions: Giving an Illustration
	   ○ 11.6 – Conclusions: Concluding with a Reference to the Introduction
	• Full Speech Videos – Several speeches provide good models for conclusions:
	   ○ Full Speech #6 ("Animal Helpers II") has a good summary.
	   ○ Full Speech #15 ("Bicycle Helmets II") features a strong challenge at the end.
	   ○ Full Speech #11 ("How to Hide Valuables") has a good summary of key steps.

| | o   Full Speech #19 ("Are You Being Overcharged?") has a pleasing conclusion. |
| | o   Full Speech #16 ("The Deadliest Natural Disaster") features a good summary and challenge at the end. |

Resources For Entire Chapter:

At End of Chapter:

- Summary
- Key Terms
- Review Questions
- Building Critical-Thinking Skills
- Building Teamwork Skills

On connectpublicspeaking.com:

- Practice test for chapter
- Checklist (for Preparing and Delivering a Speech)
- Glossary of terms
- Key-term flashcards
- Interactive exercise for chapter
- Building Internet Skills (used to be in book, now online)

On Instructor's Resource DVD-ROM:

- PowerPoint: Chapter Highlights – A PowerPoint program gives highlights of each chapter and includes some video clips. **(NOTE: Many of the PowerPoint slides have no text and require the explanation given in the accompanying script.)**
- Tests – Ready-made chapter tests and a computerized test bank are provided.

Your Thoughts?

p. 219:   In several elementary schools in recent years, visiting speakers have grabbed the attention of students by staging a fake invasion of gun-toting terrorists. Why do you think most educators have denounced this strategy?

(Answers will vary). Causing fright (and even panic) in listeners is unethical, and it puts them in a confused, distracted state of mind.

p. 224:   If you are uncertain how much background information is needed by the audience, what is the best way to find out?

(Answers will vary). Several weeks before your speech, to ascertain what listeners know and don't know about your topic, interview them or ask them to fill out a questionnaire.

p. 227:   What advice would you give a speaker who begins by saying, "I know this speech is going to bore you"?

(Answers will vary). You shouldn't give a speech that you think will bore the audience, and you should never apologize. The audience reaction would probably be, "Why, then, are you giving this speech?"

Review Questions

Key to questions on p. 232 in the textbook:

1. Why is it necessary to have attention material at the beginning of a speech?

   If you do not grab your listeners' attention and interest at the beginning of a speech, they might slip into their private world of daydreams and personal concerns.

2. What is the purpose of the orienting material in the speech introduction?

   The orienting material gives the listeners a clear sense of what the speech is about and any other information that they might need in order to understand the ideas in the speech.

3. What is a rhetorical question?

   A rhetorical question is used to stimulate audience interest, not to solicit actual answers.

4. What is an overt-response question?

   An overt-response question is asked to elicit a direct response, such as raising hands.

5. How can you give listeners an incentive to listen to a speech?

   Show listeners that they will personally benefit from the speech.

6. What is credibility?

   Credibility is an audience's perception of a speaker as believable, trustworthy, and competent.

7. In what way does a preview of main points reassure the audience?

   A preview lets the audience know that you are well-organized and focused – you are not going to ramble off the subject.

8. Why is it a mistake to end a speech abruptly?

   An abrupt ending jars the listeners and deprives them of a sense of finality.

9. What is a clincher?

   A clincher is a memorable finale, such as a quotation or a story, which reinforces the central idea of the speech.

10. Why should you restate your main points in the conclusion?

    Research shows that restating your main points increases the likelihood that listeners will remember them.

Building Critical-Thinking Skills

Key to questions on p. 232 in the textbook:

1. What advice would you give a speaker who says, in the introduction, "This speech may be too technical for you."

   You should not be speaking on a topic that is too technical (find out in advance via an audience survey), and you should not apologize in an introduction.

2. Create a rhetorical question concerning the destruction of the Central American rain forest.

   (Answers will vary.) Example: "How long will the world ignore the destruction of the forest?"

Activities

1. Assign skill builders at the end of the chapter in the text (Building Critical-Thinking Skills and Building Teamwork Skills).

2. Ask students to analyze the introductions and conclusions of three speeches in the text or in the *Supplementary Readings and Worksheets* book, discussing the techniques used and their effectiveness or ineffectiveness. This can be done orally or as a written assignment.

3. For a class discussion, you can write some topics on the board and have the class brainstorm possible introductions and conclusions for speeches on those topics.

Objective Tests

Four ready-to-print tests for Chapter 11 (Forms A, B, C, D), and answer keys for all tests are provided in this instructor's manual. The four forms cover the same material, but are sufficiently different to permit one test to be used as the class test, and the others as makeup tests for absentees. Form A features true-false questions, Forms B and C have multiple-choice questions, while Form D is more difficult, requiring students to fill in missing words or phrases. Instructors may want to combine Form D with some of the essay questions listed below.

Essay & Discussion Questions

The following can be used as essay questions for tests or as stimuli for class discussions.

1. Discuss some of the effective ways in which a speaker can gain the attention and interest of the listeners at the beginning of a speech.

2. Why is orienting material important and what should it contain?

3.   What should be contained in the conclusion of a speech?

4.   What is meant by ending a speech with a "clincher?" What kind of endings can be used as clinchers?

Chapter 12
Outlining the Speech

Chapter Objectives and Resource Integrator

After studying this chapter, students should be able to:

Objectives	Resources
1. Understand the importance of developing an outline for a speech.	**In the Text:** • Pages 236-237 **On connectpublicspeaking.com:** • Supplementary Readings: o "Using Your Subconscious Mind"—This article shows part of the creative process that one goes through in devising material.

2. Create a coherent outline for a speech.	**In the Text:**
	
	• Pages 238-246
	• Key terms: topic outline, complete-sentence outline
	
	On connectpublicspeaking.com:
	
	• Outline Tutor – This software program helps students organize their material in outline format. This interactive program shows the various parts of an outline and makes it easy to insert content into the appropriate sections of the outline.
	
	• Outlines: Most of the Full Speeches are accompanied by:
	
	  o Complete Outlines: These outlines can be viewed and printed out.
	
	  o Outline Exercises: By dragging and dropping parts of a scrambled outline into a properly sequenced outline, students can practice outlining with actual content, and become skilled at outlining five types of speeches: informative, persuasive, demonstration, speech of tribute, and self-introduction.
	
	• Bibliography Formats—For the sake of convenience, the same illustrations of MLA and APA style formats that are printed in the chapter are also included on connectpublicspeaking.com.

- Interactive Exercises:
  - "Fill in the Missing Parts"

  - Outline Exercise—Students can practice using the correct labels and numbering system for outlines.

- Supplementary Readings
  - Outline Template—This form can be used for preliminary outlines. If students are required to do their outlines in stages, they can fill in the appropriate items at the scheduled times (for example, specific purpose statement first). The advantage of this form is that students are obliged to complete all aspects of an outline; it discourages them from omitting such items as transitions. In my classes, I use this template for early drafts and encourage students to use Post-It stick-on slips—to make it easy to add, delete, and experiment. For their final outlines, I recommend that they transfer their material over to the Outline Tutor and print out a copy to turn in.

  - Speech Organizer—This template is for 3 x 3 stick-on slips, giving students a systematic way to do their preliminary work.

  - Using Cards for Outlines—As with the Speech Organizer, the card system can be used for preliminary work or for final outlines.

In the Instructor's Manual (on Instructor's Resource DVD-ROM):

- Sheet 12.1, Completion of Outline—This form can be used to prod students to include all parts of an outline. (Some students need the threat of a grade in order to do a thorough job on their outlines.) The form grades only on whether items are included; it does not grade on the quality of work in each item. The form is based on the idea that the student has 100 points to start with; 5 or 10 points are then deducted from 100 for every item that is missing. (If you wish, you can deduct less than the full amount— 3 points out of 10, say, if the student has only one main point.) You may want to let each grade count the same as a chapter quiz grade.
- Evaluation Forms – In the "Evaluation Forms" section in the front of this manual can be found the following:
  - E-1, Checklist for Revising an Outline—This form can be used by the instructor to evaluate outlines and point out what changes the student should make.

  - E-2, Checklist for Revising an Outline—This is just like E-1 except it adds a grading scheme.

  - E-21, Evaluation of Sample Outline—This form can be used to force students to study sample outlines in the book. You can pass out E-21 and assign a sample outline. You might want to

	do this in class and take up the papers to make sure that all items are filled in.
3. Create effective speaking notes based on their outline.	**In the Text:** • Pages 247-249 • Key terms: speaking notes **On Speeches DVD and on connectpublicspeaking.com:** • Videos – Several speeches provide good models of speakers using notes: o Full Speech #2 ("The Four-Day Work Week") shows a speaker who uses notes effectively. An outline and transcript of this speech appear in Chapter 12. o Full Speech #19 ("Are You Being Overcharged?") illustrates the correct way to use notes. **On connectpublicspeaking.com:** • Supplementary Readings o "How to Use Check-Off Notes"

Resources For Entire Chapter:

At End of Chapter:

- Summary
- Key Terms
- Review Questions
- Building Critical-Thinking Skills
- Building Teamwork Skills

On Speeches DVD and on connectpublicspeaking.com:

o Full Speech #2 ("The Four-Day Work Week") shows a speaker who uses notes effectively. An outline and transcript of this speech appear in Chapter 12.

On connectpublicspeaking.com:

- Practice test for chapter
- Checklist (for Preparing and Delivering a Speech)
- Glossary of terms
- Key-term flashcards
- Interactive exercise for chapter
- Building Internet Skills (used to be in book, now online)

On Instructor's Resource DVD-ROM:

- PowerPoint: Chapter Highlights – A PowerPoint program gives highlights of each chapter and includes some video clips. **(NOTE: Many of the PowerPoint slides have no text and require the explanation given in the accompanying script.)**
- Tests – Ready-made chapter tests and a computerized test bank are provided.
- Building an Outline – This PowerPoint program demonstrates the step-by-step creation of an outline. It is also available on the Instructor's section of connectpublicspeaking.com.

Your Thoughts?

p. 238:   For an outline on the different breeds of dogs, which major headings would you create?

(Answers will vary). Some students might choose Purebred Dogs/Mixed-breed Dogs....or Companion Dogs/Guard Dogs/Hunting Dogs...and so on

p. 241:   On an Internet discussion forum, a student wanted to entice as many people as possible to read his argument for the vegetarian diet, so he used this title: "How to Make a Million Dollars." Is this a blunder or a clever strategy?

(Answers will vary). A title can be catchy, but it should never be deceptive. The audience will be irritated, and the student's credibility will be severely damaged.

p. 250:   If you practice in front of friends, why is it better to say "Tell me the parts that need improvement" instead of "Tell me if you like this"?

(Answers will vary). "Tell me the parts that need improvement" will elicit helpful advice, while "Tell me if you like this" will elicit compliments "(Oh, it's great!).

Review Questions

Key to questions on p. 253 in the textbook:

1.   Why is an outline recommended for all speeches?

    An outline helps the speaker organize thoughts into a logical sequence and include all necessary information.

2.   What is a topic outline?

    A topic outline is a systematic arrangement of ideas, using words and phrases—rather than complete sentences—for headings and subheadings.

3.   What are the advantages of using complete sentences in an outline?

    Writing complete sentences forces you to sharpen your thinking, and if another person helps you with your outline, complete sentences will be easier for him or her to understand than mere phrases.

4.   What are the parts of an outline?

    Title, general purpose, specific purpose, central idea, introduction, body, conclusion, transitions, bibliography, and visual aids

5.   The text says that the title of an outline should not be spoken in the speech. Why, then, should you have one?

    In some situations, a title might be needed to publicize a speech in advance.

6.   Why should each subdivision of an outline have at least two parts?

    Logically, an item cannot be subdivided into just one piece (just as an orange cannot be cut into one piece; there must be at least two subdivisions).

7.   What are the advantages of using cards for speaking notes?

    Cards are compact, inconspicuous, and easy to hold. Their small size forces the speaker to use just a few key words.

8.   What are the disadvantages of using a full sheet of paper for speaking notes?

    (1) A speaker might be tempted to write down too many notes, causing him or her to look extensively at the sheet rather than at the audience. (2) A full sheet makes it easy for the speaker's eyes to glide over key points. (3) If the sheet is brought to the speech rolled up, it can curl up on the lectern. (4) If no lectern is available, and the sheet is hand-held, it can shake and rustle. (5) It is harder to make last-minute changes on a full sheet than on note cards because the entire sheet has to be rewritten.

9. You are advised to "revise for continuity." What does this mean?

   Practice your speech and listen for a smooth, even flow. When parts of the speech seem clunky and rough, revise until you achieve smoothness.

10. What are the advantages of using visual aids as prompts?

   You can focus on the audience and walk around the room, projecting confidence.

Building Critical-Thinking Skills

Key to questions on p. 253 in the textbook:

1. Sort out the items [in the text] and place them into a coherent topic outline. In addition to a title, the scrambled list includes four major headings, with three subheadings under each.

   The title should be Hobbies & Interests. In any order, the following should be major headings (with subheadings in parentheses): Games (Scrabble, Bingo, Paintball), Photography (Cameras, Digital Imagery, Darkroom), Cooking (Recipes, Kitchenware, Stoves), and Gardening (Annuals, Perennials, Ornamentals)

2. Transform the topic outline [in the text] into a complete-sentence outline. Create a central idea for the outline.

   (Answers will vary.)

Activities

1. Assign skill builders at the end of the chapter in the text (Building Critical-Thinking Skills and Building Teamwork Skills).

2. Lead students through the "Building an Outline" PowerPoint program (available in the Instructor's Resource DVD-ROM and on the instructor's section of connectpublicspeaking.com, which shows how to create an outline step by step.

Objective Tests

Four ready-to-print tests for Chapter 12 (Forms A, B, C, D), and answer keys for all tests are provided in this instructor's manual. The four forms cover the same material, but are sufficiently different to permit one test to be used as the class test, and the others as makeup tests for absentees. Form A features true-false questions, Forms B and C have multiple-choice questions, while Form D is more difficult, requiring students to fill in missing words or phrases. Instructors may want to combine Form D with some of the essay questions listed below.

Essay & Discussion Questions

The following can be used as essay questions for tests or as stimuli for class discussions.

1. Why is outlining important in the construction of a speech?

2. Why are complete sentences recommended for outlines?

3. Describe the key features of effective speaking notes.

4. Discuss the three options suggested by the text for speaking notes.

5. What are the parts of an outline?

6. Why should each subdivision of an outline have at least two parts?

Name _____

Completion Of Outline

Speech assignment:_____

	starting point:	100
no title	-5	
no general purpose	-5	
no specific purpose	-5	
no central idea	-10	
no attention material in introduction	-10	
no orienting material in introduction	-10	
no transition between introduction and body	-5	
no main points	-10	
no supports for main points	-10	
no transitions between main points	-5	
no transition between body and conclusion	-5	
no conclusion	-10	
no bibliography	-5	
no visual aids (if required)	-5	
FINAL GRADE		

Chapter 13
Wording the Speech

Chapter Objectives and Resource Integrator

After studying this chapter, students should be able to:

Objectives	Resources
1. Explain the importance of choosing words that are appropriate for the audience and the occasion.	**In the Text:** • Pages 256-259 • Key term: sex-related stereotype **On Instructor's Resource DVD-ROM:** "Lessons from the Movies" – An illustrated narrative based on the movie *Erin Brockovich* shows the damage that can be caused by using crude language. **On Speeches DVD and on connectpublicspeaking.com:** • Full Speech #22 ("Three Celebrity Heroes") illustrates the use of artful, appropriate language in a speech.

2. Define two types of doublespeak (euphemisms and inflated language).	**In the Text:**
	
	• Pages 263-265
	• Key terms: doublespeak, euphemism, inflated language
	
	On connectpublicspeaking.com:
	
	• Interactive Exercises
	  o "Can You Translate Doublespeak?"
	
	  o Doublespeak—A good follow-up to a class discussion of doublespeak, this worksheet stimulates students to figure out the meanings of euphemisms and inflated words.

3. Describe the two significant differences between oral and written language.	**In the Text:** • Pages 268-269
4. Explain the value of using correct grammar.	**In the Text:** • Pages 261-262

5. Explain the importance of using words that are clear, accurate, and vivid.	**In the Text:**
	
	• Pages 259-263
	• Key terms: denotation, connotation, concrete words, abstract words, doublespeak, euphemism, inflated language, jargon, imagery, metaphor, simile, mixed metaphor, cliché, parallel structure, repetition, alliteration, antithesis
	
	On Speeches DVD and on connectpublicspeaking.com:
	
	• Video clip 13.1, shows a speaker using words effectively.
	
	On connectpublicspeaking.com:
	
	• Supplementary Readings
	  o "I Have A Dream" by Dr. Martin Luther King, Jr. – Commentary on a speech that is famous, among other things, for its powerful use of language.
	
	  o Oral Interpretation of Literature—This material includes tips for oral reading and a few sample passages.
	
	  o Finding Literature for Oral Readings—Tips and Internet addresses for locating good material for oral interpretation.
	
	• Interactive Exercises
	  o "Can You Translate Doublespeak?"
	
	  o Doublespeak—A good follow-up to a class discussion of doublespeak, this exercise stimulates students to figure out the meanings of euphemisms and inflated words.
	
	  o Clichés—This simple, entertaining exercise shows students the predictability of clichés.
	
	  o Gobbledygook—Though the term gobbledygook (pompous, stuffy language) is not used in the textbook, students may enjoy learning the term (if they don't already know it) and translating gobbledygook into plain English.
	
	  o Avoiding Repetition—While students should recognize that oral language requires more elaboration than written language, they should nevertheless avoid unneeded repetition.
	
	  o Eliminating Wordiness—Students can learn to reduce windy phrases to one word.
	
	In the Instructor's Manual (on Instructor's Resource DVD-ROM):
	
	• Sheet 13.1, Clichés–Classroom Activity—The instructor can use these clichés as an oral activity for the whole class, saying the first part of the cliché and letting students say the final word in unison.

Resources For Entire Chapter:

At End of Chapter:

- Summary
- Key Terms
- Review Questions
- Building Critical-Thinking Skills
- Building Teamwork Skills

On connectpublicspeaking.com:

- Practice test for chapter
- Checklist (for Preparing and Delivering a Speech)
- Glossary of terms
- Key-term flashcards
- Interactive exercise for chapter
- Building Internet Skills (used to be in book, now online)

On Instructor's Resource DVD-ROM:

- PowerPoint: Chapter Highlights – A PowerPoint program gives highlights of each chapter and includes some video clips. **(NOTE: Many of the PowerPoint slides have no text and require the explanation given in the accompanying script.)**
- Tests – Ready-made chapter tests and a computerized test bank are provided.

Your Thoughts?

p. 261:   A publishing company was embarrassed when a receptionist, responding to a request to speak to an executive, said, "He don't work here no more." Why do you think the company was embarrassed?

> *(Answers will vary). A representative of a publishing house who makes two grammatical mistakes in one sentence spoils the image that a publisher wants to project – literate people who are careful with language.*

p. 264:   In referring to poor people, a government official once spoke of "fiscal underachievers." Why do you think he chose this term?

> *(Answers will vary). He may have wanted to avoid wincing while speaking blunt truth. He may have wanted to avoid admitting that the country has people living in poverty. Or perhaps he wanted to come across as someone who possessed profound knowledge.*

p. 268:   While effective in speeches, repetition is sometimes used in oral communication for unethical – even evil – purposes. Give some examples from history or contemporary culture.

History and current events abound with examples, such as Nazi propaganda, which repeated over and over again the assertion that Jews were a degenerate race of people.

Review Questions

Key to questions on p. 270 in the textbook:

1. Why did Dr. Martin Luther King use different words with different audiences?

   He wanted to reach each audience on its own terms, using language that was appropriate for each.

2. What is the difference between the denotation and the connotation of a word?

   The denotation of a word is the thing or idea that it refers to—its dictionary definition. The connotation of a word is the emotional meaning that is associated with it.

3. Why is incorrect grammar a handicap for a speaker?

   Some listeners devalue speakers who use poor grammar and consider them as not very intelligent.

4. What is a euphemism? Give an example.

   A euphemism is a mild, indirect, or vague word used in place of one that is harsh, blunt, or offensive. (Examples will vary.)

5. What is inflated language? Give an example.

   Inflated words are designed to puff up the importance of the person or thing being described. (Examples will vary.)

6. "Her life was a whirlwind of meetings, deadlines, and last-minute decisions." Change this metaphor to a simile.

   "Her life was like a whirlwind of meetings, deadlines, and last minute decision."

7. "My love," said poet Robert Burns, "is like a red, red rose." Change this simile to a metaphor.

   "My love is a red, red rose."

8. This sentence commits a mistake: "Learning is a spark in a person's mind that must be watered constantly." What is the term used for this error?

   Mixed metaphor

9. "Louise languished in the land of lilies and lilacs." Which rhetorical device is used in this sentence?

   Alliteration

10. In what way should oral language be treated differently from written language?

    Oral language requires more elaboration and repetition than written language.

Building Critical Thinking Skills

Key to questions on p. 270 in the textbook:

1. Some sports teams are named after birds— in football, Philadelphia Eagles, Atlanta Falcons, Seattle Seahawks, and Phoenix Cardinals; in baseball, Toronto Blue Jays, St. Louis Cardinals, and Baltimore Orioles. Why are teams named after these birds, and yet no teams are named after vultures, crows, or pigeons?

   The names of the first set of birds have positive connotations (or emotional associations), suggesting beauty, grace, and power; the latter birds have negative connotations (for example, the name "vulture" suggests an unsavory predator).

2. A book on automobile repair was once advertised under the headline "How to Repair Cars." When the advertising agency changed the headline to read, "How to Fix Cars," sales jumped by 20 percent. Why do you think sales increased?

   Although "fix" and "repair" mean the same thing, "fix" is obviously more effective than "repair," probably because fixing a car sounds easier than repairing it.

Activities

1. Assign skill builders at the end of the chapter in the text (Building Critical-Thinking Skills and Building Teamwork Skills).

2. Have students read the "I Have a Dream" speech by Martin Luther King and prepare for a class discussion on the use of language. If possible, let students hear an audiotape or videotape of the speech as they follow the transcript. (You may purchase an audiotape or videotape from a local bookstore or Amazon.com Web site.)

3. Have a "cliché hunt" by asking students to listen to a TV talk show at home and write down the clichés that they hear.

4. To demonstrate the difference between written and oral language, have students find a written passage that is concise and terse and then rewrite it in the amplified style of oral language.

Objective Tests

Four ready-to-print tests for Chapter 13 (Forms A, B, C, D), and answer keys for all tests are provided in this instructor's manual. The four forms cover the same material, but are sufficiently different to permit one test to be used as the class test and the others as makeup tests for absentees. Form A features true-false questions, Forms B and C have multiple-choice questions, while Form D is more difficult, requiring students to fill in missing words or phrases. Instructors may want to combine Form D with some of the essay questions listed below.

The following can be used as essay questions for tests or as stimuli for class discussions.

1. "They say that too much salt is bad for you." What is wrong with this sentence as a statement in a speech?

2. Discuss the difference between the denotation and the connotation of words, giving examples of both.

3. How should a public speaker use language differently from the way an essay writer would use language?

4. Define euphemisms and give at least two examples.

5. Define inflated language and give at least two examples.

6. Why should crude language be omitted from speeches?

Clichés—Classroom Activity

Say the following clichés, pausing to let the class fill in the final word:

absence makes the heart grow	fonder
add insult to	injury
bark up the wrong	tree
take the bull by the	horns
a chip off the old	block
never a dull	moment
out of sight, out of	mind
pay through the	nose
turn over a new	leaf
your guess is as good as	mine
if push comes to	shove
never look a gift horse in the	mouth
as sly as a	fox
as quiet as a	mouse
a needle in a	haystack
take this with a grain of	salt
we awoke at the crack of	dawn

Chapter 14
Delivering the Speech

Chapter Objectives and Resource Integrator

After studying this chapter, students should be able to:

Objectives	Resources
1. Explain the four methods of delivery.	**In the Text:** • Pages 275-278 • Key terms: manuscript, impromptu, extemporaneous **In the Instructor's Manual (on Instructor's Resource DVD-ROM):** • Impromptu Speech Topics are listed in Topic Helper **Activities for Impromptu Speaking:** • Sheet 14.2, "Humorous Impromptu Speaking" by Jan Caldwell • Sheet 14.3, Impromptu Critique Sheet – Jan Caldwell • Sheet 14.4, "Impromptu Speech Ideas," courtesy of Deb Maddox • Sheet 14.5, Template for Playing Cards – Deb Maddox

2. Practice and deliver an extemporaneous speech.	**In the Text:**
	
	• Pages 277-278
	• Key terms: extemporaneous
	
	On Speeches DVD and on connectpublicspeaking.com:
	
	• Video Clips:
	  o 14.1 – Extemporaneous Method
	
	  o 14.2 – Conversational Style of Speaking
	
	  o 14.3 – Speaking with Notes
	
	• Videos – The following illustrate both good and bad examples of delivery:
	  o Full Speech #3 ("One Slip – and You're Dead") shows a speaker who has a strong desire to communicate with her audience.
	
	  o Full Speech #5 ("Animal Helpers I – Informative Speech That Needs Improvement") shows delivery that is clumsy and apologetic because of poor preparation.
	
	  o Full Speech #6 ("Animal Helpers II – Improved Version")

	shows the same speaker as in Speech 5, but this time she has animated delivery and vocal variety.

	On connectpublicspeaking.com:
	
	• Supplementary Readings:
	  o "How to Use Check-Off Notes"—A handy system that is becoming popular in business and professional presentations.
	  o "Can You Practice Too Much?"—This handout helps students avoid the wrong kind of rehearsal and delivery.
	  o "Speaking in Front of a Camera"—Tips for live and taped TV and video productions.
	  o "Tips for ESL Students" – This article provides friendly suggestions for students who speak English as a second language.

3. Use effective vocal techniques in a speech.	**In the Text:**
	
	• Pages 278-284
	• Key terms: articulation, pronunciation, pitch, intonation, verbal fillers
	
	On Speeches DVD and on connectpublicspeaking.com:
	
	• Full Speech #7 ("Humanoid Robots") shows a speaker who has a strong, pleasant voice.
	
	On connectpublicspeaking.com:
	
	• Supplementary Readings
	
	  o "Oral Interpretation of Literature"—This material includes tips for oral reading and a few sample passages. Oral readings help some students to use their voices expressively and dramatically.
	  o "Finding Literature for Oral Readings"—Tips and Internet addresses for locating good material for oral interpretation.
	  o "Voice Production"—This article gives basic information about the human voice and the production of sound.
	  o "Common Pronunciation Mistakes"—This list of pronunciation problem words is a supplement to the list in Chapter 14 of the text.
	
	In the Instructor's Manual (on Instructor's Resource DVD-ROM):
	
	• Sheet 14.1, Vocal Exercises for Public Speakers (by Sandi

	Jenkins Goodridge)—These exercises help students loosen up and speak naturally and forcefully.

4. Demonstrate effective nonverbal communication in a speech.	**In the Text:**
	
	• Pages 284-291
	• Key terms: nonverbal communication, posture
	
	On Speeches DVD and on connectpublicspeaking.com:
	
	• Video Clips:
	   o 14.1 – Extemporaneous Method
	   o 14.2 – Conversational Style of Speaking
	   o 14.3 – Speaking with Notes
	   o 14.4 – Using Gestures
	• Full Speeches – The following show speakers giving lively, conversational speeches with effective nonverbal communication skills:
	   o Full Speech #10 ("How to Make Avocado Salsa")
	   o Full Speech #19 ("Are You Being Overcharged?")
	   o Full Speech #22 ("Three Celebrity Heroes")
	   o Full Speech #1 ("Scars and Bruises")
	
	On Instructor's Resource DVD-ROM:
	
	• "Lessons from the Movies" – An illustrated narrative based on the movie *Philadelphia* shows the effective use of gestures.
	
	On connectpublicspeaking.com:
	
	• Interactive Exercise:
	   o "Evaluate Nonverbal Communication"

5. Conduct a question-and-answer period in a manner that encourages audience participation.	**In the Text:** • Pages 291-292
6. Utilize productive methods in practicing a speech.	**In the Text:** • Page 293

Resources For Entire Chapter:

At End of Chapter:

- Summary
- Key Terms
- Review Questions
- Building Critical-Thinking Skills
- Building Teamwork Skills

On connectpublicspeaking.com:

- Practice test for chapter
- Checklist (for Preparing and Delivering a Speech)
- Glossary of terms
- Key-term flashcards
- Interactive exercise for chapter
- Building Internet Skills (used to be in book, now online)

On Instructor's Resource DVD-ROM:

- PowerPoint: Chapter Highlights – A PowerPoint program gives highlights of each chapter and includes some video clips. **(NOTE: Many of the PowerPoint slides have no text and require the explanation given in the accompanying script.)**
- Tests – Ready-made chapter tests and a computerized test bank are provided.

Your Thoughts?

p. 275: Is perfect delivery necessary in order for a speech to be considered highly successful? Defend your answer.

> *(Answers will vary). Perfection is rare. A perfect delivery of lousy content does not make a speech great. And a speech can be successful even if the content is brilliant and the delivery is ragged.*

p. 285: What nonverbal message is given by a person who goes to a funeral dressed in a T-shirt and jeans?

> *(Answers will vary). Disrespect – even if the person intended no such message.*

p. 288: Italians tend to use big gestures, and they gesture more frequently than the typical American. Should an American speaker try to imitate the style of Italian speakers? Defend your answer.

> *(Answers will vary). American speakers should not try to imitate speaker in other cultures. If speakers are concentrating on getting a message across, gestures are made without conscious effort.*

Key to questions on pp. 294-295 in the textbook:

1. What are the disadvantages of impromptu, manuscript, and memorized speeches?

   Impromptu speeches are unplanned, so the speaker often gives a rambling, poorly organized, poorly delivered speech. Manuscript speeches are often dull because speakers read them in a monotone and fail to maintain good eye contact with the audience. Memorized speeches sometimes sound mechanical, as if the speaker is speaking from memory and not from the heart; furthermore, the speaker runs the risk of forgetting his or her lines.

2. What ingredient is essential for the success of an extemporaneous speech?

   Preparation

3. Why is it a serious mistake to speak too rapidly at the beginning of a speech?

   The listeners need time to get accustomed to your voice and to get into the groove of your speech.

4. What are the characteristics of good eye contact?

   Good eye contact involves looking at the audience 95 percent of the time and looking at all parts of the audience.

5. What can speakers do with their hands to make sure that they are free for gesturing?

   Speakers can let their hands rest lightly on the lectern or they can allow them to hang naturally by their sides.

6. Why should a speech be learned and practiced point-by-point, instead of word for word?

   Extemporaneous speakers should learn and practice only their ideas, so that the words used to express those ideas will sound fresh, spontaneous, and conversational.

7. What form of visual aids can cause you to lose eye contact with your audience?

   Handouts

8. How many times should a speaker practice going through the entire speech?

   At least four times

9. How should you handle a listener who casts doubt on some of your facts and figures?

   Try to avoid being defensive. See if the listener's point has some merit, and if it does, say so. In some cases, you can promise to look into the matter and let the listener know later what you discovered.

10. If there is a discrepancy between your words and your nonverbal behavior, which will the audience believe?

    Listeners will interpret the nonverbal behavior as being the real message. In other words, if you say "I'm happy to be here," but your facial expression seems to contradict your words, the audience will think you are uncomfortable or a liar, or both.

Key to questions on p. 295 in the textbook:

1. "If a man takes off his sunglasses, I can hear him better," says writer Hugh Prather. Explain the meaning of this statement in terms of public speaking.

    Eye contact is an important accompaniment to words. A listener who can't see the speaker's eyes has difficulty in assessing the sincerity and conviction of the speaker.

2. Tennis coaches observe a phenomenon called "analysis equals paralysis." Novice players become so fixated on holding the racket correctly and swinging properly that they miss the ball. What lessons could public speakers draw from this phenomenon?

    If a speaker is fixated on delivery techniques, such as gestures, he or she will fail to give full energy to the most important part of speechmaking—connecting with the audience.

Activities

1. Assign skill builders at the end of the chapter in the text (Building Critical-Thinking Skills and Building Teamwork Skills).

2. Impromptu Speaking—Some instructors give students short impromptu speaking assignments to help them learn to "think on their feet" and to help them sharpen their delivery skills. There are also two other varieties of impromptu speaking that are widely used:

    Oral Evaluations of Class Speeches: Some instructors assign several students to give oral critiques of a classmate's speech immediately following the speech. This assignment can be given to selected students before the speech begins, or—to keep all listeners on their toes—it can be assigned at random after the speech.

    Question-and-Answer Period: If you require your students to hold question-and-answer periods after each major speech, they will gain experience in a form of impromptu speaking.

3. Students can develop a sensitivity to good delivery techniques by critiquing their fellow students, and also by evaluating speakers in the community. You may want to assign students to evaluate a community speaker, using the section "Speech Evaluations" in Chapter 3 and one of the evaluation forms published in the front part of this manual.

Objective Tests

Four ready-to-print tests for Chapter 14 (Forms A, B, C, D), and answer keys for all tests are provided in this instructor's manual. The four forms cover the same material, but are sufficiently different to permit one test to be used as the class test, and the others as makeup tests for absentees. Form A features true-false questions, Forms B and C have multiple-choice questions, while Form D is more difficult, requiring students to fill in missing words or phrases. Instructors may want to combine Form D with some of the essay questions listed below.

Essay & Discussion Questions

The following can be used as essay questions for tests or as stimuli for class discussions.

1. What is the most effective method of delivery for most speeches and why is it so effective?

2. Why is eye contact so important in a speech?

3. Discuss the effective use of gestures during a speech.

4. Describe how you should conduct yourself at the beginning of your speech and at the end.

5. Discuss how you should conduct a question-and-answer period.

Vocal Exercises for Public Speakers

Sandi Jenkins Goodridge

I.   To loosen up your vocal cords and "stretch" the diaphragm muscles, work up to 5 repetitions of the following exercises. Don't start doing them the day before your big speech. Say them once or twice a day out loud, in a normal, conversational voice.

The rain in Spain falls mainly on the plain.

Fah	Mah	Pah	Lah	Dah	Tah
Mest	Best	Lest	Jest	Test	Rest
Doe	Roe	Sow	Poe	Low	Foe
Loo	Doo	Soo	Foo	Too	You
Run	Fum	Ton	Sun	Pun	Yun
Me	Tee	Lee	See	Dee	Ree
Say	Fay	Ray	Lay	Tay	May
Si	Pie	Tie	Lie	My	Rie

II. To exercise your vocal cords, you must learn to project your voice. Try these techniques:

  A. Using a room larger than 20 feet long, speak to someone on the other end of the room while remaining conversational. Don't "raise" your voice or scream or screech. Try to remain natural and sound normal.

  B. Record your voice on a tape recorder from 3 feet, 6 feet, etc. Keep playing back the tape, without turning up the volume, until you can be heard from 20 feet away.

  C. Try speaking naturally over a loud distraction (dishwasher, television) until your partner says that you are clear and distinct.

III. Exercise neck and facial muscles prior to giving your speech. Don't overdo!

  A. Slowly lower your chin to your chest and hold for five seconds. Avoid movement to the rear.

  B. Pantomime the words oh! ah! wee! wow! in front of the mirror until you can see a difference in all four facial expressions.

  C. Take several deep breaths, while pulling up your shoulders as far as possible toward your ears. Exhale and slowly release your shoulders. Grasp your fingers in front of you; pull hands over and behind your head as far as possible; return to the front of your body. Repeat.

Now, you're ready to speak!

© Sandi Jenkins Goodridge—used with permission

Humorous Impromptu Speaking

Jan Caldwell

First, refer students to the text pages on impromptu delivery and the use of humor.

Second, remind them of the following:
- Impromptu speeches vary in degree of formality just like other speeches, from casual conversation to answers in class to job interviews to actual speeches.
- You can anticipate when it's likely you'll be called on and prepare a quick response.
- You can buy thinking time by restating the question in a full sentence form.
- You can keep good stories/examples in mind and practice them for just such a time to use as openers, clinchers, or support (for example, stories from comedians or plots/examples from literature, songs, movies, TV, and your own life.
- You can organize by using the motivated sequence to sell it to us, statement of reasons to convince us, topical list of uses/benefits to educate us, chronological organization to show us how it works, etc.
- You can lengthen the speech by including an attention grabber, incentive to listen, credibility, background, clear thesis, preview, review of points/thesis, clincher.
- You must avoid standing there giving a long list of uses with no development for any of the ideas.
- You should never begin without knowing how you'll end.
- You have permission to laugh at each other and should.
- You should bring a pen and an outline shell with the parts labeled to remind you what you have to fill in.
- As you search through the bag, be thinking what you'd do with each item you touch.
- You can use the items as springboards to lead in other directions such as a plastic bottle leading to a speech on recycling, modern day conveniences, the liquid metric system, etc.
- You can prepare by thinking of possible scenarios and how you'd develop them. For example:
  - ❖ Think of what you'd say about a bottle of liquid, a box, a stuffed animal, a writing utensil, etc.
  - ❖ Practice picking up random articles and speaking about them or finding random quotes and speaking about them.
  - ❖ Practice using silly arguments to refute a politician or commercial.

Procedure for in-class humorous impromptu speeches
- The first speaker may have 5 minutes to prepare after choosing his/her topic. After the 5 minutes and before the first person speaks, the second person draws so that he/she may go out in the hall and prepare while the first student speaks and is critiqued. This continues until all are done.
- Speaking order is voluntary but when students quit volunteering, the speeches are over with no chance to speak later.
- The students may choose an object from a bag of items without looking or choose three topics from an envelope and select the one he/she thinks can be best

developed. Students may not decide to choose from the other source once they've checked out the first source.
- Students may make a quick key word outline if they prefer – but mustn't try to read it.
- Fabrication is permitted. Students may make up creative new uses for the items found in the bag. They may claim responsibility for inventing it. They may lie about sources and credibility.
- Speaking time is 2-3 minutes. Time cards will be visible the entire time.

Sources of topics for the envelope:
- For informative speeches or more serious minded speakers, quotes found in daily pocket calendars make good topics.
- Make up silly stuff such as:
    Explain how to train a chicken to dance.
    Explain how to prepare crickets for a formal dinner.
    Explain three good places to store rubber bands.
    Debate: Peanut butter is better than jelly.
    Recount the most memorable spaghetti you've ever met.
    Explain how to build up the muscles in your nose.
    Teach the rules for elevator basketball.
    Tell us the real story of Little Red Riding Hood.
    Self-actualization through tattooing
- For the bag of stuff, wander around the house/office and find interesting items without much writing on them (students tend to stand and read them as part of the speech) such as:
    ❖ chirping Easter chicken (this became a disguised hand grenade)
    ❖ an ink pen (this became an anti-aging serum injector)
    ❖ a mouse nose (this became a safety mask, a costume and a Speedo as three uses given during the same speech)
    ❖ a plastic tablecloth (this became a cloaking device)
    ❖ a fuzzy mitten (this became a strange hairy disease which the student told us the cause and cure for)
    ❖ a pack of McCormick stir fry seasoning (this became a springboard for the story of how this portable food was invented by Mr. McCormick for his ailing wife who couldn't get out of bed)
    ❖ a pot holder (this became a portable flying carpet)
    ❖ a bottle of vanilla extract (this became a weight control syrup which would never run out)

Impromptu Critique Sheet

On the following page is a critique sheet developed by public speaking instructor Jan Caldwell

14.3

_____   _____
Speaker   Topic/ Title

_____   Comments:
Assignment

Choice of Subject (10)

Supporting Material (10)

Introduction (10)

Body / Organization/ Development (10)

Conclusion (10)

Bodily Action (10)

Eye Contact / Rapport (10)

Voice (10)

Language / Style (10)

Overall Effect (such as appearance, control of environment, style, etc.) (10)

Grade_____   Time_____

Ideas for Impromptu Speaking

courtesy of Deb Maddox

Public speaking instructor Deb Maddox shares some of her time-tested strategies for impromptu speeches:

1. Use a designated emotion

Students draw slips of paper from a cup. Each slip has a specific emotion written on it. Students must tell an impromptu narrative of a time when they've experienced the emotion. Emphasis is on a good narrative: attention to detail, cohesive story, specifics.

Here are some samples of the emotions: worry, vindictive, frightened, grossed out, jealous, ashamed, shocked, anxious, embarrassed, annoyed, desperate, frustrated, distraught, overwhelmed, over-the-moon joy, disappointed, intimidated, resentful, victorious, despair.

2. Deck of cards

Create a "playing cards" chart with each slot listing an impromptu topic. *(The template for the chart is on the next page.)* From a deck of cards, students draw a card, which will lead them to their topic. For example, if they draw the Jack of Spades, they look at the chart and see the corresponding topic.

Any kind of topics can be inserted into the chart. Maddox uses "advantages" and "disadvantages" (such as "Advantages to living by a dump" and "Disadvantages of finding buried treasure"). "Students have a lot of fun and creativity with the assignments," she says. "They are required to come up with 3 advantages or disadvantages for each topic. They can make up the support material. That's where a lot of the laughs come from."

See next page for the template that Maddox uses.

14.5

	Spades	Hearts	Clubs	Diamonds
2				
3				
4				
5				
6				
7				
8				
9				
10				
J				
Q				
K				
A				

Chapter 15
Speaking to Inform

Chapter Objectives and Resource Integrator

After studying this chapter, students should be able to:

Objectives	Resources

1. Prepare an informative speech.	**In the Text:**
	• Pages 298-299
	• Pages 250-252 (sample speech in Ch. 12)
	• Pages 310-316 (sample speech in Ch. 15)
	
	On Speeches DVD and on connectpublicspeaking.com:
	• Video Clip 15.1 – Relate a Speech to the Listeners' Self-Interest
	• Full Speech Videos – The following are models of informative speaking:
	  o Full Speech #3 ("One Slip – and You're Dead") – An outline and transcript of this speech appear in Chapter 15.
	
	  o Full Speech #2 ("The Four-Day Work Week – Pros and Cons) – An outline and transcript of this speech appear in Chapter 12.
	
	  o Full Speech #4 ("Wedding Crashers")
	
	  o Full Speech # 6 ("Animal Helpers II")
	
	  o Full Speech # 7 ("Humanoid Robots")
	
	  o Full Speech # 8 ("Indian Weddings")
	
	  o Full Speech # 10 ("How to Make Avocado Salsa")
	
	  o Full Speech # 11 ("How to Hide Valuables")
	
	On connectpublicspeaking.com:
	• Topic Helper—Students can browse through sample topics for demonstration and informative speeches.
	• Supplementary Readings
	  o Informative Speech – Sample outline and speech ("How to Handle Losing Your Job")

2. Identify four types of informative speeches.	**In the Text:** • Pages 299-305

	- Key terms: extended definition, definition speech, description speech, process speech, explanation speech **On Speeches DVD and on connectpublicspeaking.com:** - Full Speech # 10 ("How to Make Avocado Salsa") is a process (demonstration) speech. - Full Speech #3 ("One Slip – and You're Dead") is a definition speech that defines the term "free solo climbing." - Full Speech #2 ("The Four-Day Work Week – Pros and Cons) is an explanation speech.
3. Explain how to make information interesting.	**In the Text:** - Pages 305-309 **On Speeches DVD and on connectpublicspeaking.com:** - Video Clip 15.1 – Relate a Speech to the Listeners' Self-Interest - Full Speech # 5 ("Animal Helpers I – Informative Speech That Needs Improvement") shows a speaker who fails to offer listeners new and interesting material. - Full Speech # 6 ("Animal Helpers II – Improved Version") shows the same speaker as in Speech 5, but this time she gives interesting material. **On connectpublicspeaking.com:** - Interactive Exercise: o "Which Topics are Boring and Which Are Interesting?"
4. Explain how to help listeners understand and remember key information.	**In the Text:** - Pages 309-310

Your Thoughts?

p. 299:   How can you avoid giving listeners information that all of them already know?

(Answers will vary). By using interviews and surveys beforehand to find out what they know and don't know.

p. 308:   A survey found that one-third of adult Americans did not know which countries the U.S. fought in World War II. Are these people stupid? Defend your answer.

(Answers will vary). Not necessarily. Intelligent people have different storehouses of knowledge.

p. 310:   It is important to avoid overdosing on the fat-soluble vitamins K, A, D, and E. Create a memory aid to help an audience remember them.

(Answers will vary). An acronym – KADE – would make a handy memory aid.

Review Questions

Key to questions on p. 317 in the textbook:

1. What is an extended definition? Why is it preferable in a speech to a dictionary definition?

    An extended definition gives a full, richly detailed picture of the meaning of a term. This is obviously preferable to a dictionary definition, which is terse and dry.

2. Which two organizational patterns would be most appropriate for a speech on the life and achievements of astronaut Sally Ride?

    Chronological and topical

3. What are the two kinds of process speeches?

    One kind shows the listeners how to perform a process so that they can actually use the skills later; the other kind explains a process so that the listeners understand it, not necessarily so that they can perform it themselves.

4. In a process speech, at what point should you give listeners a warning?

    Give warning whenever you approach a difficult or tricky step.

5. Which organizational pattern would be most appropriate for a speech aimed at dispelling misconceptions about wolves?

    Fallacy-fact pattern (or myth-reality)

6. Why is it important to relate a speech, if possible, to the listeners' self-interest?

    Relating a speech to their self-interest increases their motivation to listen to the speech carefully.

7. Why is the issue of generalities versus specifics an important matter in informative speaking?

    Generalities tend to be tedious and boring, while specifics can make a speech interesting.

8. What should you do if some members of an audience know the meaning of a term but others do not?

    Explain the term—in a casual, unobtrusive way, if possible.

9. A speaker says, "The lungs of a heavy smoker look like charred meat." What principle of informative speaking is the speaker using?

    Using the familiar to explain the unfamiliar.

10. "ASAP" is an example of what kind of memory aid?

    Acronym.

Key to questions on p. 318 in the textbook:

1. A student who wanted to teach his classmates how to perform CPR (cardiopulmonary resuscitation) began his speech by asking, "How many of you know CPR?" Everyone raised a hand. What error did the speaker make?

    Failure to find out what the audience already knew.

2. A handout from a dog-obedience class says, "Training a well-behaved dog takes time and practice. The more repetitions you do on a regular basis, the quicker your dog will understand. However, do not bore him. Keep your training sessions fun and interesting." Do you think this advice would apply to training humans? Justify your answer.

    (Answers will vary.) Possibility: Humans, like dogs, learn best when they are not bored and when they have a chance to practice or use the new knowledge.

Speeches

Here are some of the varieties of speech assignments that some instructors give for informative speaking:

Informative Speech: Speaking extemporaneously, the student informs the audience about a well-investigated or well-researched topic. Details about this kind of speech may be found in Chapters 5 and 15 of the text. Some instructors let their students choose from among the variety of informative speeches (discussed in the paragraphs below).

Informative Speech with Visual Aids: This speech is like the one just discussed, except that the student is required to use at least one visual aid, as discussed in Chapter 9 of the text. If the student is unable to find a particularly exciting or unusual aid, he or she can, at the very least, put the main points of the speech on posters, one point per poster.

Definition Speech: Students go beyond dictionary definitions to give an extended definition of a concept. Examples of this kind of speech are given in Chapter 15 of the text.

Description Speech: The entire speech is devoted to describing a person, place, object, or event. See examples in Chapter 15 of the text.

Process (or Demonstration) Speech: Some instructors feel that this speech, in which students show how something is done or made, is a good speech to require early in the course because it usually involves manipulation or display of visual aids, which helps dissipate the speaker's nervous tension. Examples of this kind of speech are given in Chapter 15 of the text. (You may want to require visual aids for this speech.)

Explanation Speech: This speech, also called an oral report or lecture, involves explaining a concept or situation to an audience. Many instructors who assign this speech require research into an area that is relatively new to the student, and they may even assign the topic themselves.

Book Analysis: The student reports on a book he or she has read. Key questions that the student should answer: What was the author's purpose? Was the purpose achieved?

Personal Experience Speech: The speaker tells a long story or extended narrative of an event in his or her own life.

Activities

1. Assign skill builders at the end of the chapter in the text (Building Critical-Thinking Skills and Building Teamwork Skills).

2. Hold a class discussion on the informative speech at the end of Chapter 15, focusing on how it is organized and developed.

Objective Tests

Four ready-to-print tests for Chapter 15 (Forms A, B, C, D), and answer keys for all tests are provided in this instructor's manual. The four forms cover the same material, but are sufficiently different to permit one test to be used as the class test, and the others as makeup tests for absentees. Form A features true-false questions, Forms B and C have multiple-choice questions, while Form D is more difficult, requiring students to fill in missing words or phrases. Instructors may want to combine Form D with some of the essay questions listed below.

Essay & Discussion Questions

The following can be used as essay questions for tests or as stimuli for class discussions.

1. Discuss guidelines (as given in the text) for explaining a complicated process to listeners who know little about your subject.

2. "Relate the familiar to explain the unfamiliar." Explain what this means.

3. How can you relate a speech to the listeners' self-interest?

4. How can information be made interesting to an audience?

5. Why should generalities be used sparingly in a speech?

Chapter 16
Speaking to Persuade

Chapter Objectives and Resource Integrator

After studying this chapter, students should be able to:

Objectives	Resources
1. Prepare a persuasive speech.	**In the Text:** • Pages 322-323 • Pages 333-338 (sample speech in Appendix) **On Speeches DVD and on connectpublicspeaking.com:** • Full Speech #18 ("Inmates and Tomatoes") illustrates the motivated sequence. An outline and speech appear in Chapter 16. • Full Speech #20 ("Would You Vote for Aardvark?") uses the problem-solution pattern. An outline and speech appear in Chapter 17. • Full Speech #19 ("Are You Being Overcharged?") uses the motivated sequence. • Full Speech #21 ("Too Much of a Good Thing") uses the problem-solution pattern. • Full Speech #14 ("Bicycle Helmets I – Persuasive Speech That Needs Improvement") shows a speaker who does lots of research, but fails to connect with his listeners. • Full Speech #15 ("Bicycle Helmets II – Improved Version") shows the same speaker as in Speech 14, but this time he gives a powerful persuasive appeal. • Full Speech #16 ("The Deadliest Natural Disaster") uses the motivated sequence. • Full Speech #17 ("Native American Crafts") uses the problem-solution pattern. **On connectpublicspeaking.com:** • Topic Helper—Students can browse through sample topics for persuasive speeches. • Checklist for Preparing and Delivering a Speech—This checklist can be used for both classroom and career speeches. • Supplementary Readings o Persuasive Speech – Sample outline and speech ("Pumping Iron: A Necessity for Everyone")

2. Identify two major types of persuasive speeches.	**In the Text:** • Pages 323-326 • Key terms: speech to influence thinking, speech of refutation, speech to motivate action

3. Identify four patterns for organizing a persuasive speech.	**In the Text:**
	
	• Pages 326-333
	• Key terms: motivated sequence, problem-solution pattern, statement-of-reasons pattern, comparative-advantages pattern
	
	On Speeches DVD and on connectpublicspeaking.com:
	
	• Full Speech #18 ("Inmates and Tomatoes") illustrates the motivated sequence. An outline and speech appear in Chapter 16.
	• Full Speech #20 ("Would You Vote for Aardvark?") uses the problem-solution pattern. An outline and speech appear in Chapter 17.
	• Full Speech #19 ("Are You Being Overcharged?") uses the motivated sequence.
	• Full Speech #21 ("Too Much of a Good Thing") uses the problem-solution pattern.
	• Full Speech #16 ("The Deadliest Natural Disaster") uses the motivated sequence.
	• Full Speech #17 ("Native American Crafts") uses the problem-solution pattern.
	
	On connectpublicspeaking.com:
	
	• Interactive Exercise
	  o "The Motivated Sequence"
	
	  o The Motivated Sequence—Worksheet

Resources For Entire Chapter:

At End of Chapter:

- Summary
- Key Terms
- Review Questions
- Building Critical-Thinking Skills
- Building Teamwork Skills

On Speeches DVD and on connectpublicspeaking.com:

- Full Speech #18 ("Inmates and Tomatoes") illustrates the motivated sequence. An outline and speech appear in Chapter 16.
- Full Speech #20 ("Would You Vote for Aardvark?") uses the problem-solution pattern. An outline and speech appear in Chapter 17.
- Full Speech #19 ("Are You Being Overcharged?") uses the motivated sequence.
- Full Speech #21 ("Too Much of a Good Thing") uses the problem-solution pattern.
- Full Speech #14 ("Bicycle Helmets I – Persuasive Speech That Needs Improvement") shows a speaker who does lots of research, but fails to connect with his listeners.
- Full Speech #15 ("Bicycle Helmets II – Improved Version") shows the same speaker as in Speech 14, but this time he gives a powerful persuasive appeal.
- Full Speech #16 ("The Deadliest Natural Disaster") uses the motivated sequence.
- Full Speech #17 ("Native American Crafts") uses the problem-solution pattern.

On connectpublicspeaking.com:

- Interactive exercise for chapter
- Building Internet Skills (used to be in book, now online)
- Practice test for chapter
- Checklist (for Preparing and Delivering a Speech)
- Glossary of terms
- Key-term flashcards
- Supplementary Readings
  - "Job Interviews" – Tips for handling one of the most important oral communication events in a person's life.

  - "Frequently Asked Questions" – Some of the most popular questions asked during a job interview and suggestions on how to answer them.

  - "Letter of Application" – Guidelines and a sample letter.

  - "Résumé" – Guidelines and a sample résumé.

On Instructor's Resource DVD-ROM:

- PowerPoint: Chapter Highlights – A PowerPoint program gives highlights of each chapter and includes some video clips. **(NOTE: Many of the PowerPoint slides have no text and require the explanation given in the accompanying script.)**
- Tests – Ready-made chapter tests and a computerized test bank are provided.

Your Thoughts?

p. 323:   Is it acceptable for speakers to pretend to be "just giving the facts" when they are secretly trying to sway the audience to accept a certain belief? Defend your answer.

(Answers will vary). An ethical speaker will be upfront in sharing his or her motives with the audience.

p. 330:   TV commercials for headache remedies often use the problem-solution pattern. Why do you think this pattern is chosen?

(Answers will vary). Narratives (or stories) are very effective on television, and the problem part of the problem-solution pattern is usually cast in the form of a story. Also, once viewers identify with the problem, they are eager to see the solution.

Review Questions

Key to questions on p. 340 in the textbook:

1.   What is the goal of the speech of refutation?

   Your main goal is to knock down arguments or ideas that you feel are false.

2.   In a speech to motivate action, why should you try to get listeners to take action immediately?

   Listeners are more likely to take action if it can be done immediately (instead of in the future). And taking action strengthens a listener's commitment to the speaker's cause.

3.   Give three examples of immediate, on-the-spot audience action.

   Possible answers include petition, show of hands, sign-up sheet, and written assignment.

4.   What is the goal of the *need* step of the motivated sequence?

   To show the audience that there is a serious problem that needs action.

5.   What is the goal of the *satisfaction* step of the motivated sequence?

   To satisfy the need by presenting a solution, and showing how it works.

6.   What is the goal of the *visualization* step of the motivated sequence?

   To paint a picture of results.

7.   What is the goal of the *action* step of the motivated sequence?

   To request action from the audience.

8.   Which organizational pattern is useful when listeners don't know how serious a problem is?

   Problem-solution

9.   When is the statement-of-reasons pattern especially effective?

This pattern is effective when an audience leans toward the speaker's position, but needs some justification for that leaning.

10. When is the comparative advantages pattern most effective?

    This pattern is useful when listeners already agree with the speaker that a problem exists, but aren't sure which solution is best.

Building Critical-Thinking Skills

Key to questions on p. 340 in the textbook:

1. Charities often give instructions like these to their fund-raisers: "If people decline to contribute, ask them to give just a token amount, such as a quarter or one dollar." These instructions are sometimes effective in building support for an organization because they follow one of the successful persuasive techniques discussed in this chapter. What is the technique?

   A response—even a small, token action—helps to increase a listener's commitment to a cause.

2. Which organizational pattern is used in this partial outline, which shows the two main points of a speech?
   I. Car thefts have risen in frequency throughout the U.S.
   II. The number of thefts can be dramatically reduced if owners make their cars less vulnerable.

   Problem-solution

Activities

1. Assign skill builders at the end of the chapter in the text (Building Critical-Thinking Skills and Building Teamwork Skills).

2. Students can be assigned to read persuasive speeches for a subsequent class discussion. One such speech appears at the end of chapter 16 in the text. Other persuasive speeches appear on connectpublicspeaking.com.

Speeches

Here are some of the varieties of speech assignments that some instructors give for persuasive speaking:

Persuasive Speech: Speaking extemporaneously, the student attempts to get the listeners to think or act a certain way. Because of its importance and relative difficulty, many instructors assign this speech in the latter part of the course, after students have sharpened their research and organizational skills.

Speech to Influence Thinking: This variety of persuasive speech aims at convincing listeners to adopt the speaker's position on a particular subject. Examples of this kind of speech are given in Chapter 16 of the text.

Speech of Refutation: The speech of refutation, which is a sub-category of the speech to influence thinking, tries to knock down arguments or ideas that the speaker feels are false. Examples of this kind of speech are given in Chapter 16 of the text.

Speech to Motivate Action: This speech tries to get people to take action. The motivated sequence is one of the possible patterns that can be used to develop this speech. Examples are given in Chapter 16 of the text.

Speech Using the Motivated Sequence: This is a speech to motivate action, with the motivated sequence required as the pattern of development. Examples are given in Chapter 16 of the text, and a sample speech using this pattern is at the end of the chapter.

Speech Using Problem-Solution Pattern: In this persuasive speech, the speaker shows a problem, then provides a solution.

Speech Using Statement-of-Reasons Pattern: This pattern is discussed in Chapter 16.

Speech Using the Comparative-Advantages Pattern: This pattern is discussed in Chapter 16.

Objective Tests

Four ready-to-print tests for Chapter 16 (Forms A, B, C, D), and answer keys for all tests are provided in this instructor's manual. The four forms cover the same material, but are sufficiently different to permit one test to be used as the class test, and the others as makeup tests for absentees. Form A features true-false questions, Forms B and C have multiple-choice questions, while Form D is more difficult, requiring students to fill in missing words or phrases. Instructors may want to combine Form D with some of the essay questions listed below.

Essay & Discussion Questions

The following can be used as essay questions for tests or as stimuli for class discussions:

1. Name and discuss at least three token actions that listeners can be asked to take before they leave the room.

2. Name and explain the five steps of the motivated sequence.

3. What is the pitfall in hinting or implying the action you want listeners to take?

4. When is the comparative advantages pattern most effective in persuasive speaking?

5. When is the problem-solution pattern most effective in persuasive speaking?

Chapter 17
Persuasive Strategies

Chapter Objectives and Resource Integrator

After studying this chapter, students should be able to:

Objectives	Resources
1. Describe how to analyze listeners, using a persuasion scale.	**In the Text:** • Pages 345-348 **On connectpublicspeaking.com:** • Interactive Exercise o Persuasion Scale and Sample Scale—This scale can be used to analyze an audience for a persuasive speech. The instructor may want to assign students to fill in a sheet for each of their persuasive speeches.
2. Explain how to build credibility with an audience in a persuasive speech.	**In the Text:** • Pages 348-351 • Key terms: credibility **On Instructor's Resource DVD-ROM:** • "Lessons from the Movies" – An illustrated narrative based on the movie *The Man Who Shot Liberty Valence* shows how a lack of credibility can undermine a speaker's effectiveness. **On Speeches DVD and on connectpublicspeaking.com:** • Full Speech #8 ("Indian Weddings") – The speaker has high credibility because she herself was a recent bride in an arranged marriage.
3. Explain how to marshal convincing evidence in a persuasive speech.	**In the Text:** • Pages 351-352 • Key terms: evidence **On Speeches DVD and on connectpublicspeaking.com:** • Full Speech #20 ("Would You Vote for Aardvark?") shows use of ample evidence. • Full Speech # 21 ("Too Much of a Good Thing") has a variety of good evidence.

	On connectpublicspeaking.com:
	• Interactive Exercise o "Which is More Persuasive?"

4. Distinguish between deduction and induction as tools of reasoning in a persuasive speech.	**In the Text:**
	• Pages 352-356
	• Key terms: reasoning, deduction, syllogism, induction
	
	On Speeches DVD and on connectpublicspeaking.com:
	• Video Clips
	   o 17.1 – Using Deductive Reasoning
	   o 17.2 – Using Inductive Reasoning

5. Identify nine fallacies in reasoning.	**In the Text:** • Pages 356-358 • Key terms: bandwagon, fallacy, hasty generalization, red herring, attack on a person, false cause, building on an unproven assumption, false analogy, either-or fallacy, straw man
6. Select motivational appeals for a persuasive speech.	**In the Text:** • Pages 358-360 • Key term: motivations, self-actualization, Maslow's hierarchy of needs **On Speeches DVD and on connectpublicspeaking.com:** • Video Clip o 17.3 – Appealing to Motivations
7. Explain how to arouse emotions in a persuasive speech.	**In the Text:** • Pages 360-362

At End of Chapter:

- Summary
- Key Terms
- Review Questions
- Building Critical-Thinking Skills
- Building Teamwork Skills

On Speeches DVD and on connectpublicspeaking.com:

- Full Speech #18 ("Inmates and Tomatoes") illustrates the motivated sequence. An outline and speech appear in Chapter 16.
- Full Speech #20 ("Would You Vote for Aardvark?") uses the problem-solution pattern. An outline and speech appear in Chapter 17.
- Full Speech #19 ("Are You Being Overcharged?") uses the motivated sequence.
- Full Speech #21 ("Too Much of a Good Thing") uses the problem-solution pattern.
- Full Speech #14 ("Bicycle Helmets I – Persuasive Speech That Needs Improvement") shows a speaker who does lots of research, but fails to connect with his listeners.
- Full Speech #15 ("Bicycle Helmets II – Improved Version") shows the same speaker as in Speech 14, but this time he gives a powerful persuasive appeal.
- Full Speech #16 ("The Deadliest Natural Disaster") uses the motivated sequence.
- Full Speech #17 ("Native American Crafts") uses the problem-solution pattern.

On connectpublicspeaking.com:

- Interactive exercise for chapter
- Practice test for chapter
- Checklist (for Preparing and Delivering a Speech)
- Glossary of terms
- Key-term flashcards
- Building Internet Skills (used to be in book, now online)

On Instructor's Resource DVD-ROM:

- PowerPoint: Chapter Highlights – A PowerPoint program gives highlights of each chapter and includes some video clips. **(NOTE: Many of the PowerPoint slides have no text and require the explanation given in the accompanying script.)**
- Tests – Ready-made chapter tests and a computerized test bank are provided.

Your Thoughts?

p. 350: According to *Harvard Business Review*, many listeners are afraid of being "bowled over and manipulated" by a persuasive speaker. How can a speaker reassure such listeners?

(Answers will vary). Speakers can reassure audiences of their honesty by being careful with facts and figures, by using reliable sources, by avoiding exaggeration and wild claims, by

being fair in examining the arguments of "the other side" of an issue, by being eager and willing to reveal sources, and by showing respect for any listeners who might disagree.

p. 357:   The "attack on a person" fallacy is often effective in political battles. Why do you think this is so?

(Answers will vary). Unfortunately, many voters make decisions based on personality and background of a candidate – not on the issues.

Review Questions

Key to questions on p. 369 in the textbook:

1. Why are sarcastic remarks inappropriate when directed toward listeners who are hostile to your view?

    Sarcastic remarks make people defensive and all the more committed to their side.

2. Why is it a good idea in many cases to tell the audience why you are competent to speak on your particular subject?

    Telling about your special competence enhances your credibility; it says, in effect, "I've been there—I know what I'm talking about."

3. How is an audience likely to react if you are careless with your facts and ideas?

    Listeners may discount everything you say.

4. Which is more persuasive with the typical audience—one vivid personal narrative or a series of statistical data?

    "All other things being equal," says social psychologist Elliot Aronson, "most people are more deeply influenced by one clear, vivid personal example than by an abundance of statistical data."

5. What is the difference between deduction and induction?

    Deduction moves from the general to the specific, while induction proceeds from the specific to the general.

6. Why should a speaker never use the logical fallacy called "attack on a person"?

    You weaken your credibility if you attack a person rather than his or her ideas.

7. What is the "straw man" fallacy?

    Trying to win an argument by creating a straw man (a ridiculous caricature of what opponents believe) and then beating it down with great ease.

8. What is a "red herring" argument?

    This fallacy diverts listeners from the real issue to an unrelated matter.

9. List at least five motivations that all listeners have.

    Answers will vary; possibilities include love, happiness, health, social acceptance, financial security, adventure, and creativity.

10. Why should emotional appeals always be accompanied by rational appeals?

If you appeal only to emotions, you give the audience only one underpinning for a belief. People like to think of themselves as rational. They need to have reasons for the feelings and passions they embrace in their heart.

Building Critical-Thinking Skills

Key to questions on p. 369 in the textbook:

1. One of the most influential books in American history, *Silent Spring*, was published in 1962 as a warning against the health hazards of pesticides. Its author, Rachel Carson, was attacked by a scientist who questioned her concern for future generations because she was an unmarried woman with no children. What fallacy of reasoning was the scientist using? Why was the criticism invalid?

    Attack on a person. The scientist should have limited his criticism to Carson's ideas.

2. A TV commercial shows a video of an attractive young couple running barefoot on a beach, while a voice says, "ABC multivitamin supplements – just one a day for the rest of your life." Identify the motivational appeals in the commercial.

    Health, physical fitness, being attractive, appearing youthful, romantic love, happiness

Activities

1. Assign skill builders at the end of the chapter in the text (Building Critical-Thinking Skills and Building Teamwork Skills).

2. In a class discussion on logical fallacies, ask students to come up with examples (other than those given in the text) of each fallacy.

Objective Tests

Four ready-to-print tests for Chapter 17 (Forms A, B, C, D), and answer keys for all tests are provided in this instructor's manual. The four forms cover the same material, but are sufficiently different to permit one test to be used as the class test, and the others as makeup tests for absentees. Form A features true-false questions, Forms B and C have multiple-choice questions, while Form D is more difficult, requiring students to fill in missing words or phrases. Instructors may want to combine Form D with some of the essay questions listed below.

Here are essay questions for tests or stimuli for class discussions:

1. Should a speaker feel defeated if he or she fails to persuade every listener? Explain your answer.

2. How should a speaker approach those listeners who are hostile to the speaker's argument?

3. Discuss how speakers can enhance their credibility with an audience.

4. Describe and give examples of three of the following fallacies in reasoning: (a) hasty generalization, (b) red herring, (c) straw man, (d) attack on a person, (e) false cause, (f) either-or reasoning, (g) building on an unproven assumption, (h) bandwagon

5. Discuss how a speaker can appeal to the motivations of an audience.

6. What are the characteristics of good evidence in a persuasive speech?

7. What is the most effective way to evoke fear in a persuasive speech?

8. What is the difference between induction and deduction?

Chapter 18
Special Types of Speeches

Chapter Objectives and Resource Integrator

After studying this chapter, students should be able to:

Objectives	Resources
1. Prepare an entertaining speech.	**In the Text:** • Pages 373-377 • Key term: entertaining speech **On Speeches DVD and on connectpublicspeaking.com:** • Video: Although Full Speech #22 ("Three Celebrity Heroes") is listed as a speech of tribute, it can also be classified as an entertaining speech. It is light, enjoyable, and easy to listen to. • Video: Full Speech #1 ("Scars and Bruises") is a self-introduction speech that uses self-deprecating humor effectively. **On connectpublicspeaking.com:** • Supplementary Readings: o Entertaining Speech—Transcript of a student's speech, "Spoonerisms, Goldwynisms, and Malapropisms."
2. Prepare a speech of introduction.	**In the Text:** • Pages 377-378 • Key term: speech of introduction
3. Prepare a speech of presentation.	**In the Text:** • Pages 378-379 • Key term: speech of presentation
4. Prepare a speech of acceptance.	**In the Text:** • Page 379 • Key term: speech of acceptance

5. Prepare a speech of tribute.	**In the Text:**
	
	• Pages 379-382
	• Key terms: speech of tribute, eulogy, toast, wedding speech
	
	On Speeches DVD and on connectpublicspeaking.com:
	
	• Full Speech #22 ("Three Celebrity Heroes") pays tribute to three unusual American celebrities.
	
	On connectpublicspeaking.com:
	
	• Supplementary Readings
	   o The Most-Watched Speech in Human History
	
	• Interactive Exercise
	   o "Which Statement is Inappropriate in a Eulogy?"

6. Prepare an inspirational speech.	**In the Text:** • Pages 382-383 • Key term: inspirational speech **On connectpublicspeaking.com:** • Commentary on "I Have a Dream" by Dr. Martin Luther King, Jr.
7. Identify potential pitfalls in using humor in a speech.	**In the Text:** • Pages 373-375

Resources For Entire Chapter:

At End of Chapter:

- Summary
- Key Terms
- Review Questions
- Building Critical-Thinking Skills
- Building Teamwork Skills

On connectpublicspeaking.com:

- Interactive exercise for chapter
- Practice test for chapter
- Checklist (for Preparing and Delivering a Speech)
- Glossary of terms
- Key-term flashcards
- Building Internet Skills (used to be in book, now online)

On Instructor's Resource DVD-ROM:

- PowerPoint: Chapter Highlights – A PowerPoint program gives highlights of each chapter and includes some video clips. **(NOTE: Many of the PowerPoint slides have no text and require the explanation given in the accompanying script.)**
- Tests – Ready-made chapter tests and a computerized test bank are provided.

Your Thoughts?

p. 375: Psychologists have discovered that humor can improve a person's problem-solving abilities. Why do you think this happens?

> *(Answers will vary). Humor relaxes us and reduces our tension, making us more nimble mentally.*

p. 382: A new trend is to deliver a eulogy in the presence of an elderly person *before* he or she dies. Do you think this is a good idea? Explain your answer.

> *(Answers will vary). One obvious advantage is that the person gets to hear the praise while still alive.*

Review Questions

Key to questions on p. 384 in the textbook:

1. Why would an informative speech on a difficult, highly technical subject usually be inappropriate for an after-dinner audience?

After-dinner audiences want to be entertained; they are not receptive to speeches that require mental exertion.

2. In what situation is self-deprecating humor inadvisable?

   Don't use self-deprecating humor when you have not yet established your competence or won the audience's confidence.

3. List four guidelines for the speech of acceptance.

   (1) Thank those who played a part in your achieving the honor, (2) Thank the organization giving you the award and recognize the work they are doing, (3) Do not exaggerate, and (4) Be brief.

4. What is the function of the speech of tribute?

   A speech of tribute praises or celebrates a person, a group, an institution, or an event.

5. What are the risks that a speaker takes when telling a joke?

   Listeners may have heard the joke before, or they may not be in a receptive mood.

6. If you are asked to introduce a speaker, why should you coordinate your remarks beforehand with those of the speaker?

   If you do not coordinate your remarks, you may say something that spoils or contradicts what the speaker is planning to say, or you may unwittingly steal the speaker's material.

7. When introducing a speaker, some introducers use the speaker's first name; others use the last name. What advice does the text give on this issue?

   Ask the speaker beforehand what name he or she prefers that you use.

8. In which kind of special occasions speech does the speaker often withhold an honoree's name until the last sentence?

   The speech of presentation

9. What should be the focus of a eulogy?

   The significance of the person's life.

10. What is the main difference between an inspirational speech and a persuasive speech?

    In the inspirational speech, you devote yourself almost solely to stirring emotions, while in the persuasive speech, you use emotional appeals as just one of many techniques.

Building Critical-Thinking Skills

Key to questions on p. 384 in the textbook:

1. One speaker told his audience, "Before I left for this speech, my wife gave me some advice: 'Don't try to be charming, witty, or intellectual. Just be yourself.'" What kind of humor is the speaker using?

   Self-deprecating humor

2. "Our speaker tonight," says the master of ceremonies, "will outline the five key steps in rescuing a person who is danger of drowning. Let me give you a quick preview of these steps." What mistake is the master of ceremonies making?

Stealing the speaker's material

Activities

1. Assign skill builders at the end of the chapter in the text (Building Critical-Thinking Skills and Building Teamwork Skills).

2. Students can be assigned to read special-occasion speeches for a subsequent class discussion. One entertaining speech appears in Chapter 18 of the text and another, "Spoonerisms, Goldwynisms, and Malapropisms," appears in the *Supplementary Readings* on connectpublicspeaking.com.

Speeches

Here are some assignments that can be given for special speeches:

Entertaining (or After-Dinner) Speech: The entertaining speech, as explained in Chapter 18 of the text, comes in many varieties. One simple approach is to assign the students to "tell an entertaining story—either true or fictional." In such a case, the elaborate outline system recommended (in Chapter 12 of the text) for informative and persuasive speeches can be substituted by a simpler scheme: (1) opening of the story, (2) middle of the story, and (3) ending.

Speech of Introduction: When students give their major speeches in class, some instructors assign others students to give a brief speech of introduction to set the stage for the speech and the speaker. Guidelines are presented in Chapter 18 of the text.

Speech of Presentation: In a role-playing situation, one student makes a few remarks in presenting an honor or an award to another student. Guidelines are presented in Chapter 18 of the text.

Speech of Acceptance: Often paired with the above type, the speech of acceptance gives students a chance to practice what one should say in acknowledging an honor or an award. Guidelines are presented in Chapter 18.

Speech of Tribute: A speech of tribute praises or celebrates a person, a group an institution, or an event. One of the most popular types is the eulogy, which is discussed in Chapter 18. Also discussed are toasts and wedding speeches.

Inspirational Speech: The inspirational speech is designed to stir positive emotions—to cause people to feel excited, uplifted, encouraged. This type of speech, which is discussed briefly in Chapter 18, could be assigned in conjunction with a study of Chapter 13 (Wording the Speech).

Objective Tests

Four ready-to-print tests for Chapter 18 (Forms A, B, C, D), and answer keys for all tests are provided in this instructor's manual. The four forms cover the same material, but are sufficiently different to permit one test to be used as the class test, and the others as makeup tests for absentees. Form A features true-false questions, Forms B and C have multiple-choice questions, while Form D is more difficult, requiring students to fill in missing words or phrases. Instructors may want to combine Form D with some of the essay questions listed below.

Essay & Discussion Questions

The following can be used as essay questions for tests or as stimuli for class discussions.

1. Discuss the characteristics of a good speech of introduction.
2. Discuss what features should be included in a speech of acceptance.
3. Discuss what features should be included in a speech of presentation.
4. Discuss the characteristics of a good entertaining speech.
5. Discuss the characteristics of a good inspirational speech.

Chapter 19
Speaking in Groups

Chapter Objectives and Resource Integrator

After studying this chapter, students should be able to:

Objectives	Resources
1. Serve as a leader or a participant in a small group meeting.	**In the Text:** • Pages 389-395
2. Describe responsibilities of both leaders and participants in small groups.	**In the Text:** • Pages 389-393 • Key terms: agenda, minutes, hidden agenda **On connectpublicspeaking.com:** • Interactive Exercise o "What is Wrong with This Agenda?" **In the Instructor's Manual (on Instructor's Resource DVD-ROM):** • **Sheet 19.1, Panel Discussion**—This handout gives rules for panel discussions, duties of both moderator and panelists, and suggested topics.
3. Identify and explain the seven steps of the reflective-thinking method.	**In the Text:** • Pages 393-395 • Key terms: reflective-thinking method, brainstorming **In the Instructor's Manual (on Instructor's Resource DVD-ROM):** • **Sheet 19.2, Sample Discussion**—A student discussion using the reflective-thinking method is summarized.
4. Prepare and deliver a presentation as a member of a team.	**In the Text:** • Pages 396-397 • Key terms: team presentation

5. Participate in a symposium.	**In the Text:** • Page 397 • Key terms: symposium
4. Serve as moderator or panelist in a panel discussion.	**In the Text:** • Pages 397-400 • Key terms: panel discussion

Resources For Entire Chapter:

At End of Chapter:

- Summary
- Key Terms
- Review Questions
- Building Critical-Thinking Skills
- Building Teamwork Skills

On connectpublicspeaking.com:

- Practice test for chapter
- Glossary of terms
- Key-term flashcards
- Interactive exercise for chapter
- Building Internet Skills (used to be in book, now online)

On Instructor's Resource DVD-ROM:

- PowerPoint: Chapter Highlights – A PowerPoint program gives highlights of each chapter and includes some video clips. **(NOTE: Many of the PowerPoint slides have no text and require the explanation given in the accompanying script.)**
- Tests – Ready-made chapter tests and a computerized test bank are provided.

Your Thoughts?

p. 390:   Why do you think that some managers hold short meetings with everyone standing up?

(Answers will vary). This arrangement discourages long-winded, unnecessary discussions, and it makes participants eager to wrap up the meeting and get back to work.

p. 396:   How should a team handle the possibility of one member being sick and absent on presentation day?

(Answers will vary). Contingencies such as illness should be built into the team's plan. A substitute speaker should be assigned for each part of the presentation.

Key to questions on p. 401 in the textbook:

1. Why is an agenda necessary for a meeting?

    An agenda prevents a group from pursuing irrelevant matters or wasting time on minor issues.

2. Why is nonverbal behavior important in a group meeting?

    Nonverbal behavior, such as facial expressions and posture, speaks more powerfully than words.

3. If you disagree with what everyone else in the group is saying, what should you do?

    You should speak up, but avoid personal attacks.

4. What does a group do when it brainstorms?

    Participants rapidly contribute ideas without fear of ridicule or judgment.

5. In what ways does a team presentation resemble an individual speech?

    A team's presentation is similar to an individual's speech, except the parts are divided among team members.

6. What is a hidden agenda?

    Unannounced private goals that conflict with the group's goals.

7. What are the seven steps of the reflective-thinking method?

    (1) Define the problem, (2) Analyze the problem, (3) Establish criteria for evaluating solutions, (4) Suggest possible solutions, (5) Choose the best solution, (6) Decide how to implement the solution, (7) Decide how to test the solution.

8. What should a group leader do after a meeting?

    Make sure that minutes are written and distributed to each participant and that all participants carry out their assignments.

9. What are the duties of the moderator in a panel discussion?

    The moderator must keep the discussion moving along smoothly, restrain the long-winded or domineering panelist from hogging the show, draw out the reticent panelist, and field questions from the audience.

10. What are the duties of panelists in a panel discussion?

    Panelists should prepare for the discussion by finding out all they can about the audience and the occasion. They should prepare notes, not a written statement. They should respect time limits, be brief in their comments, stay on the subject, and be respectful of the views of other panelists and members of the audience.

Key to questions on p. 401 in the textbook:

1. A football huddle is a type of group meeting. Fran Tarkenton, former star quarterback for the Minnesota Vikings, says, "Many of my best plays were the result of input by other team members. For example, outside receivers often told me that they could run a specific pattern against the defense, and we adjusted to run those plays. I would guess that 50 percent of my touchdowns came about by my receivers suggesting pass patterns." How could Tarkenton's insights be applied to business meetings?

   Just as a quarterback welcomes the insights of other players, a group leader welcomes and solicits the input of participants.

2. Some communication experts say that group meetings lose a great deal of their effectiveness when group members number more than twelve. Assuming that this statement is true, what would account for a decline in effectiveness?

   When a group has a large number of members, it can lose effectiveness because members don't feel as spontaneous, comfortable, and interactive as they would in a small group.

Activities

1. Assign skill builders at the end of the chapter in the text (Building Critical-Thinking Skills and Building Teamwork Skills).

2. Problem-Solving Group Project: In-group projects, students are assigned to groups of 4 to 8 members and told to investigate a problem and find possible solutions to it. Each group should select a leader and follow the roles described in Chapter 19. In solving the assigned problem, the groups should use the reflective-thinking method, as explained in Chapter 19. The findings of the group can be presented in either a symposium or panel discussion (see next two items).

3. Symposium: A symposium is a series of brief speeches on a common topic. A symposium can feature a problem-solving group (see above) presenting its findings to the entire class.

4. Panel Discussion: A panel is usually made up of three to eight members and is led by a moderator. The panelists usually discuss an issue among themselves, with the moderator acting as a referee, and then the listeners are invited to ask questions. The problem-solving group (discussed above) could use a panel discussion as a way of presenting the group's findings in an informal way.

5. Team Presentation: Members of a team prepare a speech that is similar to the speech that an individual would deliver, except that the parts of the speech are divided among team members.

Objective Tests

Four ready-to-print tests for Chapter 19 (Forms A, B, C, D), and answer keys for all tests are provided in this instructor's manual. The four forms cover the same material, but are sufficiently different to permit one test to be used as the class test, and the others as makeup tests for absentees. Form A features true-false questions, Forms B and C have multiple-choice questions, while Form D is more difficult, requiring students to fill in missing words or phrases. Instructors may want to combine Form D with some of the essay questions listed below.

Essay & Discussion Questions

The following can be used as essay questions for tests or as stimuli for class discussions.

1. What advantages do small groups have over individuals and over large groups?

2. In keeping a group on track, how should a leader deal with difficult participants?

3. Participants in a meeting are often advised to "disagree without being disagreeable." Explain what this means.

4. What is a hidden agenda and why should it be avoided?

5. Describe the steps of the reflective-thinking method.

6. Describe how a panel discussion should be conducted.

Panel Discussion

Rules governing panel discussion:

1. State your topic as a question.

2. Seek to answer the question in the discussion.

3. Preparation should be based on research.

4. Information must be documented.

5. You may give your opinion, but this should be based on research.

6. Panel may be designed to give the pro's and con's of a topic (example: Should the U.S. leave the U.N.?) or various aspects of a topic (for example, What can be done to help the alcoholic?)

7. Notes and visual aids may be used. (Be careful not to read too much.)

Duties of Moderator:

1. Introduce panel members.

2. Introduce topic—give overview.

3. Ask members questions.

4. Interact with panelists.

5. Keep panel on the subject.

6. See that all members participate.

7. Summarize remarks.

8. Open the floor for questions at the end.

9. Keep control of the audience and keep it on the topic.

Duties of Panelists:

1. Show evidence of preparation.

2. Participate by answering questions and volunteering information.

3. Define terms.

4. Respect the opinions of others.

5. Listen to other panel members.

6. Be creative and try not to sound too "bookish."

Suggested Topics

- ☐ Alternate energy sources
- ☐ Bioterrorism
- ☐ Social Security
- ☐ Forced retirement
- ☐ Gay rights
- ☐ Dangers of food additives
- ☐ Cloning
- ☐ High school competency tests
- ☐ Problems of the mentally ill
- ☐ Decreasing auto accidents
- ☐ Abuse of medicines
- ☐ Beneath the ocean
- ☐ Job opportunities in the future
- ☐ Increase in divorce
- ☐ Mass transit
- ☐ Drunken drivers
- ☐ Global climate change
- ☐ Mercury levels in seafood
- ☐ Strip mining
- ☐ Acid rain
- ☐ Vegetarianism
- ☐ Teenage runaways
- ☐ Food labeling
- ☐ Sex education in schools
- ☐ Taxing of church property
- ☐ A sensible exercise program
- ☐ Survey of diets
- ☐ Take a trip/cruise to _____
- ☐ Revitalization of inner city housing
- ☐ Housing options (condos)
- ☐ Home furnishings for smaller living space
- ☐ My favorite castles
- ☐ Religions of the world
- ☐ Uses of asbestos
- ☐ What does (city or county) offer you?
- ☐ Your choice

[These instructions are adapted and reprinted, by permission, from a handout provided by Bob Sampson, Central Piedmont Community College.]

Sample Discussion

A group of students was assigned to use the reflective-thinking method to suggest solutions to a troubling social problem in America: the plight of mentally ill patients who roam the streets of many American cities without adequate food, shelter, or medical treatment. Here is a summary of the group's work:

Define the problem

The first matter the group discussed was, "Is there really a problem?" If mentally ill people are happy roaming the streets, rather than being confined to institutions, isn't this their right in a free society? After doing research on this issue, the group agreed that while some mentally ill persons adapt to conditions in society, thousands of them are too disoriented to cope effectively with life on the streets. They go hungry, their psychiatric problems worsen, they are exploited by others, and some even freeze to death.

After concluding that a just and humane society should intervene and care for these people, the group defined the problem by phrasing it in the form of a question, "What should be done with the mentally ill who live on the streets?"

Analyze the problem

Group members carried out research to answer two key questions:

How severe is the problem? One student quoted an American Psychiatric Association's report that between 250,000 and 3 million Americans are homeless, with as many as 50 percent suffering from serious mental disorders, such as schizophrenia. From this, the group concluded that the problem is quite severe.

What are the causes of the problem? The students discovered that thousands of patients once confined to the "back" wards of state mental institutions have been released because (1) powerful antipsychotic drugs are available to control patients' hallucinations, (2) it is believed by many mental health experts that the mentally ill fare better in their own communities than in institutions, and (3) many states cut back on mental-health services to save money.

Establish criteria for evaluating solutions	The group decided that a solution would be unacceptable unless it met two criteria: (1) It must provide food, shelter, and psychiatric treatment, and (2) It must preserve the dignity and self-respect of the patients.
Suggest possible solutions	The group held a brainstorming session, and came up with 14 potential solutions, ranging from "return the patients to state hospitals" to "set up more soup kitchens and hostels for the homeless."
Choose the best solution	Using its two criteria as yardsticks, the group rejected many solutions. For example, the idea of returning patients to large, understaffed state hospitals was rejected because it could mean a loss of dignity and self-respect. Finally, the group decided that the best solution would be to commit the patients to "group homes" in residential settings. The first criterion would be met by requiring the homes to provide psychiatric treatment in addition to basic amenities. The second criterion would be met by requiring the homes to treat the patients as full-fledged members of the community.
Decide how to implement the solution	To put the solution into action, the group recommended that state legislatures pass laws mandating quality psychiatric care for the mentally ill in group homes. Each home would be assigned a psychiatrist to care for the patients' mental disorders and a social worker to help the patients integrate themselves into the mainstream of society. To make sure that the patients receive quality care in a dignified setting, the group recommended that a state board of examiners be formed to monitor the homes and revoke the charters of any homes that fail to provide adequate care.
Decide how to test the solution	To determine whether the plan truly solved the problem, the group recommended that each state create a review panel, made up of mental health professionals, to assess the group homes after one year of operation by inspecting facilities, interviewing patients, and conducting public hearings. The panel could then decide whether the plan has been successful.

Stop Sign

If you want to avoid the disruption caused by late-arriving students coming into class while a classmate is giving a speech, try putting the following sign on the classroom door. You can laminate it or enclose it in a plastic sheet protector so that it will last for many years.

Thanks to David Holcombe for this idea.

STOP!

Speech in Progress

Please Do Not Enter Until End of Speech

Objective Tests

On the following pages are four tests (Forms A, B, C, and D) for each chapter. The tests are ready to reproduce. Simply tear out at the perforation and make photocopies. Answer keys are provided on the pages that immediately follow the tests.

The forms are sufficiently different to permit one test to be used as the class test and the others as makeup tests for absentees.

Form A features true-false questions, Forms B and C consist of multiple-choice questions, while Form D is more difficult, requiring students to fill in missing words or phrases.

On the following page is a blank answer sheet, offered as an alternative to having students write on the actual test sheet.

Instructors also have two other options for tests:

1. Download the chapter tests from the Instructor's Resource CD and alter them by adding, deleting, or modifying questions before printing out.

2. Create chapter tests using the computerized test bank on the Instructor's Resource CD.

Answer Sheet

Chapter _____ Form _____

Name _____

1.

2.

3.

4.

5.

6.

7.

8.

9.

10.

Name _____

True or False If the statement is true, circle T; if false, circle F.

T F 1. If speakers send nonverbal signals that contradict their verbal message, listeners will typically accept the nonverbal behavior as the true message.

T F 2. The speaker's message consists entirely of what the speaker says with words.

T F 3. A speaker should work harder to communicate to an audience of 500 people than to an audience of five people.

T F 4. When an applicant seeks a job, employers place heavier emphasis on oral communication skills (speaking and listening) than on the person's technical knowledge.

T F 5. Abstract words usually mean the same thing to all listeners.

T F 6. Television is an example of a channel of communication.

T F 7. Time of day plays a part in how receptive an audience is to a speech.

T F 8. Everything that a speaker expresses in a message is in the form of symbols.

T F 9. If, while giving a speech, you observe that some of your listeners seem confused by your last remark, you should wait until the end of the speech to explain yourself better.

T F 10. A speaker can cause interference in the speech communication process.

Name _____

Multiple-Choice Questions Each question has only one correct answer.

____ 1. When hiring, employers are MOST likely to be influenced by an applicant's (a) grade point average, (b) letters of reference, (c) technical knowledge of the field, (d) oral communication skills (speaking and listening), (e) written communication skills (reading and writing)

____ 2. Radio and television are examples of (a) feedback, (b) interference, (c) channels, (d) messages

____ 3. A speaker who blames doctors for the rise in lung cancer deaths is engaging in (a) scapegoating, (b) stereotyping, (c) distortion, (d) harassment

____ 4. Who bears the responsibility for communication actually taking place? (a) the speaker, (b) the listener, (c) both the speaker and the listener, (d) neither the speaker nor the listener

____ 5. An oversimplified mental picture is known as a (a) generalization, (b) cliché, (c) scapegoat, (d) stereotype

____ 6. Bizarre clothing worn by the speaker is an example of (a) interference, (b) message, (c) feedback, (d) channel

____ 7. Which of the following is bad advice for a speaker? (a) Try to meet the needs of all listeners, (b) Use visual aids when speaking to hearing-impaired listeners, (c) Avoid politics, sports, and business with a female audience, (d) Explain American slang used when addressing international students

____ 8. "Information overload" is caused by a speaker who (a) deceives the audience with erroneous information, (b) covers too much material, (c) relates boring stories, (d) provides no proof for arguments

____ 9. Which method of public speaking involves looking at the audience most of the time, while occasionally glancing at brief notes? (a) extemporaneous, (b) impromptu, (c) memorization, (d) manuscript

____ 10. The part of a speech that links one section to another is known as a (a) connection, (b) transition, (c) chain, (d) cementer

Name _____

Multiple-Choice Questions Each question has only one correct answer.

____ 1. If there are discrepancies between the verbal and nonverbal components of a speech, listeners will probably (a) reject both components as untrue, (b) accept the verbal as the true message, (c) accept the nonverbal as the true message

____ 2. Which of the following can cause a speech to be dull? (a) unattractive clothes, (b) unenthusiastic delivery, (c) disrespect for the audience, (d) obscene language

____ 3. A speech, says management consultant David W. Richardson, takes place in (a) the context of speaker-listener communication, (b) the minds of the listeners, (c) the spoken words of the speaker, (d) the memories of all participants

____ 4. When you are a speaker, which of the following is the key question to constantly ask yourself? (a) Am I getting through to my listeners? (b) Am I performing well? (c) Am I giving out good information? (d) Am I making a good impression?

____ 5. Which of the following does the text list as a component of the speech communication process? (a) originator, (b) facilitator, (c) argument, (d) situation

____ 6. In the speech communication process, the message is sent in the form of (a) inferences, (b) symbols, (c) codes, (d) approximations

____ 7. The part of a speech that you want your listeners to remember if they forget everything else is known as the (a) specific purpose, (b) central idea, (c) attention-getter, (d) conclusion

____ 8. A loudspeaker is an example of a (a) channel, (b) transmitter, (c) message, (d) situation

____ 9. The extemporaneous method of speaking involves (a) memorizing a speech, (b) reading a script, (c) using notes, (d) ad-libbing

____ 10. In the speech communication process, anything that blocks or hinders the communication of a message is called (a) blockage, (b) obstruction, (c) confusion, (d) interference

Name _____

Fill in the missing words or phrases.

1. The _____ is the context—the time and place—in which communication occurs.

2. Simplistic images that humans carry in their minds about groups of people are called _____.

3. The _____ is the medium used to communicate a message to an audience.

4. Words are not things; they are _____ of things.

5. Anything that blocks or hinders the communication of a message is known as _____.

6. Items in a speech designed to carry listeners smoothly from one section to another are called _____.

7. _____ are people who innocently bear the blame of others.

8. According to a survey, one of the biggest mistakes made by speakers is trying to cover _____ in one speech.

9. The response that listeners give the speaker is known as _____.

10. _____ interference occurs when the speaker uses words that are unfamiliar to the audience.

Name _____

True or False If the statement is true, circle T; if false, circle F.

T F 1. A shy person's shyness will block that person from giving a good, dynamic speech.

T F 2. If your hands tremble or you show some other sign of nervousness, you should apologize to your audience or try to make a joke out of your problem.

T F 3. Gesturing or walking around a bit during your speech helps siphon off excessive nervous energy.

T F 4. In preparation for a speech, a person should read over his or her notes rather than actually rehearse the speech.

T F 5. A good speaker tries very hard to eliminate all fear and nervousness.

T F 6. In filling your mind with images before a speech, you should picture yourself speaking with confidence, poise, and completely without nervousness.

T F 7. If you see people whispering during your speech, you should assume that they are exchanging negative comments about you or your speech.

T F 8. Most of your nervous symptoms are not seen by your audience.

T F 9. Memorizing a speech is a bad technique for handling nervousness.

T F 10. If you feel yourself approaching panic (your heart is beating furiously and so on), you should leave the room or ask to be excused from speaking.

Name _____

Multiple-Choice Questions Each question has only one correct answer.

_____ 1. The term used by the text for visualizing successful actions is (a) creative imagination, (b) positive imagery, (c) success orientation, (d) power visualization

_____ 2. Which of the following does the text recommend as a way to release tension? (a) inhale and exhale slowly, (b) mentally prepare for a panic attack, (c) make a joke about your nervousness, (d) arrive precisely one minute before your speech

_____ 3. According to the text, "locking" your eyes with a listener's eyes (a) intensifies your anxiety, (b) makes the listener uneasy, (c) demonstrates that you have no fear, (d) helps to calm you

_____ 4. Public speakers should regard their task as (a) communication only, (b) performance only, (c) both communication and performance, (d) communication, performance, and duty

_____ 5. When practicing your speech, devote extra time to (a) the introduction, (b) the body, (c) the conclusion, (d) the question-and-answer period

_____ 6. Acting as if you are poised and confident (a) is a pretense that the audience will immediately see through, (b) sometimes leads to actually becoming poised and confident, (c) will make you even more nervous than before

_____ 7. If, during a speech, your mind goes blank and you forget where you are in the speech, the text recommends that you (a) apologize and sit down, (b) start over from the beginning, (c) make a joke about your predicament, (d) ask the audience, "Where was I?"

_____ 8. According to the text, shyness (a) is caused by a childhood trauma, (b) is a barrier to effective public speaking, (c) can be eliminated by psychotherapy, (d) is a characteristic of some successful people in show business

_____ 9. According to the text, a sudden bolt of panic can hit speakers who (a) overprepare, (b) initially feel no fear, (c) dislike the audience, (d) have poor self-esteem

_____ 10. Which one of the following fears usually disappears as speakers gain experience? (a) fear of being stared at, (b) fear of failure, (c) fear of the unknown, (d) fear of rejection

Name _____

Multiple-Choice Questions Each question has only one correct answer.

____ 1. Striving for perfection (a) helps you to achieve almost total perfection, (b) is a necessary mental ploy to achieve success, (c) is the best way to develop a positive outlook, (d) places unnecessary pressure on yourself

____ 2. Which of the following was mentioned in the text as a way to control nervousness? (a) arrive just a few moments before your speech, (b) act as if you are already poised and confident, (c) encourage listeners to ask questions throughout the speech, (d) look at a fixed point on the wall in the back of the room

____ 3. The greatest amount of anxiety in a speech is usually experienced in the (a) introduction, (b) body, (c) conclusion, (d) question-and-answer period

____ 4. To avoid memory lapses during a speech, (a) memorize basic facts before the speech, (b) prepare a word-for-word script, (c) prepare a card with key information on it, (d) learn to eliminate nervousness

____ 5. A public speaker who tries to eliminate all fear is pursuing a goal that is (a) desirable, (b) impossible, (c) unimportant, (d) undesirable

____ 6. To gain rapport with their audiences, some comedians (a) pretend to have stage fright, (b) deliberately make mistakes, (c) go out into the audience to shake hands, (d) playfully "insult" some listeners

____ 7. Switching your thoughts from "I'm going to fail" to "I will give the audience some good information" is a technique known as changing your (a) opinion, (b) perception, (c) self-talk, (d) outlook

____ 8. The text says that worrying about yourself and your image in a speech is a kind of (a) motivation, (b) vanity, (c) self-defense, (d) awareness

____ 9. The term used by the text to describe "a zesty, enthusiastic, lively feeling with a slight edge to it" is (a) positive nervousness, (b) focused enthusiasm, (c) managed anxiety, (d) heightened sensitivity

____ 10. If you flub a sentence or mangle an idea during a speech, you should (a) stop and apologize for your blunder, (b) pause and correct yourself without apologizing, (c) apologize and sit down immediately, (d) make a joke about hating speechmaking

Name _____

Fill in the missing words or phrases.

1. The text cites an old saying, "Speakers who say they are as cool as a cucumber usually give speeches about as interesting as a _____."

2. Positive _____ is a technique used by golfers as well as public speakers to visualize success.

3. Of all parts of the speech, you should devote extra practice time to _____.

4. Of all the fears engendered by public speaking, the fear of _____ usually disappears as a speaker gets more experience.

5. According to the text, the very best precaution against excessive stage fright is _____.

6. Pretending to be confident can sometimes cause you to become a _____ speaker.

7. Making a joking, lighthearted comment about your nervousness is a _____ technique for a speaker to use.

8. Concerning most speakers, the audience is _____ of their physical symptoms such as pounding heart and trembling knees.

9. Some comedians deliberately plan _____ as a technique for gaining rapport with an audience.

10. Speakers can control nervousness and enhance their speeches if they think of speechmaking as communication, rather than as _____.

Name _____

True or False If the statement is true, circle T; if false, circle F.

T F 1. In taking notes, a listener should try to record the speaker's exact words.

T F 2. It is more important for a listener to remember the main points of a speech than to remember support materials.

T F 3. If you whisper, it is okay to talk on a cell phone while attending a presentation.

T F 4. If good listening skills are used, listening to a complex lecture should require no more mental effort than listening to a comedian tell jokes.

T F 5. In some countries, whistling by listeners is a sign of approval.

T F 6. In Japan, listeners who close their eyes during a speech might be showing respect.

T F 7. The Golden Rule of Listening is "Listen wisely and well."

T F 8. When a speaker makes a point with which you disagree, immediately prepare a rebuttal in your mind to use later in the question-and-answer period.

T F 9. In giving a speaker an evaluation of a speech, you should always note any indications of the speaker's nervousness.

T F 10. Listening occurs when your ears pick up sound waves being transmitted by a speaker.

Name _____

Multiple-Choice Questions Each question has only one correct answer.

____ 1. Ned is trying hard to pull up his grades in a class. When the instructor lectures, he furiously writes down virtually every word that is said. Which listening mistake is Ned making? (a) not being prepared, (b) mentally arguing with the speaker, (c) making prejudgments, (d) failing to take notes correctly

____ 2. In what country do listeners sometimes close their eyes to show respect for the speaker's ideas? (a) Nigeria, (b) Brazil, (c) India, (d) Japan

____ 3. Reading background material on a speaker's topic is something the listener should do (a) before the speech, (b) during the speech, (c) immediately after the speech, (d) several days after the speech

____ 4. Which of these comments would be helpful for an evaluator to make to a speaker? (a) "You looked as if you were scared of the audience," (b) "Try to speak in a conversational manner"

____ 5. In most speeches, listeners can process information at about _____ words per minute, whereas most speakers talk at 125 to 150 words a minute. (a) 150, (b) 200, (c) 300, (d) 500

____ 6. Taking notes on a laptop computer during a speech is discouraged unless (a) the laptop has a noiseless keyboard, (b) the monitor is raised only when notes are being taken, (c) the listener gets permission from the speaker beforehand, (d) everyone else in the room is using a laptop

____ 7. Two days after listening to a 10-minute oral presentation, the average person comprehends and retains _____% of the information. (a) 25, (b) 50, (c) 75, (d) 90

____ 8. Two groups of students at Cornell University listened to the same lecture, with one group allowed to use laptops to browse the Internet and the other group required to keep laptops closed. When tested, the group with Internet access remembered (a) significantly more information than the other group, (b) about the same amount of information, (c) significantly less information

____ 9. Which one of the following options does the text consider acceptable during a presentation? (a) using a laptop computer for e-mail, (b) talking on a cell phone in a whisper, (c) using the "vibrate" option of a cell phone or pager, (d) sitting in the back of the room to receive phone calls

____ 10. Taking notes while engaged in a one-on-one discussion with your supervisor (a) is a compliment to the superior, (b) is insulting because of lack of eye contact, (c) makes you appear as if you have a poor memory

Name _____

Multiple-Choice Questions Each question has only one correct answer.

____ 1. The note-taking system suggested by the text has three columns with headings for main ideas, support material, and (a) statistics, (b) examples, (c) proof, (d) response

____ 2. A headache causes which type of distraction? (a) cryptic, (b) physical, (c) alternative, (d) auditory

____ 3. Listeners who multitask (perform a variety of activities) usually retain (a) as much information as listeners who focus on just the speaker, (b) less information than listeners who focus on just the speaker

____ 4. The text quotes Keith Davis as saying, "Hearing is with the ears; listening is with the _____." (a) mind, (b) heart

____ 5. In giving a speaker an evaluation of a speech, which should be presented first? (a) positive comments, (b) negative comments, (c) neutral comments that are neither negative nor positive

____ 6. Ten minutes after listening to a 10-minute oral presentation, the average person understands and retains ____% of the information. (a) 10, (b) 25, (c) 50, (d) 75

____ 7. A speaker who asks listeners to turn off electronic devices is (a) unwisely intruding on the rights of listeners, (b) wisely improving the odds that the audience will listen to the message

____ 8. If you have the habit of engaging in fake listening, one of the best ways to force yourself to pay attention is to (a) look directly at the speaker, (b) mentally repeat the speaker's words, (c) take notes, (d) practice self-discipline skills

____ 9. To confront listeners who are immersed in their electronic devices, speakers are advised by the text to try using _____ to capture audience interest. (a) a promise of a shortened presentation, (b) a threat of revenge, (c) a quick blast of loud music, (d) an attention-getting introduction

____ 10. Hermina listened politely to a speech on zoos, but she became angry when the speaker argued for abolition of all zoos. For the rest of the speech, she tuned him out and planned the counter-arguments that she could throw at him during the question-and-answer period. What listening mistake is she making? (a) failing to control emotions, (b) giving in to distractions, (c) failing to prepare, (d) rationalizing

Name _____

Fill in the missing words or phrases.

1. State the Golden Rule of Listening:

    _____
    _____
    _____
    _____
    _____

2. While listening to a speech, you should focus on main ideas
    and _____ materials.

3. When a speaker starts a speech on a controversial issue,
    some listeners have an emotional reaction that cuts off
    listening. In their minds, they prepare a counterattack to be
    launched during the question-and-answer period. Which
    listening mistake are they committing?

    _____

4. If you engage in _____ listening, you risk
    embarrassment and ridicule.

5. Before listening to a difficult lecture, you should prepare
    yourself intellectually and
    _____.

6. Refrain from using a laptop computer during a speech
    unless you need to _____.

7. Many listeners take notes during a speech and throw them
    away at the end. They didn't waste their time because note
    taking kept them from _____.

8. The major types of distractions during a speech are mental,
    physical, visual, and _____.

9. While listening to a speech, our brain works
    _____ than the speed needed for listening.

10. Because listening is hard work, a person listening to
    complex material might have at least three bodily reactions.
    Name one of them: _____

Name _____

True or False If the statement is true, circle T; if false, circle F.

T F 1. It is acceptable to tell a joke about a certain ethnic group if no one from that ethnic group is present in the audience.

T F 2. The most understood form of nonverbal communication in the world is the smile.

T F 3. In a large auditorium, your listeners are more likely to be responsive if they are sparsely seated throughout the hall than if they are tightly packed together.

T F 4. "Taboo" is the term used to describe an act, a word, or an object that is forbidden on grounds of morality or taste.

T F 5. If you cannot persuade skeptical listeners to adopt your views, you should at least try to move them closer to your position.

T F 6. If you have handouts, it is a good idea to give one to a blind listener.

T F 7. If your audience knows little or nothing about your topic, you should limit the number of new ideas you discuss.

T F 8. Elderly members of an audience will feel stigmatized and offended if a speaker explains the meaning of terms that are popular among young people and unlikely to be known to older listeners.

T F 9. Listeners might get upset if your speech topic varies from what they had anticipated.

T F 10. For blind or visually impaired listeners with a seeing-eye dog, it is a good idea for a speaker to be friendly with the dog before the speech by talking to it in a soft voice.

Name _____

Multiple-Choice Questions Each question has only one correct answer.

___ 1. Which question is the major concern of the audience-centered speaker? (a) "Am I doing a good job?" (b) "Does everyone like me?" (c) "How do I look?" (d) "Am I getting my message across to the listeners?"

___ 2. According to advice given in the text, a speaker who is addressing hearing-impaired listeners doesn't need to (a) emphasize consonants, (b) emphasize final syllables, (c) speak loudly, (d) exaggerate words

___ 3. Some audience members know a lot about your speech topic; others know nothing. Your best approach is to (a) keep audience attention through a highly enthusiastic delivery, (b) ignore those audience members who are extremely knowledgeable about the topic, (c) ignore those audience members who know virtually nothing about the topic, (d) begin simply and add complexity throughout the presentation

___ 4. In preparing for a speech next week, you discover that one member of the audience has a visual disability. To find out how to meet her needs, whom should you consult? (a) her closest relative, (b) the person who invited you to speak, (c) the woman herself, (d) her health-care provider

___ 5. Horace noticed some listeners looking confused when he used a certain term in his speech, so he backed up and explained the term in greater detail. Horace exhibited (a) catering to an audience, (b) using demographic analysis, (c) adaptation during a speech, (d) audience analysis

___ 6. The belief that one's own cultural group is superior to other groups is known as (a) superiority complex, (b) ethnocentrism, (c) power tripping, (d) judgmentalism

___ 7. In working with an interpreter, which of the following is NOT recommended by the text? (a) Talk directly to a sign-language interpreter instead of to the audience, (b) Provide the interpreter with your outline in advance, (c) Ask the interpreter to rehearse with you, (d) Introduce the interpreter to the audience

___ 8. In the business world, the term for adapting to consumers' special needs is (a) matching, (b) accommodating, (c) customizing, (d) retrofitting

___ 9. A speaker who interviews a few members of an audience before a speech is (a) wasting time because the number of listeners is unrepresentative, (b) gaining a good sample of what the audience is like

___ 10. If listeners are already favorable toward your ideas, your task is to (a) entertain them with colorful stories, (b) heap scorn on those who don't agree with you, (c) reinforce your listeners' positive views, (d) praise the listeners for their insight

Chapter 4 (Form C)

Name _____

Multiple-Choice Questions Each question has only one correct answer.

____ 1. For listeners who are deaf or hearing-impaired, the text recommends which of the following? (a) slow your rate of speech slightly, (b) exaggerate your words, (c) look at them constantly

____ 2. If a blind listener brings a guide dog into the room where a speech will be delivered, what should the speaker do? (a) Greet the listener and speak to the dog in a soft voice to befriend it, (b) Assist the listener and the dog in finding a place in the rear of the room, (c) Do nothing unless the listener needs assistance, (d) Ask the listener to station the dog outside the room so it doesn't frighten or disturb listeners

____ 3. In analyzing an audience, which one of the following variables should NOT be considered? (a) age, (b) educational background, (c) personal appearance, (d) gender

____ 4. The textbook notes that many _____ persons prefer to think of their condition as a cultural difference rather than a disability. (a) learning-disabled, (b) mobility-impaired (wheelchair), (c) blind or visually impaired, (d) deaf or hearing impaired

____ 5. For a presentation, which approach do most international audiences prefer? (a) humorous, (b) emotional, (c) serious, (d) informal

____ 6. What is the most understood and useful form of nonverbal communication in dealing with people from all parts of the world? (a) a smile, (b) a handshake, (c) eye contact, (d) a soft voice

____ 7. Tailoring your speech to fit audience needs and interests is described in the text as (a) form-fitting, (b) shaping, (c) customizing, (d) altering

____ 8. A taboo is (a) a prohibition, (b) an insult, (c) a mystery, (d) a mistake

____ 9. An open-ended question on a questionnaire involves (a) filling in blanks, (b) writing out a sentence or paragraph, (c) answering yes or no, (d) ranking items from first to last

____ 10. The text recommends that an invitation to company employees should be worded as: a) "You and your husband or wife are invited to the company picnic." (b) "You and your spouse are invited to the company picnic." (c) "You and your guest are invited to the company picnic."

Chapter 4 (Form D)

Name _____

Fill in the missing words or phrases.

1. How can speakers know what accommodations to make to meet the special needs of listeners with disabilities?
    _____

2. To be an audience-centered speaker, your first step in preparing a speech is to _____ your listeners.

3. Your second step is to _____ your speech to the needs and interests of the audience.

4. A cultural prohibition is called a
    _____.

5. President Franklin D. Roosevelt's formula for speechmaking: "Be sincere. Be _____. Be seated."

6. The emotional baggage—the favorable or unfavorable predispositions—that a listener brings to a speech is called
    _____.

7. The text quotes a Mexican-American proverb, "Everybody in the world _____ in the same language."

8. The belief that one's own cultural group is superior to other groups is known as _____.

9. Eye contact, facial expressions, and other types of _____ communication vary from country to country.

10. A speaker who is asked to speak for 20 minutes but talks for 45 minutes has failed to respect _____ limits.

Name _____

True or False If the statement is true, circle T; if false, circle F.

T F   1.   A good way to find speech topics is to explore the Internet.

T F   2.   The central idea of a speech should begin with an infinitive.

T F   3.   Brainstorming means doing thorough research in the library.

T F   4.   The key concept that you want your listeners to remember if they forget everything else is called the specific purpose statement.

T F   5.   The three most popular types of speeches are informative, persuasive, and entertaining.

T F   6.   Hidden objectives in a speech are always undesirable.

T F   7.   Jokes are not necessary in an entertaining speech.

T F   8.   In the informative speech, your overriding concern is to win the listeners to your way of thinking.

T F   9.   The specific purpose statement should be limited to one major idea.

T F   10.   "I will discuss robots as surgeons" is an effective example of a central idea.

Name _____

Multiple-Choice Questions Each question has only one correct answer.

_____ 1. The most important task in a speech is to communicate the (a) general purpose, (b) specific purpose, (c) central idea, (d) topic

_____ 2. What is the maximum number of major ideas that can be included in a specific purpose statement? (a) one, (b) two, (c) three, (d) four

_____ 3. The textbook says that a central idea should be phrased as (a) an opinion, (b) an announcement, (c) an eternal truth, (d) an assertion

_____ 4. "A parent who reneges on child-support payments should be forced to pay or be sent to prison." This is an example of (a) a general purpose, (b) a specific purpose, (c) a central idea, (d) a topic

_____ 5. Hidden objectives in a speech (a) are always undesirable, (b) sometimes sabotage a speaker's primary goal, (c) are a necessary component of all speeches, (d) are always detected by intelligent listeners

_____ 6. "To explain how the pyramids in Egypt were constructed." According to the text, this item is (a) correctly written, (b) incorrectly written

_____ 7. Ed's objective for his speech is to get listeners to stop a certain behavior. What is his general purpose? (a) to inspire, (b) to entertain, (c) to inform, (d) to persuade

_____ 8. A verb form beginning with "to" is called (a) an infinitive, (b) a preposition, (c) a gerund, (d) a participle

_____ 9. Which one of the following is NOT listed by the text as part of overall speech design? (a) introduction, (b) transition, (c) question-and-answer period, (d) body

_____ 10. "Parrots as pets" is an example of (a) a topic, (b) a general purpose, (c) a specific purpose, (d) a central idea

Name _____

Multiple-Choice Questions Each question has only one correct answer.

_____ 1. According to the text, we should eliminate hidden purposes that (a) reveal our central idea, (b) divulge our personal secrets, (c) sabotage our true goal, (d) embarrass our listeners

_____ 2. Which of the following should give the essence of your speech? (a) introduction, (b) conclusion, (c) central idea, (d) specific purpose

_____ 3. "To entertain" is an example of a (a) general purpose, (b) specific purpose, (c) central idea, (d) target

_____ 4. Which one of the following is a synonym for central idea? (a) specific purpose, (b) thesis sentence, (c) conclusion, (d) agenda

_____ 5. "Food-borne illnesses" is an example of (a) a topic, (b) a general purpose, (c) a specific purpose, (d) a central idea

_____ 6. The three most popular types of speeches are informative, entertaining, and _____. (a) inspirational, (b) persuasive, (c) motivational, (d) introductory

_____ 7. "To explain to my listeners the chemical composition of vegetable oils." According to the text, this item is (a) appropriate for a classroom speech, (b) too technical for a classroom speech

_____ 8. "How to Make a Home Burglar-Proof" is an example of which kind of speech? (a) persuasive, (b) informative, (c) inspirational, (d) entertaining

_____ 9. A verb form beginning with "to" is called (a) a gerund, (b) a preposition, (c) an infinitive, (d) a participle

_____ 10. In brainstorming, you should (a) critically examine each idea as it springs forth, (b) deliberately avoid writing down words and phrases, (c) carefully plan the path that your mind will follow, (d) produce a flurry of ideas without any initial criticism

Name _____

Fill in the missing words or phrases.

1. A verb form that begins with "to" is called
    _____.

2. The goal of a persuasive speech is to change listeners' minds
    and/or their _____.

3. The basic message of the entire speech is called the
    _____.

4. "To explain how Egyptian pyramids were constructed" is a
    defective purpose statement because it lacks
    _____.

5. _____ is a technique for generating
    ideas by writing down whatever comes to your mind without
    censoring or criticizing.

6. A specific purpose statement should be limited to how many major
    ideas? _____

7. The three most popular general purposes for speeches are to
    inform, to entertain, and to _____.

8. How many central ideas should each speech have?
    _____

9. A central idea should make a/an _____
    rather than an announcement or a statement of fact.

10. A speech on the chemical composition of vegetable oils would be
    too _____ for a classroom speech.

Name _____

True or False If the statement is true, circle T; if false, circle F.

T F   1.   A vlog is a Web option that specializes in international news and opinions.

T F   2.   According to the text, e-mail is a good tool for interviewing experts.

T F   3.   A blog has limited value for researchers because it covers only the views of individuals.

T F   4.   Field research means gathering information first-hand, for example, by observing an event.

T F   5.   When interviewing people on controversial subjects, it is a good idea to record their comments secretly, so that they are candid and unconstrained in giving their true views.

T F   6.   With so much information available on the Internet, traditional library resources are typically not needed.

T F   7.   While advising you to set up a lifetime filing system, the text says that you need not worry about accumulating too many notes.

T F   8.   You should take notes in an interview even if you are using a video or audio recorder.

T F   9.   If you are using a computer database to search for articles on exploration of Mars, the computer can be instructed to exclude Mars articles that mention Venus and Saturn.

T F 10. A good research technique is to turn your specific purpose statement into a research question.

Name _____

Multiple-Choice Questions Each question has only one correct answer.

____ 1. An abstract is a (a) summary, (b) mystery, (c) Web address, (d) research question

____ 2. A vlog specializes in (a) virtual reality, (b) video files, (c) verbatim reports, (d) vintage news

____ 3. The main disadvantage of interlibrary loan is that (a) you have to pay for any book ordered, (b) only a few large libraries have this service, (c) you cannot be certain of a book arriving quickly, (d) you must be an expert computer user to take advantage of this service

____ 4. Before starting your research, you should decide on your (a) specific purpose, (b) central idea, (c) title, (d) introduction

____ 5. "What percentage of registered voters actually voted in the last presidential election?" is an example of _____ type of question. (a) an imprecise, (b) a follow-up, (c) an open, (d) a closed

____ 6. To find out if patients using a new headache remedy are pleased with the drug, your best approach is to use (a) expert sites, (b) search engines, (c) discussion forums, (d) subject directories

____ 7. For researchers, one of the most valuable resources in blogs is (a) corporate views, (b) links to other sites, (c) personal opinions, (d) live video

____ 8. In most libraries, the person who is best able to help you with your research is called (a) an information librarian, (b) a reference librarian, (c) a database librarian, (d) a search-and-find librarian

____ 9. The _____ for an article gives the title, author's name, magazine, date, and page numbers. (a) abstract, (b) summary, (c) listing, (d) citation

____ 10. The formats of MLA and APA are designed to help you to (a) find Web sites, (b) verify accuracy of information, (c) contact online libraries, (d) cite sources

Name _____

Multiple-Choice Questions Each question has only one correct answer.

____ 1. For hard-to-find information, use (a) Google (b) Yahoo, (c) several different search engines, (d) ObscureInfo.com

____ 2. An Internet catalog that starts off with broad categories, which are then subdivided into smaller categories, is known as (a) subject directory, (b) search engine, (c) newsgroup, (d) Usenet

____ 3. If you are looking for a book that is not available in your library, the text recommends that you (a) visit other libraries, (b) consult the World Wide Web, (c) use interlibrary loan, (d) explore discussion forums

____ 4. Basic bibliographical facts about a source, such as title and date, are contained in the (a) abstract, (b) bulletin, (c) tipsheet, (d) citation

____ 5. "Do Democrats outnumber Republicans in this state?" is an example of the _____ type of question. (a) closed, (b) open, (c) imprecise, (d) follow-up

____ 6. In research, which of the following resources is likeliest to yield the most up-to-date information? (a) a just-published book, (b) an article in the current issue of a magazine, (c) a computer database of articles and summaries, (d) an interview with an expert

____ 7. The three major research options are libraries, the Internet, and _____. (a) search engines, (b) field research, (c) reference works, (d) catalogs

____ 8. If you want to ask dog experts on the Internet about their experiences with electronic fences, your best strategy is to post a query via (a) discussion forums, (b) Web sites, (c) search engines, (d) subject directories

____ 9. The text says that interviewing an expert via e-mail is (a) an acceptable method, (b) an unacceptable method

____ 10. For a speech, your own personal experiences and observations (a) can suggest avenues of research but should not be used as source material, (b) might provide valuable material that can be used in a speech

Name _____

Fill in the missing words or phrases.

1. On the Internet, a _____ is a catalog that begins with a broad subject area, which is then subdivided into smaller categories.

2. Electronic databases often offer brief summaries of articles; these summaries are called _____.

3. Should library research be done *before* or *after* an interview?
   _____

4. In most libraries, the library _____ lists the titles and authors of books owned by the library.

5. In an interview, questions that give the interviewee wide latitude for responding are called _____ questions.

6. A blog that specializes in videos is known as a _____.

7. In an interview, questions that require only "yes" or "no" answers are called _____ questions.

8. Web sites that enable you to get information from authorities on a subject are called _____.

9. MLA and APA formats offer ways to cite _____.

10. Interviewing experts and using your own investigations are examples of _____ research.

Name _____

True or False If the statement is true, circle T; if false, circle F.

T F   1.   Researchers can trust claims that are based on testimonials.

T F   2.   "I got my information from the Internet" is an acceptable way to assure audiences that the information in your speech is valid.

T F   3.   Anything published before 1923 is no longer protected by copyright law.

T F   4.   Plagiarism in public speaking can cause public humiliation and loss of a job.

T F   5.   If you make changes in copyrighted material, it is no longer protected under copyright law.

T F   6.   The Internet domain suffix ".com" is the least objective of all domains.

T F   7.   Some Internet domain names include the country of origin.

T F   8.   To avoid plagiarism, you must give credit to the sources of your information.

T F   9.   Widespread appearance on the Internet is a strong indication that a report is accurate.

T F   10. Almost all people are honest when they reply anonymously to questions posed by pollsters.

Name _____

Multiple-Choice Questions Each question has only one correct answer.

____ 1. Which one of the following is on the textbook's list of criteria for high-quality information? (a) current, (b) widely believed, (c) appearing in Wikipedia, (d) receiving at least 1,000 hits on a search engine

____ 2. The _____ loophole in copyright laws lets scholars, writers, and public speakers disseminate information without having to get permission for small amounts. (a) public domain, (b) scholarly exemption, (c) royalty-free, (d) fair use

____ 3. To reassure an audience that his information is accurate, a speaker says, "I got my information from Google." The speaker is (a) citing a reliable source, (b) giving a vague reference, (c) injecting unnecessary humor, (d) falsifying the entire speech

____ 4. The Internet address "www.etw.org" indicates (a) a government agency, (b) a commercial operation, (c) a non-profit entity, (d) a military unit

____ 5. If you make changes in copyrighted material (a) the material is no longer protected by copyright, (b) the material retains its copyright status, (c) the material becomes your property, (d) the material reverts to public domain

____ 6. A group called "Mothers for Honest Government" issues a report on campaign financing. A researcher (a) can trust the report because of the obvious integrity of the group, (b) should consider the group reliable if it is a nonprofit organization, (c) should find out who is in the group and what motives it has, (d) should reject the group because it represents ordinary citizens instead of economic experts

____ 7. According to the text, results of polls often depend upon (a) whether individuals are paid to participate, (b) the time of day the poll is conducted, (c) how a question is asked, (d) the gender of the person conducting the poll

____ 8. Skepticism, as defined by the text, is equivalent to (a) sour negativity, (b) rejection of new ideas, (c) cynicism, (d) open-minded inquiry

____ 9. A spoken acknowledgment of the source of one's material is known as (a) an oral citation, (b) an oral footnote, (c) an oral credit, (d) an oral attribution

____ 10. If you want to reproduce a U.S. Weather Bureau pamphlet on how to protect oneself in a tornado, you are required to (a) write for permission to reproduce, (b) pay a fee, (c) write for permission and pay a fee, (d) do nothing

Name _____

Multiple-Choice Questions Each question has only one correct answer.

_____ 1. Testimonials should be handled with care because (a) they are used only for commercial gain, (b) they are by definition dishonest, (c) they are all absurd, (d) they do not constitute proof

_____ 2. Which one of the following can be reprinted without getting permission? (a) a Quaker State booklet on how to change oil in a car, (b) a Microsoft booklet on how to operate a software program, (c) a U.S. Department of Agriculture booklet on how to raise bees, (d) a Yale University booklet on how to apply for admission to the school

_____ 3. Which one of the following citations during a speech is inadequate? (a) "I got my information from Dr. Kathleen Bronson of Harvard Medical School." (b) "I got my information from the Google search engine on the Internet." (c) "I got my information from this month's issue of *Scientific American* magazine." (d) "I got my information from *Cancer Prevention*, a book published by the American Medical Association."

_____ 4. Sites at which Internet domain tend to be the least objective? (a) .edu, (b) .com, (c) .net, (d) .org

_____ 5. A book or magazine published before _____ is no longer protected by copyright and may be reproduced and distributed by anyone without violating the law. (a) 1893, (b) 1900, (c) 1923, (d) 1953

_____ 6. Until recently, the text reports, most medical experts were wrong in their understanding of the correct (a) sitting position, (b) treatment of migraine headaches, (c) stretching technique, (d) cure for eczema

_____ 7. In a survey of American attitudes, the American Jewish Committee found that a large number of respondents had a low opinion of (a) Muslims, (b) Scientologists, (c) Rastafarians, (d) Wisians

_____ 8. A speaker says, "In the latest issue of *American Health,* Dr. Emily Sanchez says that ..." This is an example of (a) an oral footnote, (b) an abstract, (c) full disclosure, (d) fair play

_____ 9. Which is the most reliable type of material? (a) evidence, (b) testimonial, (c) opinion, (d) anecdote

_____ 10. A conclusion or judgment that remains open to dispute but seems true to one's own mind is (a) a testimonial, (b) an anecdote, (c) an opinion, (d) an intuition

Name _____

Fill in the missing words or phrases.

1. Passing off someone else's words or ideas as your own is called
   _____.

2. Polls are sometimes unreliable because results often depend upon how
   a question is _____.

3. What is the Internet domain suffix denoting a non-profit organization?
   _____

4. What is the Internet domain suffix used by the vast majority of sites?
   _____

5. One reason for the unreliability of polls is that some people do not
   respond _____.

6. The legal loophole that allows researchers to use small amounts of
   copyrighted material without getting permission or paying a fee is
   known as the _____ doctrine.

7. The _____ is the equivalent of a footnote in
   a written document and its purpose is the same: to give credit for
   information or ideas that did not originate with the speaker.

8. Material that was copyrighted before 1923 is now in the
   _____ domain.

9. Experts can be a valuable source of information on any subject, but it is
   a mistake to think that they are _____.

10. Conscientious, ethical researchers are more interested in finding
    _____ than in espousing a cherished cause or
    winning an argument.

Name _____

True or False If the statement is true, circle T; if false, circle F.

T F   1.   Dictionary definitions are generally less effective than informal definitions.

T F   2.   In a speech, you should round off long numbers.

T F   3.   To paraphrase means to quote someone's words exactly.

T F   4.   If we show that two sets of data are correlated, we prove a cause-and-effect relationship.

T F   5.   If a story fails to develop the key ideas of a speech, it should not be used.

T F   6.   Support materials always constitute proof of an assertion.

T F   7.   Abbreviations such as FTC should be explained in a speech.

T F   8.   The more statistics used in a persuasive speech, the better the speech will be.

T F   9.   A narrative in a speech must always be factual.

T F   10. Sometimes one single example is enough to support a point.

Chapter 8 (Form B)

Name _____

Multiple-Choice Questions Each question has only one correct answer.

_____ 1. In a speech, which is the best use of statistics? (a) "In the last election, 96,274,564 Americans voted." (b) "In the last election, millions of Americans voted." (c) "In the last election, more than 96 million Americans voted."

_____ 2. Paraphrasing a quotation is (a) acceptable, (b) unacceptable, (c) unnecessary, (d) unethical

_____ 3. "The college's course catalog resembles a gigantic buffet table." The speaker is using which type of support material? (a) example, (b) contrast, (c) analogy, (d) definition

_____ 4. A high correlation between two sets of data (a) proves a cause-and-effect relationship, (b) does not prove a cause-and-effect relationship

_____ 5. "Jazz is a form of American music that grew out of African-American musical traditions." This sentence is (a) a definition, (b) a comparison, (c) a contrast, (d) an analogy

_____ 6. A speaker says, "According to historian Barbara Tuchman, 'Every successful revolution puts on in time the robes of the tyrant it has deposed.'" This sentence illustrates the use of (a) contrast, (b) testimony, (c) example, (d) definitions

_____ 7. "Manufacturers such as Ford, General Motors, and Toyota make sports utility vehicles." This sentence illustrates the use of (a) testimony, (b) examples, (c) comparisons, (d) definitions

_____ 8. Imagine five people of the following ages: 32, 28, 20, 18, and 17. The 20-year-old has the _____ age. (a) mean, (b) standard, (c) median, (d) statistical

_____ 9. The statistical device that identifies a portion of 100 is called the (a) correlation, (b) average, (c) mean, (d) percentage

_____ 10. "Sleet is harsh and icy, whereas snow is soft and fluffy" is an example of (a) comparison, (b) contrast, (c) hypothetical narrative, (d) statistics

Name _____

Multiple-Choice Questions Each question has only one correct answer.

_____ 1. "Punctuation marks are like traffic signs." This sentence is (a) a statistic, (b) testimony, (c) proof, (d) an analogy

_____ 2. A speaker who says, "France is 212,000 square miles—roughly the size of Texas," is using (a) testimony, (b) statistics, (c) contrast, (d) narrative

_____ 3. A speaker says, "Fresh pizza and store-bought frozen pizza are so different that I think the only thing they have in common is the name pizza. Fresh pizza is tangy, tasty, and easy to chew, whereas store-bought pizza is flat, bland, and hard to chew." This speaker is using (a) statistics, (b) comparison, (c) contrast, (d) hypothetical narrative

_____ 4. The success of vivid images as support material depends upon the good use of (a) flowery words, (b) poetic pictures, (c) specific details, (d) visual aids

_____ 5. "A feast is a meal that is rich and abundant and includes many guests." This sentence is (a) a definition, (b) a comparison, (c) a contrast, (d) an analogy

_____ 6. "Companies such as Canon, Nikon, and Olympus make digital cameras." This sentence illustrates the use of (a) comparisons, (b) testimony, (c) examples, (d) definitions

_____ 7. A speaker says, "Former Israeli prime minister Golda Meir said, 'To be successful, a woman has to be much better at her job than a man.'" This sentence illustrates the use of (a) vivid images, (b) testimony, (c) example, (d) definitions

_____ 8. The term percent means "out of _____." (a) 1, (b) 10, (c) 100, (d) 1,000

_____ 9. Support materials _____ prove a point. (a) always, (b) never, (c) sometimes

_____ 10. Imagine five people of the following ages: 45, 37, 26, 20, and 18. The 26-year-old has the _____ age. (a) median, (b) mean, (c) statistical, (d) balanced

Name _____

Fill in the missing words or phrases.

1. Numerical ways of expressing information are called _____.

2. Showing how two or more things are alike is called _____.

3. Avoid _____ definitions because they tend to be tedious and hard to grasp.

4. Taking a quotation expressed in the form of jargon and turning it into plain English is called _____.

5. A _____ narrative tells the audience about an imaginary situation.

6. Showing how two or more things are different is called _____.

7. The term _____ is used to show the relationship between two sets of data (for example, the relationship between IQ scores and grade-point averages).

8. A special type of comparison that explains a concept or an object by likening it to something that is—at first glance—quite different is known as _____.

9. Quoting verbatim means replicating a person's exact _____.

10. Regarding averages, the median is derived by listing the numbers, ranging from highest to lowest, and then locating the number that falls in the _____.

Name _____

True or False If the statement is true, circle T; if false, circle F.

T   T   F   1.   Research shows that speakers are better off using no visual aids than using poor ones.

T   T   F   2.   If you find a photo on a Web site and want to use it in a classroom speech, you can use it without asking permission from the Web site.

T   T   F   3.   Even the simplest, most easily understood visual aid should be discussed with the audience.

T   T   F   4.   A "thumbnail" on a Web site is an image with very low resolution.

F   T   F   5.   A lengthy set of handouts can be distributed during a speech if you tell your listeners to stay with you and not read ahead.

T   T   F   6.   The device known as a "visual presenter" can be used to show three-dimensional objects such as coins.

F   T   F   7.   The more visual aids used, the stronger your speech.

F   T   F   8.   Creating a graphic on a whiteboard or chalkboard during a speech is an effective way to hold the audience's attention.

F   T   F   9.   If a visual aid is small, it should be passed among the listeners during the speech so that everyone can get a good look.

T   T   F   10.   Research shows that people who are taught orally and visually can recall far more information after a presentation than those who are taught only orally.

Name _____

Multiple-Choice Questions Each question has only one correct answer.

____ 1. The text advises that you "aim for back-row comprehension." This means that you should (a) focus your attention on people in the back of the room, (b) make sure all visuals can be clearly seen by people in the back of the room, (c) speak loud enough to be heard by people in the back of the room

____ 2. Another name for an information chart is (a) fact sheet, (b) information schematic, (c) list of key ideas, (d) text file

____ 3. In a bar graph, the bars should be (a) horizontal, (b) vertical, (c) either horizontal or vertical

____ 4. In the business world, paper handouts are (a) rarely used, (b) very popular, (c) never used

____ 5. Labels on visual aids should be (a) vertical (b) horizontal, (c) either vertical or horizontal

____ 6. It is legal to download multimedia files from the Internet if they are to be used in (a) classroom speeches, (b) business presentations, (c) TV commercials, (d) Web anthologies

____ 7. Most international audiences prefer (a) visuals prepared in advance, (b) visuals prepared spontaneously during a presentation, (c) a mixture of both types of visuals

____ 8. For a pie graph in a speech, the text recommends no more than _____ wedges. (a) 3, (b) 8, (c) 16, (d) 20

____ 9. For a speech, the best time to distribute a five-page handout is (a) before you begin speaking, (b) during the body of the presentation, (c) during the conclusion, (d) after you finish speaking

____ 10. The textbook says that good models for visual aids in public speaking are (a) television commercials, (b) cereal boxes, (c) outdoor signs, (d) CD album covers

Name _____

Multiple-Choice Questions Each question has only one correct answer.

_____ 1. In considering whether and how to use PowerPoint slides, your first step is to (a) decide the ideal number of slides, (b) investigate the availability of photos on the Internet, (c) compile a list of potential slides, (d) create the outline for your speech

_____ 2. How many PowerPoint slides should you use in a speech? (a) only three, (b) no more than five, (c) as many as are needed to make key points

_____ 3. The _____ is a device that can show three-dimensional objects such as jewelry. (a) visual presenter, (b) overhead projector, (c) image enlarger, (d) multimedia projector

_____ 4. Regarding a speaker's credibility with an audience, which one of the following statements is true? (a) The more visual aids a speaker uses, the greater the credibility. (b) A speaker is better off using no visual aids at all than poor ones.

_____ 5. It is legal to download an image from the Internet without asking for permission if the use of the image is limited to (a) a sales presentation for a pharmaceutical company, (b) a Web site for a car dealer, (c) a student speech in a college classroom, (d) a brochure for a beauty salon

_____ 6. Posters are often preferred to PowerPoint slides in (a) corporate presentation rooms, (b) Army training rooms, (c) hotel conference rooms, (d) courtrooms

_____ 7. If your multimedia projector stops working during a PowerPoint presentation, your best option is to (a) distribute paper copies of the slides and continue your presentation, (b) give the audience a five-minute break while you try to fix the equipment, (c) give a summary of points covered so far and end the presentation, (d) describe the contents of the remaining slides

_____ 8. Most international audiences prefer (a) a visual that is prepared spontaneously during a presentation, (b) a visual that is prepared in advance, (c) a mixture of both types of visuals

_____ 9. The technique whereby a visual is displayed one part at a time is known as (a) gradual revelation, (b) piece-by-piece revelation, (c) incremental revelation, (d) progressive revelation

_____ 10. During a presentation, you should _____ look at your visual aids. (a) constantly, (b) occasionally, (c) never

Name _____

Fill in the missing words or phrases.

1. Circulating visual aids during a speech is a _____ idea.

2. Do thumbnail images have *high* or *low* resolution?

3. Whenever possible, appeal to the senses—sight, hearing, taste, smell, and _____.

4. The technique of revealing only one part of a visual at a time is known as _____ revelation.

5. A pie graph is a circle representing _____ percent and divided into segments of various sizes.

6. Of all graphs, a _____ graph is perhaps the easiest to read, because it visually translates information into a picture that can be grasped instantly.

7. According to the text, the most frequent audiovisual mistake is creating a graphic that is difficult for everyone to _____ clearly.

8. In books, labels on visuals can be either horizontal or vertical. In a speech, they should be _____.

9. For most international audiences, a spontaneously prepared visual aid during a presentation is interpreted as a sign of _____.

10. An information chart is also called a list of _____ ideas.

Name _____

True or False If the statement is true, circle T; if false, circle F.

T F 1. Organizing material from north to south is an example of the spatial pattern.

T F 2. Your main points should be created before you formulate your central idea.

T F 3. If you use the topical pattern, you should divide your central idea into components or categories.

T F 4. In the cause-effect pattern of organization, it is permissible to discuss effects first and then causes.

T F 5. Bridges and internal summaries should never be used together.

T F 6. In an outline, all main points should have the same number of supporting points.

T F 7. If you plan to give a speech to several different audiences, you might need to have different main points for each audience.

T F 8. Each main point should make an announcement rather than an assertion.

T F 9. For a long speech, most experienced speakers cover only two or three main points.

T F 10. Telling what happened before, during, and after an event is an example of the chronological pattern.

Name _____

Multiple-Choice Questions Each question has only one correct answer.

____ 1. Which of the following organizational pattern is a TV news reporter most likely to use in a report of an event? (a) topical, (b) cause-effect, (c) chronological, (d) analytical

____ 2. Discussing your speech's key ideas with a knowledgeable source is called (a) double checking, (b) an insurance policy, (c) a confirmation, (d) an expert check

____ 3. In a speech on redwood trees, a speaker begins by discussing the roots, proceeds to the trunk, then the branches, and finally the leaves. Which organizational pattern is being used? (a) spatial, (b) chronological, (c) cause-effect, (d) problem-solution, (e) topical

____ 4. A speaker says, "Now we come to the most important thing I have to tell you." Which device is the speaker using? (a) bridge, (b) internal summary, (c) signpost, (d) spotlight

____ 5. A speaker says, "Now that we have looked at the problem, let's turn our attention to the solution." Which device is the speaker using? (a) bridge, (b) internal summary, (c) signpost, (d) spotlight

____ 6. Which one of the following statements is true? (a) All main points need supporting materials. (b) Each main point should have the same number of supports as every other main point. (c) It is impossible to have too many supports. (d) Transitions are the most important type of supports.

____ 7. The cause-effect pattern of organization (a) must explain causes before effects, (b) must explain effects before causes, (c) can explain either causes or effects first

____ 8. For a speech on the history of a Native American family in Arizona, which organizational pattern would you be most likely to choose? (a) spatial, (b) chronological, (c) cause-effect, (d) problem-solution, (e) topical

____ 9. Which part of the speech does the text recommend that you create first? (a) title, (b) introduction, (c) body, (d) conclusion

____ 10. When you are organizing your material, each note card should be limited to how many ideas? (a) one, (b) two, (c) three, (d) four, (e) five, (f) six

Name _____

Multiple-Choice Questions Each question has only one correct answer.

_____ 1. Which organizational pattern is especially popular in persuasive speeches? (a) topical, (b) chronological, (c) spatial, (d) problem-solution

_____ 2. A speaker describes the safety features of a new car, starting at the front bumper and progressing to the rear bumper. Which organizational pattern is the speaker using? (a) spatial, (b) chronological, (c) cause-effect, (d) problem-solution, (e) topical

_____ 3. For a speech explaining how to bake bread, which organizational pattern would be used? (a) spatial, (b) chronological, (c) cause-effect, (d) problem-solution, (e) topical

_____ 4. Main points are designed to help the audience understand and remember (a) the general purpose, (b) the specific purpose, (c) the introduction, (d) the central idea

_____ 5. A speaker discusses three types of work dogs. Which pattern is the speaker using? (a) spatial, (b) chronological, (c) topical, (d) problem-solution

_____ 6. A speaker says, "So far, we have seen that carelessness is the main cause for industrial accidents." Which device is the speaker using? (a) crossroad, (b) internal summary, (c) traffic light, (d) barrier

_____ 7. A speaker says, "What I am going to explain now will help you understand the rest of the speech." Which device is the speaker using? (a) crossroad, (b) internal summary, (c) external summary, (d) spotlight

_____ 8. A speaker discusses why some people abuse animals, and then describes the effects of abuse on the animals. Which pattern is the speaker using? (a) cause-effect, (b) chronological, (c) spatial, (d) topical

_____ 9. Which of the following shows a parallel grammatical form? (a) If you are trapped outdoors in a thunderstorm, avoid being the tallest object in a field, stay away from poles and fences, and do not touch any metal. (b) If you are trapped outdoors in a thunderstorm, avoid being the tallest object in a field, poles and fences should be avoided, and no metal should be touched.

_____ 10. The first thing speakers should create for their speech is the (a) title, (b) introduction, (c) body, (d) conclusion

Name _____

Fill in the missing words or phrases.

1. If main points are organized according to the way in which they relate to each other in physical space, the _____ pattern is being used.

2. Main points are used to drive home the _____ of a speech.

3. If you speak on the federal government and create main points based on the three branches (executive, legislative, and judicial), you are using the _____ pattern of organization.

4. Which should a main point make—an assertion or an announcement? _____

5. How many main points should you have for a 5-minute speech? _____

6. If main points are organized according to a cause-and-effect relationship, the _____ pattern is being used.

7. If main points are organized in a time sequence, the _____ pattern is being used.

8. Spotlights, bridges, and signposts are examples of what component of a speech?

    _____

9. Speakers who discuss a problem in the first part of a speech and then give a solution in the second part are using the _____ pattern of organization.

10. In the middle of your speech, if you give a summary of what you have discussed up to that point, you are using the device called _____.

Name _____

True or False If the statement is true, circle T; if false, circle F.

T F   1.   In the introduction, it is acceptable to tell a hypothetical narrative (a story that did not actually happen).

T F   2.   In the conclusion, the speaker should never repeat ideas or information contained in the introduction.

T F   3.   It is possible for an introduction to be too short.

T F   4.   The part of the introduction that is designed to get your audience's attention and interest is called the orienting material.

T F   5.   The introduction should be prepared before the body of a speech is developed.

T F   6.   All members of an audience listen attentively for the first 30 seconds of a speech.

T F   7.   Saying "In conclusion. . ." as you wrap up your speech is not acceptable in good speechmaking.

T F   8.   You should never bring new main points into the conclusion.

T F   9.   Rhetorical questions should be avoided in introductions.

T F   10. If you didn't have enough time to prepare your speech, the conclusion is a good place to apologize to the audience.

Name _____

Multiple-Choice Questions Each question has only one correct answer.

_____ 1. Which one of the following is an acceptable option in a conclusion? (a) discussing a new main point, (b) apologizing for inadequate preparation, (c) referring to the introduction, (d) promising to give a better speech next time

_____ 2. A speaker says, "How long will America continue to be plagued with child abuse?" This is an example of _____ question. (a) a rhetorical, (b) an overt-response

_____ 3. Telling a story, asking a question, and using a visual aid are examples of (a) orienting material, (b) attention material, (c) evidence, (d) enticement

_____ 4. Which one of the following is an acceptable option in an introduction? (a) a convincing clincher, (b) a sincere apology, (c) a hypothetical narrative

_____ 5. Most attorneys believe that courtroom battles are won because of the effectiveness of (a) the opening statement, (b) the closing argument, (c) both the opening statement and the closing argument, (d) the supporting evidence

_____ 6. It is _____ for an introduction to be too short. (a) possible, (b) impossible

_____ 7. In a speech, which one of the following is a mistake if used in the conclusion? (a) a quotation by a reputable authority, (b) a new main point, (c) a repetition of key points, (d) a reference to the introduction

_____ 8. You can signal the end of a speech with (a) verbal signals, (b) nonverbal signals, (c) both verbal and nonverbal signals

_____ 9. For the first few sentences in a speech, which one of the following options would be a mistake? (a) a rhetorical question, (b) a surprising statistic, (c) an announcement of the topic, (d) a narrative

_____ 10. Issuing an appeal or a challenge at the end of a speech is an example of (a) a summary, (b) a clincher, (c) orienting material, (d) attention material

Name _____

Multiple-Choice Questions Each question has only one correct answer.

____ 1. According to most attorneys, courtroom battles are usually won on the effectiveness of (a) the opening statement, (b) the closing argument, (c) both the opening statement and the closing argument

____ 2. A speaker says, "Please raise your hands to answer this: How many of you know how to swim?" What kind of question is this speaker using? (a) overt-response, (b) rhetorical

____ 3. The best place to reassure your listeners that you are well-prepared and that you are not going to waste their time is in (a) the attention material, (b) the orienting material

____ 4. Which one of the following options fails to serve as orienting material? (a) grabbing the listeners' attention, (b) previewing the body of the speech, (c) giving background information, (d) establishing credibility

____ 5. The text quotes the old speechmaking formula, "Tell 'em what you're going to tell 'em. Tell 'em. Then tell 'em what you told 'em." The last sentence refers to (a) the clincher, (b) the orienting material, (c) the summary, (d) the attention material

____ 6. In career speeches, a few words spoken before your attention material is called (a) a prologue, (b) an icebreaker, (c) a welcome, (d) an opener

____ 7. "Today I'd like to tell you how to grow vegetables." This sentence is most appropriate for (a) attention material, (b) orienting material

____ 8. The best way to indicate that you have finished with a quotation is to (a) say "End of quotation" (b) pause as an "oral" punctuation device, (c) use both hands to make "finger quotes" in the air, (d) crumple the card on which the quotation is written

____ 9. Informing the audience of your qualifications to speak on a topic is (a) a form of bragging to be avoided, (b) recommended to build credibility, (c) not advised unless you are an expert

____ 10. The text says, "Quotations usually work best when they are _____." (a) cryptic, (b) from an ancient philosopher, (c) risqué, (d) short

Name _____

Fill in the missing words or phrases.

1. Telling the audience about your expertise on your topic is a good way to establish _____.

2. If you ask your listeners a question, but you don't want them to answer overtly by raising their hands or speaking, you are asking what kind of question?

   _____

3. The part of the introduction in which you prepare your audience intellectually and psychologically for the body of the speech is known as _____.

4. The part of the introduction in which you capture and hold your audience's attention is known as

   _____.

5. When is a clincher used in a speech?

   _____

6. The text says that it is acceptable to use fresh material in your conclusion as long as the material does not constitute

   _____.

7. At the end of a speech, instead of coming to an abrupt halt, a speaker should use verbal signals and

   _____.

8. The text says that when you prepare a speech, you should work on which part first: the introduction, the body, or the conclusion? _____

9. If you use a quotation in a speech, what oral punctuation device does the text recommend that you use at the end of the quotation? _____

10. "I guess that's all I have to say" is a _____ ending for a speech.

Name _____

True or False If the statement is true, circle T; if false, circle F.

T F 1. Speaking notes should be written in complete sentences.

T F 2. The textbook recommends that you make a fresh set of speaking notes on the eve of your speech.

T F 3. Main points in outlines are represented by Roman numerals (I, II, III, and so on).

T F 4. According to the text, the body of a speech should have its own numbering sequence in the outline, independent of the introduction and conclusion.

T F 5. An outline has a title, but the speaker does not actually say it in the speech.

T F 6. It is acceptable to write quotations in full on your speaking notes.

T F 7. In an outline, transitions should be placed between each main point.

T F 8. In an outline, one of the places where you should put a transition is between the body of the speech and the conclusion.

T F 9. A topic outline has more words than a complete-sentence outline.

T F 10. Although you can use notes if you need them, the most desirable technique for public speaking is to use no notes.

Name _____

Multiple-Choice Questions Each question has only one correct answer.

____ 1. Roman numerals (I, II, III, and so on) should be used in an outline for (a) major divisions, (b) first-level subdivision, (c) second-level subdivision, (d) third-level subdivision

____ 2. For speaker's notes, the text recommends that _____ should be written in large letters and contrasting colors. (a) the introduction, (b) main points, (c) transitions, (d) delivery reminders

____ 3. A disadvantage of using a full sheet of paper for speaking notes is (a) a sheet can contain notes for an entire speech, (b) a sheet can cause a speaker's eyes to glide over key points, (c) a sheet is larger than an index card, (d) a sheet can appear to be a computer printout

____ 4. An outline should include (a) delivery reminders, (b) every word that you will say during the speech, (c) transitions, (d) an audience analysis

____ 5. Donald Macleod of Princeton Theological Seminary tells his seminarians that the maximum time for an effective sermon is (a) 8 minutes, (b) 18 minutes, (c) 28 minutes, (d) 38 minutes

____ 6. Using notes in a speech (a) is a sign of weakness in communicating, (b) shows a lack of confidence in speaking ability, (c) shows preparedness and respect for the audience

____ 7. A good time to use a topic outline is (a) in the early stages of preparation, when you are brainstorming and putting down your ideas, (b) in the later stages, when you are refining and polishing your ideas

____ 8. "Czech It Out! Why You Should Visit Prague" is an _____ title for a speech. (a) acceptable, (b) unacceptable

____ 9. For your speaking notes on a piece of paper or note card, you should (a) write on only one side, (b) write on both sides

____ 10. A speech should have _____ the complete-sentence outline. (a) about the same number of words as, (b) fewer words than, (c) more words than

Name _____

Multiple-Choice Questions Each question has only one correct answer.

_____ 1. An outline helps you to see the relationship between (a) ideas, (b) subjects and verbs, (c) formats, (d) topics

_____ 2. In an outline, which of the following places would be unnecessary for inserting a transition? (a) between each main point, (b) between the introduction and the body, (c) between the body and the conclusion, (d) between the conclusion and documentation

_____ 3. For an outline, which one of the following is unnecessary? (a) title, (b) bibliography, (c) list of visual aids, (d) speaker's notes

_____ 4. In an outline, it is incorrect to have _____ under a heading. (a) only one subheading, (b) more than 10 subheadings, (c) a subheading labeled "example"

_____ 5. Writing complete sentences in your outline (a) will guarantee a better speech than if you write phrases, (b) will make it easier for another person to help you than if you write phrases, (c) will help you memorize the speech, (d) will be necessary in order for you to read your speech

_____ 6. When no time limit is set for a speech, the speaker should talk (a) briefly, (b) as long as the speaker wants

_____ 7. When you deliver your speech, you should use (a) your outline, (b) your speaking notes, (c) both your outline and your speaking notes

_____ 8. "Ouch! How to Treat a Bee Sting" is an _____ title for a speech. (a) acceptable, (b) unacceptable

_____ 9. A topic outline uses (a) complete sentences, (b) only one word per line, (c) key words or phrases, (d) a topic analysis

_____ 10. Concerning a complete-sentence outline and the speech itself, which one of the following statements is true? (a) The speech itself should have about the same number of words as the outline. (b) The speech itself should have more words than the outline. (c) The speech itself should have fewer words than the outline.

Name _____

Fill in the missing words or phrases.

1. A speaker begins by saying, "The title of my speech is 'How to Lose Weight Permanently.'" What mistake is the speaker making?
_____

2. In the standard system of subdivisions in an outline, you mark your main points with _____.

3. In an outline, each heading should have at least _____ subdivisions or none at all.

4. If you practice your speech and discover that you are running four minutes over the time limit, what should you do?
_____

5. The text says that the two most popular formats for outlines are the topic outline and the _____ outline.

6. Some people have the mistaken notion that using notes is a sign of _____ weakness.

7. The text says that _____ is a common-sense way of arranging information in a logical pattern.

8. You should make indentations in your speaking notes that correspond to those in your _____.

9. Which should have more words—the outline or the actual speech? _____

10. Are speeches today generally shorter or longer than in the past?
_____

Name _____

True or False If the statement is true, circle T; if false, circle F.

T F   1.   "The deafening din of dynamite" is an example of antithesis.

T F   2.   "Her and me went to Chicago" is grammatically correct.

T F   3.   "Just between you and I" is grammatically correct.

T F   4.   If your listeners share your specialized vocation, you can use jargon in a speech.

T F   5.   Abstract words are more likely to be remembered by an audience than concrete words.

T F   6.   Oral language requires more amplification and elaboration than written language.

T F   7.   Words like *new, improved,* and *easy* in advertising can cause an increase in sales of a product.

T F   8.   The best way to convey complex ideas is to use complex language.

T F   9.   "Passed away" instead of "died" is an example of a euphemism.

T F   10. "A deferred dream dries up like a raisin in the sun" is an example of a metaphor.

Name _____

Multiple-Choice Questions Each question has only one correct answer.

_____ 1. If the person who sends your car through a car wash is called "a corrosion control specialist," what type of language is being used? (a) doublespeak, (b) cliché, (c) mixed metaphor, (d) simile, (e) metaphor

_____ 2. "This is a government by the people, of the people, and for the people." This is an example of (a) a euphemism, (b) jargon, (c) a metaphor, (d) parallel structure

_____ 3. "The Indonesians have a tough row to hoe to keep their economic heads above water." This is an example of a (a) euphemism, (b) jargon word, (c) mixed metaphor, (d) simile

_____ 4. "They don't care about people, but they do care about possessions." This sentence illustrates (a) alliteration, (b) metaphor, (c) euphemism, (d) antithesis

_____ 5. Friendship is (a) an abstract word, (b) a concrete word, (c) a phony word, (d) a meaningless word

_____ 6. "The stars are diamonds in the sky." This is an example of (a) a simile, (b) a metaphor, (c) a euphemism, (d) jargon

_____ 7. Which one of the following is incorrect grammatically? (a) He and Mary strolled on the beach. (b) This news is just between you and I. (c) For me and Jack, the raise was welcome. (d) Please give the files to me and Susan.

_____ 8. "Last, but not least" is an example of (a) a euphemism, (b) jargon, (c) a cliché, (d) parallel structure

_____ 9. The emotional meaning attached to a word is its (a) denotation, (b) connotation

_____ 10. The text says that grammatical errors in a speech distract the audience and can cause the speaker to lose (a) self-confidence, (b) an aura of expertise, (c) credibility with the audience, (d) a tone of seriousness

Name _____

Multiple-Choice Questions Each question has only one correct answer.

____ 1. "After you open a can of worms, they always come home to roost." This is an example of (a) mixed metaphor, (b) euphemism, (c) jargon, (d) simile

____ 2. "The sad sister sat on a silver seat" is an example of (a) antithesis, (b) euphemism, (c) alliteration, (d) metaphor

____ 3. "The stars are like diamonds in the sky." This is an example of (a) a metaphor, (b) a simile, (c) jargon, (d) a euphemism

____ 4. Which one of the following is incorrect grammatically? (a) Please give the files to me and Susan. (b) He and Mary strolled on the beach. (c) For me and Jack, the raise was welcome. (d) This news is just between you and I.

____ 5. "Blind as a bat" is an example of (a) euphemism, (b) jargon, (c) cliché, (d) parallel structure

____ 6. When politicians raise taxes, but call their action "revenue enhancement," they are using (a) jargon, (b) a euphemism, (c) poor grammar, (d) parallel language

____ 7. Honesty is (a) an abstract word, (b) a concrete word, (c) a phony word, (d) a meaningless word

____ 8. If a funeral director is called a "grief therapist," what type of language is being used? (a) doublespeak, (b) cliché, (c) mixed metaphor, (d) simile, (e) metaphor

____ 9. A dictionary definition of a word is its (a) connotation, (b) denotation

____ 10. "We want justice for ourselves, for our friends, and for our children." This is an example of (a) euphemism, (b) jargon, (c) metaphor, (d) parallel structure

Name _____

Fill in the missing words or phrases.

1. A euphemism is harmful when it is used to _____ the listener.

2. If you say, "Your bread and butter will be snatched from under your feet," you are guilty of using mixed _____.

3. Trite, worn-out words or phrases are called _____.

4. The connotation of a word is the _____ meaning that is associated with it.

5. When the person who sends your car through a car wash is called a "corrosion control specialist," what kind of doublespeak is being used? _____.

6. When people use the specialized language of a group or profession—for example, using terms such as AWOL—they are using _____.

7. The text quotes an Arab proverb, "The best speaker is one who can turn the ear into _____."

8. "The tame tiger teased the tiny tot" is an example of the rhetorical device known as _____.

9. The text says that poor grammar can hurt you because it makes you sound (to some people) as if you are not _____.

10. A person who says, "You was late" has made a _____ error.

Name _____

True or False If the statement is true, circle T; if false, circle F.

T F 1. If you are not feeling enthusiastic about giving a speech, you should pretend to be enthusiastic.

T F 2. When you speak into a microphone, you should raise your voice slightly.

T F 3. Pauses in speeches should be avoided because they make you look indecisive.

T F 4. The extemporaneous method of delivery involves speaking on the spur of the moment with no chance to prepare.

T F 5. When speaking to a small audience, you should establish eye contact with every listener.

T F 6. If you don't receive any questions during the question-and-answer period, you must have failed to stimulate the audience's interest in the topic.

T F 7. Some speeches call for few or no gestures.

T F 8. The memorized method of delivery has the virtue of allowing the speaker to figure out exact wording ahead of time.

T F 9. It is a good idea to speak fast at the beginning of your speech so that the audience doesn't get bored.

T F 10. A speech should be practiced point by point, not word for word.

Name _____

Multiple-Choice Questions Each question has only one correct answer.

____ 1. Which aspect of nonverbal communication is considered a "figurative handshake?" (a) personal appearance, (b) gestures, (c) eye contact, (d) posture

____ 2. The key to effective delivery is (a) good eye contact with each member of the audience, (b) effective use of gestures and body movement, (c) a winning smile and enthusiastic attitude, (d) a strong desire to communicate with the audience

____ 3. If nonverbal communication contradicts verbal messages, listeners will accept _____ as the true message. (a) the nonverbal, (b) the verbal, (c) neither the nonverbal nor the verbal

____ 4. A speaker's clothes should be (a) about as dressy as the listeners' clothes, (b) a bit dressier than the listeners' clothes, (c) less dressy than the listeners' clothes

____ 5. If you fear that you will cry while telling a painful personal story in a speech, you should (a) omit the story to avoid embarrassment, (b) tell the story after alerting the audience that you might cry, (c) videotape yourself telling the story and play the video during the speech, (d) put the story on a handout that is distributed at the end of the speech

____ 6. A few audience members are rudely chatting among themselves during your speech, distracting other listeners. Which one of the following solutions is unacceptable? (a) Ignore the talkers. (b) Ask the talkers to please give you their attention. (c) Stop speaking and look directly at the talkers.

____ 7. "Uh" and "um" are examples of what the text calls (a) meaningless pauses, (b) impromptu utterances, (c) oral distracters, (d) verbal fillers

____ 8. During a question-and-answer session, which one of the following responses is undesirable? (a) "That's a good question." (b) "I don't know." (c) "I don't understand your question." (d) "I'll find out the answer and get back to you soon."

____ 9. If you practice your speech and find that you are two minutes over the time limit, you should (a) cut out material by using your outline and speaking notes, (b) practice your speech with a faster rate of speaking, (c) do nothing about it because the information is the priority, (d) plan on delivering your speech as quickly as possible

____ 10. "Cannahepya?" for "Can I help you?" is an example of poor (a) vowelizaton, (b) articulation, (c) intonation, (d) sound production

Name _____

Multiple-Choice Questions Each question has only one correct answer.

_____ 1. Which one of the following statements about pauses is false? (a) Pauses should last a minimum of ten seconds. (b) Pauses give audiences a chance to digest what you have said. (c) Pauses give you a moment to think of what you are going to say next. (d) Pauses let the listeners know when you have finished one thought and are ready to go to the next. (e) Pauses can be used to emphasize an important statement.

_____ 2. Which method of delivery involves speaking on the spur of the moment with no chance to prepare? (a) extemporaneous, (b) manuscript, (c) memorized, (d) impromptu

_____ 3. In a manuscript speech, the text recommends inserting slanting lines to indicate (a) a louder voice, (b) a softer voice, (c) a glance at the audience, (d) a pause

_____ 4. If you as a speaker do not know the answer to a listener's question, you should (a) give as strong an answer as you can manage under the circumstances, (b) deflect the question by telling the audience that there is not enough time to answer the question adequately, (c) admit that you do not know the answer

_____ 5. The text recommends that you look at the audience what percentage of the time? (a) 50%, (b) 75%, (c) 85%, (d) 95%

_____ 6. The PREP (Position, Reason, Example, Position) template is recommended for _____ speeches. (a) manuscript, (b) extemporaneous, (c) impromptu, (d) memorized

_____ 7. If you are asked to speak impromptu in five minutes, the first thing you should do is decide (a) your introduction, (b) your main points, (c) your conclusion, (d) your opening joke.

_____ 8. In an oral presentation, if you say, "I'm happy to speak to you today," but your facial expression shows unhappiness, your audience is most likely to assume that (a) you are happy to be speaking, (b) you are unhappy about speaking, (c) you are happy in some ways and unhappy in others, (d) you are a troubled and deceitful person

_____ 9. Which method of delivery is a person most likely to use in delivering a paper at a scientific conference? (a) extemporaneous, (b) memorized, (c) manuscript, (d) impromptu

_____ 10. "Watchadoin?" for "What are you doing?" is an example of poor (a) articulation, (b) vowelization, (c) intonation, (d) sound production

Name _____

Fill in the missing words or phrases.

1. To sound conversational in a speech, you should be yourself but intensify the emotional tones and vibrancy of your _____.

2. The text recommends that you follow the maxim "Practice ideas, not _____."

3. The text recommends that you practice your speech at least _____ times.

4. If, before a speech, you do not feel confident, the text recommends that you _____ to be confident.

5. If you don't want your speech interrupted by questions but you do want questions in the question-and-answer period, you should advise your audience of your desire. When should you make your announcement?

   _____

6. The text says that the key to good speech delivery is

   _____.

7. If the verbal signals and the nonverbal signals in your speech contradict each other, which will the audience accept as the true message?

   _____

8. The _____ method of speaking is the most popular style of speaking in America today.

9. Speaking on the spur of the moment—without a chance to prepare—is called the _____ method of delivery.

10. The text says that the biggest spoiler of eye contact is

    _____.

Name _____

True or False If the statement is true, circle T; if false, circle F.

T F   1. One of the goals of informative speaking is to convey fresh information.

T F   2. A definition speech focuses on giving a dictionary definition of a concept.

T F   3. In a process speech, the goal is always to teach the listeners how to perform the process themselves.

T F   4. "To explain to my listeners the meaning of capitalism in modern society" is a specific purpose statement for a process speech.

T F   5. "To tell my audience about the life of Malcolm X" is an example of a specific purpose statement for a definition speech.

T F   6. "To inform my audience how a thunderstorm forms" is an example of a specific purpose statement for a process speech.

T F   7. In a speech to a graduating high school class, you can assume that all the students know basic information, such as the fact that Alaska and Hawaii were the last states admitted to the United States.

T F   8. Of the three main channels for learning information, the visual is the strongest.

T F   9. An explanation speech is not appropriate for a college classroom speech.

T F   10. Calling on people at random is a technique that the text recommends for long presentations.

Name _____

Multiple-Choice Questions Each question has only one correct answer.

_____ 1. Which one of these channels for learning information is the strongest? (a) auditory, (b) visual, (c) physical activity

_____ 2. "To inform my audience of the reasons for the near extinction of mountain gorillas" is a specific purpose statement for which type of speech? (a) analytical, (b) topical, (c) process, (d) explanation

_____ 3. "To tell my audience about the life of Florence Nightingale" is a specific purpose statement for which type of speech? (a) definition, (b) description, (c) process, (d) topical

_____ 4. "To tell my listeners how porpoises are trained to do out-of-water stunts" is a specific purpose statement for which type of speech? (a) definition, (b) analytical, (c) process, (d) spatial

_____ 5. "To explain to my listeners the meaning of feminism in modern America" is a specific purpose statement for which type of speech? (a) definition, (b) description, (c) process, (d) topical

_____ 6. Which one of the following specific purpose statements is appropriate for an informative speech? (a) "To demonstrate to my listeners how to build kites." (b) "To prove to my listeners that they should stop drinking soda." (c) "To help my listeners see that they should buy cars made in Detroit." (d) "To talk my listeners into voting for Republican candidates."

_____ 7. The text says that for a long presentation that lasts all afternoon, it is best to give a coffee or stretch break after every ____-minute period. (a) 30, (b) 45, (c) 60, (d) 90

_____ 8. To provide variety during a long presentation, you can ask questions of listeners. The best technique is to (a) ask for volunteers, (b) call a listener's name before you ask the question, (c) call a listener's name after you ask the question, (d) pull a name from a hat

_____ 9. Explaining Adolf Hitler's identity to a college audience (a) is insulting to the intelligence of the listeners, (b) can be carried out indirectly, without insulting anyone's intelligence, (c) is unnecessary for listeners at the college level, (d) is necessary for about 60 percent of a typical college audience

_____ 10. A speech recounting the history of the attack on Pearl Harbor would be which type of speech? (a) persuasive, (b) informative, (c) entertaining, (d) demonstration

Name _____

Multiple-Choice Questions Each question has only one correct answer.

____ 1. According to the text, one of the goals of informative speaking is to convey what kind of information? (a) substantial, (b) fresh, (c) unusual, (d) indisputable

____ 2. In a first aid class, a nurse says, "To control bleeding, remember RED, which stands for Rest, Elevation, and Direct pressure." Which learning device is the nurse using? (a) shortcut, (b) linguistic trick, (c) acronym, (d) alliteration

____ 3. "To inform my listeners how a guitar makes music" is a specific purpose statement for which type of speech? (a) definition, (b) description, (c) process, (d) spatial

____ 4. "A tornado's funnel is like the vortex you see when you let water go down a drain." This is an example of which principle? (a) Relate the speech to the listeners' self-interest. (b) Assess the knowledge of the listeners. (c) Use the familiar to explain the unfamiliar.

____ 5. Nina Totenberg, a nationally known TV and radio reporter, says the most important element in an effective speech is _____ information. (a) humorous, (b) controversial, (c) interesting, (d) timely

____ 6. A speaker explains why most car thieves steal 10-year-old cars rather than new cars. The speaker is likely to use the _____ pattern of organization. (a) problem-solution, (b) chronological, (c) spatial, (d) statement-of-reasons

____ 7. "To inform my audience about living conditions in an institution for autistic children" is a specific purpose statement for which type of speech? (a) definition, (b) description, (c) process, (d) topical

____ 8. "To inform my audience about the dangers of quicksand" is a specific purpose statement for which type of speech? (a) innovative (b) topical, (c) explanation, (d) analytical

____ 9. The text quotes Voltaire as saying, "The secret of being tiresome is in _____." (a) repeating yourself, (b) talking only about yourself, (c) recounting boring stories, (d) telling everything

____ 10. An ancient Chinese proverb says, "I hear, and I forget. I see, and I remember. I do, and I _____." (a) understand, (b) enjoy, (c) ask questions, (d) appreciate

Name _____

Fill in the missing words or phrases.

1. A teacher is an example of a(n) _____
   speaker, not a persuasive speaker.

2. In a process speech, you should give advance warning of
   _____.

3. The text quotes an ancient Chinese proverb that applies to modern
   communication: "I hear, and I forget. I see, and I remember. I do, and
   I_____."

4. If you describe a robot from top to bottom, you are using the
   _____ pattern of organization.

5. "To explain to my listeners how to refinish furniture" is a purpose
   statement for which type of informative speech?
   _____

6. The kind of definition that is richer and fuller than a dictionary definition is
   a(n) _____ definition.

7. Many speeches are boring because speakers deal primarily with
   generalities instead of _____.

8. The text advises you to "use the familiar to explain the
   _____."

9. Of the three main channels for learning new information, the auditory is
   weakest, the visual is stronger, and _____ is
   strongest of all.

10. To motivate listeners to pay attention to your speech, you should relate
    your remarks to their _____.

Name _____

True or False If the statement is true, circle T; if false, circle F.

T F 1. In a speech of refutation, deeply held beliefs are easier to demolish than a set of erroneous facts.

T F 2. The statement-of-reasons pattern is a good method of organization when the audience leans toward your position but needs some justification for that leaning.

T F 3. The text advocates applying pressure to those listeners who are reluctant to take action on a proposal.

T F 4. Role play can be used to change people's behavior.

T F 5. According to the text, petition drives are almost never successful in persuading lawmakers to change their positions.

T F 6. The speech to motivate action can try to stimulate either positive or negative action.

T F 7. Persuasion in one's career often requires weeks, months, or even years.

T F 8. Speakers should ask for a show of hands only when they are sure that most listeners will be eager and unembarrassed to make a public commitment.

T F 9. Implying what you want your listeners to do is more effective than asking for precisely what action you want them to take.

T F 10. A leave-behind is a handout distributed at the end of a meeting.

Name _____

Multiple-Choice Questions Each question has only one correct answer.

____ 1. In which one of the following situations is the problem-solution pattern a bad choice? (a) when listeners don't realize the existence of a particular problem, (b) when listeners don't realize the seriousness of a problem, (c) when listeners already accept your solution

____ 2. A good persuasive speech _____ contains sections that look like sections of an informative speech. (a) never, (b) often

____ 3. According to the text, whether you succeed in persuasion often comes down to one key question: (a) Are you sincere? (b) Are you likeable? (c) Are you trustworthy?

____ 4. In a speech of refutation, you are more likely to demolish opposing arguments if (a) the opposing arguments are based on a set of erroneous facts, (b) the opposing arguments are based on deeply held beliefs

____ 5. To encourage listeners to call the Red Cross to volunteer for blood donation, you should try to get them to use their cell phones (a) before the speech is finished, (b) at the end of the speech, (c) as soon as they leave the room, (d) sometime before they go to sleep that evening

____ 6. The first step in the motivated sequence is (a) need, (b) satisfaction, (c) attention, (d) action, (e) motivation, (f) visualization

____ 7. The final step in the motivated sequence is (a) need, (b) satisfaction, (c) attention, (d) action, (e) motivation, (f) visualization

____ 8. Persuasion in one's careers (a) usually demands high-pressure sales techniques, (b) often requires weeks, months, or even years

____ 9. The visualization step of the motivated sequence offers a scenario that can be (a) positive, (b) negative, (c) either positive or negative

____ 10. Which of the following would be a mistake if offered as take-home material? (a) a transcript of the speech, (b) a summary of key ideas, (c) a list of new points, (d) a bibliography of sources, (e) a printout of graphics

Name _____

Multiple-Choice Questions Each question has only one correct answer.

_____ 1. Convincing your audience that democracy is expanding in China is an example of a (a) speech of curtailment, (b) speech to influence thinking, (c) speech to motivate action

_____ 2. It is _____ for a persuasive speech to include sections that seem identical to sections of an informative speech. (a) acceptable, (b) unacceptable

_____ 3. Persuading people to stop smoking is an example of a (a) speech to influence thinking, (b) speech to motivate action, (c) speech of curtailment

_____ 4. In the motivated sequence, the first step is "attention" and the second step is (a) visualization, (b) need, (c) satisfaction, (d) action

_____ 5. If you explain the three factors that contribute to the rise in asthma cases, you are using which organizational pattern? (a) motivated sequence, (b) statement-of-reasons, (c) chronological, (d) problem-solution

_____ 6. If you show the audience the impact of brain injuries in child athletes and then tell how to improve the situation, you are using which organizational pattern? (a) spatial, (b) statement-of-reasons, (c) chronological, (d) problem-solution

_____ 7. In a persuasive speech, you should reveal to the audience (a) your true goals and motives, (b) the weaknesses in your argument, (c) your feelings about those who disagree with you, (d) your difficulty in preparing the speech

_____ 8. A DVD about your speech topic, given to listeners at the end of your speech, is an example of what the book calls (a) a hidden persuader, (b) an enticement, (c) a leave-behind, (d) a gimmick

_____ 9. The technique of changing one's behavior by performing scenarios and receiving critiques is called (a) sensitivity training, (b) role play, (c) peer modeling, (d) assertiveness skill building

_____ 10. "To convince listeners to reject the idea that tornadoes are incapable of striking large cities." This is an example of a specific purpose statement for (a) a speech to motivate action, (b) a speech of refutation, (c) a speech of argumentation

Name _____

Fill in the missing words or phrases.

1. The speech that has five steps—attention, need, satisfaction, visualization, and action—uses a pattern that is known as _____.

2. If you list three reasons why zoos should be preserved, you are using the _____ pattern of organization.

3. If you show the advantages of alternative sentences over prison terms, you are using the _____ pattern of organization.

4. A speaker who describes a problem and then advocates a solution is using the _____ pattern of organization.

5. Many speakers fail to move an audience to take action because they are reluctant to _____.

6. The _____ is the type of speech in which your main goal is to knock down arguments or ideas that you feel are false.

7. In the speech to motivate action, you can urge listeners to start doing certain things or to _____ doing certain things.

8. Handouts that are distributed at the end of a meeting are called _____.

9. In your career, persuasion is often a long-term process requiring weeks, months, or even _____.

10. The process of influencing or changing attitudes, beliefs, values, or behavior is known as _____.

Name _____

True or False If the statement is true, circle T; if false, circle F.

T F 1. The text recommends using deductive reasoning when your audience is skeptical or hostile to your central idea.

T F 2. Inductive reasoning is never used by scientists.

T F 3. Aiming sarcastic remarks at listeners who disagree with you will make them defensive at first, but will eventually increase their respect for your courage and integrity.

T F 4. Deductive reasoning is convincing only if both the major and minor premises are accepted by the audience as true.

T F 5. According to the text, some emotional appeals are inherent in pieces of evidence.

T F 6. Most people are more deeply influenced by one clear, vivid personal example than by an abundance of statistical data.

T F 7. In persuasive speaking, it is unethical for the speaker to stir up both positive and negative emotions.

T F 8. Explaining your expertise on your subject matter is a good way to build credibility with an audience.

T F 9. In a persuasive speech, your credibility is strengthened if you concede that your ideas sometimes do not work.

T F 10. In Maslow's hierarchy of needs, physiological needs must be met before a person can try to satisfy esteem needs.

Name _____

Multiple-Choice Questions Each question has only one correct answer.

____ 1. "Everyone is drinking strawberry lemonade for good health, and so should you." This is an example of which type of logical fallacy? (a) either-or reasoning, (b) bandwagon, (c) red herring, (d) deduction

____ 2. A pediatrician sees five children in her office one winter morning. Because all five have symptoms of influenza, the pediatrician concludes that her community is experiencing an influenza epidemic. The pediatrician has used (a) faulty reasoning, (b) deductive reasoning, (c) emotional reasoning, (d) inductive reasoning

____ 3. In Maslow's hierarchy of needs, the highest level of needs is (a) self-actualization, (b) esteem, (c) love and belonging, (d) physiological

____ 4. A speaker wants to persuade an audience to stop engaging in unhealthy behavior. Which level of fear is most effective in accomplishing this objective? (a) no fear, (b) a small amount of fear, (c) a moderate amount of fear, (d) a high level of fear

____ 5. In a persuasive speech, conceding that your ideas do not work in all cases (a) undermines your credibility, (b) strengthens your credibility

____ 6. "Because Germans are the smartest engineers in the world, you should buy a German-made car." This speaker is guilty of using what kind of fallacy in reasoning? (a) building on an unproven assumption, (b) either-or reasoning, (c) attack on a person, (d) straw man

____ 7. A speaker says, "We must adopt a vegetarian diet, or we will all die of cancer." This speaker is guilty of using which fallacy in reasoning? (a) straw man, (b) either-or reasoning, (c) attack on a person, (d) induction

____ 8. A speaker says, "Jackson says he believes that there is intelligent life on some other planet in the universe, but how can you believe him? He's not an astronomer; in fact, he is not a scientist at all. The only degree he has is a masters in business administration." This speaker is guilty of using which kind of fallacy in reasoning? (a) false cause, (b) either-or reasoning, (c) hasty generalization, (d) attack on a person

____ 9. A speaker says, "People who favor gun control want to turn our society over to the criminals. Therefore, we must ignore these gun-control advocates." This speaker is guilty of using which kind of fallacy in reasoning? (a) straw man, (b) either-or reasoning, (c) false cause, (d) induction

____ 10. A speaker says, "I knew a red-headed kid in third grade who was always getting into fights on the playground. And I know two red heads who are easily angered. I guess you can say that red heads are quick-tempered people." The speaker is guilty of using which kind of fallacy in reasoning? (a) straw man, (b) hasty generalization, (c) attack on a person, (d) either-or reasoning

Name _____

Multiple-Choice Questions Each question has only one correct answer.

____ 1. Which type of logical fallacy diverts listeners from the real issue to an unrelated matter? (a) either-or reasoning, (b) induction, (c) red herring, (d) deduction

____ 2. A speaker says, "I owned a Ford and had nothing but trouble with it. My cousin had a Ford that was a lemon. And my best friend is unhappy with her Ford. I tell you, Ford is a lousy automobile." What fallacy in reasoning is the speaker using? (a) straw man, (b) false cause, (c) hasty generalization, (d) attack on a person

____ 3. A speaker says, "Because the Japanese make the best stereo sound systems in the world, you should consider buying a Japanese-made sound system." This speaker is guilty of using which kind of fallacy in reasoning? (a) building on an unproven assumption, (b) straw man, (c) either-or reasoning, (d) attack on a person

____ 4. A speaker says, "Scientists who perform operations on animals in laboratories are not interested in getting scientific knowledge—they enjoy inflicting suffering on animals. Therefore, we must stop the use of animals in experiments." This speaker is guilty of using which kind of fallacy in reasoning? (a) straw man, (b) either-or reasoning, (c) false cause, (d) induction

____ 5. Which type of logical fallacy asserts an argument that is based on popularity rather than on evidence and reasoning? (a) either-or reasoning, (b) bandwagon, (c) red herring, (d) deduction

____ 6. In Maslow's hierarchy, the human need to help others falls into the _____ category of needs. (a) physiological, (b) safety, (c) esteem, (d) self-actualization

____ 7. According to research, which is the more persuasive type of evidence? (a) a clear, vivid personal example, (b) an abundance of statistical data

____ 8. Reasoning that moves from a generalization to a specific conclusion is (a) deductive reasoning, (b) inductive reasoning

____ 9. A speaker says, "We must change to the metric system or we will fall behind the rest of the world in science and industry." This speaker is guilty of using which kind of fallacy in reasoning? (a) straw man, (b) attack on a person, (c) either-or reasoning, (d) induction

____ 10. A speaker says, "There is no need for me to refute Senator Smith's ideas about regulating professional baseball. Senator Smith is unqualified to speak on baseball because he has never played any sport on the high school, collegiate, or professional level." This speaker is guilty of using which type of fallacy in reasoning? (a) false cause, (b) either-or reasoning, (c) hasty generalization, (d) attack on a person

Name _____

Fill in the missing words or phrases.

1. In reasoning, the chain of logic that goes from specific instances to a generalization is called _____.

2. _____ is the degree to which a speaker is perceived to be believable, trustworthy, and competent.

3. Some speakers try to win an argument by attacking a person rather than the person's ideas. This fallacy in reasoning is known as _____.

4. In a speech, which appeal—high-fear or low-fear—has been found by researchers to be the more effective? _____

5. Emotional appeals should always be combined with _____ appeals.

6. In Maslow's hierarchy of needs, the highest level is called _____.

7. When your audience is skeptical or hostile to your central idea, which form of reasoning should you use—inductive or deductive?

8. The _____ herring fallacy occurs when a speaker tries to divert listeners from the real issue to an irrelevant matter.

9. In reasoning, the chain of logic that carries you from a generalization to a specific instance to a conclusion is called _____.

10. When a speaker states that there are only two alternatives, when in fact there are many, the speaker is using which fallacy in reasoning? _____

Name _____

True or False If the statement is true, circle T; if false, circle F.

T F 1. Humor can sometimes be used in a eulogy.

T F 2. To be successful, an entertaining speech must have at least three jokes.

T F 3. Overstating a speaker's credentials is common and acceptable procedure in speeches of introduction.

T F 4. In a speech of presentation, the name of the recipient must always be given at the beginning of the remarks.

T F 5. A eulogy should be dignified, without exaggerated sentimentality.

T F 6. An entertaining speech should contain no elements of persuasion, information, or inspiration.

T F 7. A rule of thumb for speeches of introduction is to keep them under ten minutes.

T F 8. In a speech of tribute to a great person, it adds to your credibility if you point out some negative features of the person.

T F 9. In a wedding toast, it is acceptable to tease the bride and groom.

T F 10. When you give a speech of introduction, you should ask the speaker ahead of time what kind of introduction the speaker would like.

Name _____

Multiple-Choice Questions Each question has only one correct answer.

____ 1. In a speech of introduction, you should (a) use the speaker's full name, (b) use the speaker's first name only, (c) use the speaker's last name only, (d) use the name the speaker prefers

____ 2. A key objective of the _____ speech is to get the speaker and audience interested in each other. (a) entertaining, (b) inspirational, (c) tribute, (d) acceptance, (e) introduction

____ 3. The speech of introduction should (a) give background information about the speaker, (b) give no background information because that would take away from the speaker's speech

____ 4. Which one of the following is inappropriate for a best man's speech at a wedding celebration? (a) reciting a poem, (b) showing a video, (c) telling a joke about the groom's ex-girlfriend, (d) focusing the entire remarks on the bride and groom

____ 5. A speech of introduction should be kept under _____ minutes. (a) 3, (b) 8, (c) 12, (d) 15

____ 6. A toast offered at a celebration should avoid (a) teasing, (b) wishes for happiness, (c) warm reminiscences, (d) anecdotes about the bride or groom

____ 7. Which kind of liquid can be used for a toast in the United States and Canada, but should be avoided in some other cultures? (a) wine, (b) champagne, (c) water, (d) soda

____ 8. An important dimension of inspirational speaking is (a) sarcasm, (b) delivery, (c) grandiloquence, (d) personal appearance

____ 9. An inspirational speech is often similar to (a) an informative speech, (b) a persuasive speech, (c) an entertaining speech

____ 10. A speech of tribute is defined as a speech that praises (a) only a living person, (b) only a dead person, (c) either a dead or living person

Name _____

Multiple-Choice Questions Each question has only one correct answer.

____ 1. The safest kind of joke is (a) satirical, (b) a play on words, (c) self-deprecating, (d) ironic

____ 2. According to the text, a rule of thumb is that a speech of introduction should be (a) under three minutes, (b) at least five minutes, (c) one-tenth of the estimated length of the speech that is about to be delivered, (d) no more than ten minutes

____ 3. Which kind of speech would you be most likely to deliver to an evening banquet? (a) entertaining, (b) acceptance, (c) tribute

____ 4. A speaker says, "It is easy to quit smoking. I have done so a thousand times." This is an example of what the text calls _____ humor. (a) witty (b) low-key, (c) perceptive, (d) indirect

____ 5. A spine-tingling tale of adventure would be most appropriate for which kind of speech? (a) entertaining speech (b) speech of introduction, (c) speech of acceptance, (d) inspirational speech

____ 6. Before you give a speech of introduction, you should coordinate your remarks with the speaker's. The primary reason for doing so is to avoid (a) divulging embarrassing personal details, (b) inadvertently antagonizing the audience, (c) pretending you know more about the subject than the speaker, (d) stealing the speaker's material

____ 7. To introduce a speech filled with humor, what kind of speech of introduction would be appropriate? (a) a humorous speech of introduction to set a light tone, (b) a serious speech of introduction to avoid upstaging the speaker

____ 8. A speech of tribute should (a) focus on the significance of a person's life and deeds, (b) give a comprehensive history of the person's biographical events, (c) focus on the person's career achievements, (d) focus on the person's family and friends

____ 9. A speech designed to formally bestow an award of honor is known as the speech of (a) acceptance, (b) honor, (c) presentation, (d) entertainment

____ 10. A coach giving a pep talk to her team is delivering which type of speech? (a) entertaining, (b) introduction, (c) tribute, (d) inspirational, (e) acceptance

Name _____

Fill in the missing words or phrases.

1. A eulogy should focus on the _____ of a person's life and deeds.

2. Can humor sometimes be appropriate in a eulogy?
   _____

3. If you are giving a speech of introduction, you should not discuss the speaker's _____ unless the speaker gives prior permission.

4. A rule of thumb for speeches of introduction is to keep them under _____ minutes.

5. The goal of the inspirational speech is to stir _____ emotions.

6. Saying a few words while giving an award to a dedicated worker is an example of the speech of _____.

7. A eulogy is an example of the speech of
   _____.

8. If listeners are spread apart in a large room, try to
   _____.

9. Are jokes appropriate or inappropriate for an entertaining speech?
   _____

10. Who should be consulted before a speech of introduction is delivered?
    _____

Name _____

True or False If the statement is true, circle T; if false, circle F.

T F 1. A team presentation is like a speech given by an individual except that the content is divided among the team members.

T F 2. For panel moderators, open-ended questions are the best way to stimulate discussion.

T F 3. A group often has an IQ (or intelligence level) that is higher than the IQ of any individual in the group.

T F 4. A participant should not express views in a meeting if they are clearly contrary to the views of the majority.

T F 5. Meetings should not begin until all participants have arrived.

T F 6. At the beginning of a meeting, the leader should review the purpose of the meeting and the scope of the group's power.

T F 7. In a meeting, the leader should periodically summarize the group's work.

T F 8. Members of a small group can catch and correct errors that might slip past an individual.

T F 9. A hidden agenda is an effective technique for small group meetings.

T F 10. Minutes of the preceding meeting should be reviewed at every meeting.

Name _____

Multiple-Choice Questions Each question has only one correct answer.

____ 1. A speech that is divided into parts, with each part delivered by a different person, is known as a (a) team presentation, (b) symposium, (c) panel, (d) split speech

____ 2. A group spends all its time on minor issues and never gets around to the major issues. The group could solve the problem by (a) establishing and following an agenda, (b) choosing a forceful leader, (c) allotting extra time for each meeting

____ 3. If you are part of a team and one of your team members is speaking to an audience, what signal would you send the audience if you review your notes? (a) "I want to be well-prepared when I get my turn to speak." (b) "What's being said is not very important."

____ 4. What is the first step in the reflective-thinking method? (a) Establish criteria for evaluating solutions. (b) Decide how to implement the solution. (c) Define the problem. (d) Analyze the problem. (e) Choose the best solution. (f) Decide how to test the solution. (g) Suggest possible solutions.

____ 5. A series of brief speeches on a common topic is known as (a) a panel, (b) a symposium

____ 6. Alterations to an agenda should be made by participants (a) one day before the meeting, (b) one hour before the meeting, (c) at the start of the meeting, (d) at the end of the meeting

____ 7. A written record of the group's activities during a meeting is called the (a) agenda, (b) minutes, (c) record, (d) dossier

____ 8. In a meeting, the group leader should forbid (a) spontaneous ideas from participants, (b) attacks on people or ideas, (c) disagreements between members of the group, (d) efforts to add new items to the agenda

____ 9. Brainstorming by a small group resulted in which successful product? (a) Image-capture chips in digital cameras, (b) Nike Air Max shoes, (c) Hershey's Candy Kisses, (d) YouTube video clips

____ 10. Writer H.L. Mencken is quoted as saying that for every human problem, "there is always an easy solution—neat, plausible, and _____." (a) ingenious, (b) workable, (c) hopeless, (d) wrong

Name _____

Multiple-Choice Questions Each question has only one correct answer.

_____ 1. The secret of a successful team, says Dean Kamen, "is not to assemble the largest team possible, but rather to assemble a team that can _____." (a) reach goals quickly, (b) operate without disagreements, (c) work well together, (d) follow the directives of the leader

_____ 2. A document that summarizes what transpired at a meeting is known as the (a) minutes, (b) agenda, (c) synopsis, (d) draft

_____ 3. When you are a participant in a panel discussion, you should (a) stand firm on your position, (b) be willing to alter your position.

_____ 4. Jack Smith works hard on a committee preparing a plan for action. At the sixth meeting, he finds out that the committee can only advise; it does not have the power to take action. Jack is distraught because he feels that much of his work has been in vain. Whose fault is it that Jack has labored under a misconception? (a) Jack himself, for not inquiring about the scope of the group's power, (b) the group leader, for not making clear the scope of the group's power

_____ 5. Ideally, participants in a meeting should receive the agenda (a) well before the meeting, (b) at the start of the meeting, (c) in the middle of the meeting, (d) at the end of the meeting

_____ 6. In a team presentation, the text says, the most important part is (a) the introduction, (b) the visual aids, (c) the conclusion, (d) the question-and-answer period

_____ 7. In an agenda, items should be rank ordered (a) from least important to most important, (b) from most important to least important

_____ 8. Meetings are sometimes sabotaged by participants who have (a) a hidden agenda, (b) a private vendetta, (c) a legitimate grievance, (d) an unwillingness to work closely with others

_____ 9. In the famous Coca-Cola fiasco involving "New Coke" in the 1980s, the soft drink maker erred by choosing a solution that was _____ but wrong. (a) clever, (b) lucrative, (c) easy, (d) radical

_____ 10. Meetings should always begin (a) at the designated time, (b) five minutes after the designated time, (c) 10 minutes after the designated time, (d) only when all the participants have arrived

Name _____

Fill in the missing words or phrases.

1. What do you call a speech that is divided into sections, with each section delivered by a different person?

2. In a panel discussion, should panelists use notes or a written statement? _____

3. The moderator of a panel should ask what type of questions? _____

4. A list of items that need to be covered in a meeting is called the _____.

5. The _____ method is the problem-solving technique derived from the writings of the American philosopher John Dewey.

6. Unannounced private goals that conflict with the group's goals are called _____.

7. In group meetings, one of the best ways to generate ideas is _____, a technique wherein participants rapidly throw out ideas and the group leader writes them on a chalkboard.

8. At the designated time for a meeting, if some group members have not arrived yet, what should the chairperson do? _____

9. A record of what was discussed and accomplished during a meeting is known as the _____.

10. A _____ is a series of brief speeches on a common topic.

KEY

Name _____

True or False If the statement is true, circle T; if false, circle F.

					page
T	T F	1.	If speakers send nonverbal signals that contradict their verbal message, listeners will typically accept the nonverbal behavior as the true message.		9
F	T F	2.	The speaker's message consists entirely of what the speaker says with words.		9
F	T F	3.	A speaker should work harder to communicate to an audience of 500 people than to an audience of five people.		14
T	T F	4.	When an applicant seeks a job, employers place heavier emphasis on oral communication skills (speaking and listening) than on the person's technical knowledge.		6
F	T F	5.	Abstract words usually mean the same thing to all listeners.		9
T	T F	6.	Television is an example of a channel of communication.		9
T	T F	7.	Time of day plays a part in how receptive an audience is to a speech.		11
T	T F	8.	Everything that a speaker expresses in a message is in the form of symbols.		9
F	T F	9.	If, while giving a speech, you observe that some of your listeners seem confused by your last remark, you should wait until the end of the speech to explain yourself better.		10
T	T F	10.	A speaker can cause interference in the speech communication process.		10

 Name _____

page

Multiple-Choice Questions Each question has only one correct answer.

d ___ 1. When hiring, employers are MOST likely to be influenced by an applicant's (a) grade point average, (b) letters of reference, (c) technical knowledge of the field, (d) oral communication skills (speaking and listening), (e) written communication skills (reading and writing)　**6**

c ___ 2. Radio and television are examples of (a) feedback, (b) interference, (c) channels, (d) messages　**9**

a ___ 3. A speaker who blames doctors for the rise in lung cancer deaths is engaging in (a) scapegoating, (b) stereotyping, (c) distortion, (d) harassment　**13**

c ___ 4. Who bears the responsibility for communication actually taking place? (a) the speaker, (b) the listener, (c) both the speaker and the listener, (d) neither the speaker nor the listener　**8**

d ___ 5. An oversimplified mental picture is known as a (a) generalization, (b) cliché, (c) scapegoat, (d) stereotype　**13**

a ___ 6. Bizarre clothing worn by the speaker is an example of (a) interference, (b) message, (c) feedback, (d) channel　**10**

c ___ 7. Which of the following is bad advice for a speaker? (a) Try to meet the needs of all listeners, (b) Use visual aids when speaking to hearing-impaired listeners, (c) Avoid politics, sports, and business with a female audience, (d) Explain American slang used when addressing international students　**13**

b ___ 8. "Information overload" is caused by a speaker who (a) deceives the audience with erroneous information, (b) covers too much material, (c) relates boring stories, (d) provides no proof for arguments　**18**

a ___ 9. Which method of public speaking involves looking at the audience most of the time, while occasionally glancing at brief notes? (a) extemporaneous, (b) impromptu, (c) memorization, (d) manuscript　**16**

b ___ 10. The part of a speech that links one section to another is known as a (a) connection, (b) transition, (c) chain, (d) cementer　**18**

KEY

page

Multiple-Choice Questions Each question has only one correct answer.

c ___ 1. If there are discrepancies between the verbal and nonverbal components of a speech, listeners will probably (a) reject both components as untrue, (b) accept the verbal as the true message, (c) accept the nonverbal as the true message — **9**

b ___ 2. Which of the following can cause a speech to be dull? (a) unattractive clothes, (b) unenthusiastic delivery, (c) disrespect for the audience, (d) obscene language — **18**

b ___ 3. A speech, says management consultant David W. Richardson, takes place in (a) the context of speaker-listener communication, (b) the minds of the listeners, (c) the spoken words of the speaker, (d) the memories of all participants — **8**

a ___ 4. When you are a speaker, which of the following is the key question to constantly ask yourself? (a) Am I getting through to my listeners? (b) Am I performing well? (c) Am I giving out good information? (d) Am I making a good impression? — **7**

d ___ 5. Which of the following does the text list as a component of the speech communication process? (a) originator, (b) facilitator, (c) argument, (d) situation — **11**

b ___ 6. In the speech communication process, the message is sent in the form of (a) inferences, (b) symbols, (c) codes, (d) approximations — **9**

b ___ 7. The part of a speech that you want your listeners to remember if they forget everything else is known as the (a) specific purpose, (b) central idea, (c) attention-getter, (d) conclusion — **17**

a ___ 8. A loudspeaker is an example of a (a) channel, (b) transmitter, (c) message, (d) situation — **10**

c ___ 9. The extemporaneous method of speaking involves (a) memorizing a speech, (b) reading a script, (c) using notes, (d) ad-libbing — **16**

d ___ 10. In the speech communication process, anything that blocks or hinders the communication of a message is called (a) blockage, (b) obstruction, (c) confusion, (d) interference — **10**

Name _____

Fill in the missing words or phrases.   page

situation   1. The _____ is the context—the time   **11**
                        and place—in which communication occurs.

stereotypes   2. Simplistic images that humans carry in their minds about   **13**
                        groups of people are called _____.

channel   3. The _____ is the medium used to   **9**
                        communicate a message to an audience.

symbols   4. Words are not things; they are   **9**
                        _____ of things.

interference   5. Anything that blocks or hinders the communication of a   **10**
                        message is known as _____.

transitions   6. Items in a speech designed to carry listeners smoothly from   **18**
                        one section to another are called
                        _____.

scapegoats   7. _____ are people who innocently   **13**
                        bear the blame of others.

too much   8. According to a survey, one of the biggest mistakes made by   **18**
                        speakers is trying to cover _____
                        in one speech.

feedback   9. The response that listeners give the speaker is known as   **10**
                        _____.

Speaker-   10. _____ interference occurs when   **10**
generated   the speaker uses words that are unfamiliar to the audience.

KEY

Name _____

True or False If the statement is true, circle T; if false, circle F.

Page

F   T F   1. A shy person's shyness will block that person from giving a good, dynamic speech.   **28**

F   T F   2. If your hands tremble or you show some other sign of nervousness, you should apologize to your audience or try to make a joke out of your problem.   **34**

T   T F   3. Gesturing or walking around a bit during your speech helps siphon off excessive nervous energy.   **37**

F   T F   4. In preparation for a speech, a person should read over his or her notes rather than actually rehearse the speech.   **27**

F   T F   5. A good speaker tries very hard to eliminate all fear and nervousness.   **25**

F   T F   6. In filling your mind with images before a speech, you should picture yourself speaking with confidence, poise, and completely without nervousness.   **28**

F   T F   7. If you see people whispering during your speech, you should assume that they are exchanging negative comments about you or your speech.   **35**

T   T F   8. Most of your nervous symptoms are not seen by your audience.   **33**

T   T F   9. Memorizing a speech is a bad technique for handling nervousness.   **27**

F   T F   10. If you feel yourself approaching panic (your heart is beating furiously and so on), you should leave the room or ask to be excused from speaking.   **31**

KEY

Name _____

Multiple-Choice Questions Each question has only one correct answer.

page

b ___ 1. The term used by the text for visualizing successful actions is (a) creative imagination, (b) positive imagery, (c) success orientation, (d) power visualization

28

a ___ 2. Which of the following does the text recommend as a way to release tension? (a) inhale and exhale slowly, (b) mentally prepare for a panic attack, (c) make a joke about your nervousness, (d) arrive precisely one minute before your speech

30

d ___ 3. According to the text, "locking" your eyes with a listener's eyes (a) intensifies your anxiety, (b) makes the listener uneasy, (c) demonstrates that you have no fear, (d) helps to calm you

36

a ___ 4. Public speakers should regard their task as (a) communication only, (b) performance only, (c) both communication and performance, (d) communication, performance, and duty

31

a ___ 5. When practicing your speech, devote extra time to (a) the introduction, (b) the body, (c) the conclusion, (d) the question-and-answer period

29

b ___ 6. Acting as if you are poised and confident (a) is a pretense that the audience will immediately see through, (b) sometimes leads to actually becoming poised and confident, (c) will make you even more nervous than before

36

d ___ 7. If, during a speech, your mind goes blank and you forget where you are in the speech, the text recommends that you (a) apologize and sit down, (b) start over from the beginning, (c) make a joke about your predicament, (d) ask the audience, "Where was I?"

37

d ___ 8. According to the text, shyness (a) is caused by a childhood trauma, (b) is a barrier to effective public speaking, (c) can be eliminated by psychotherapy, (d) is a characteristic of some successful people in show business

28

b ___ 9. According to the text, a sudden bolt of panic can hit speakers who (a) overprepare, (b) initially feel no fear, (c) dislike the audience, (d) have poor self-esteem

26

c ___ 10. Which one of the following fears usually disappears as speakers gain experience? (a) fear of being stared at, (b) fear of failure, (c) fear of the unknown, (d) fear of rejection

25

KEY

Name _____

Multiple-Choice Questions Each question has only one correct answer.   **page**

d ____ 1.   Striving for perfection (a) helps you to achieve almost total perfection, (b) is a necessary mental ploy to achieve success, (c) is the best way to develop a positive outlook, (d) places unnecessary pressure on yourself   **37**

b ____ 2.   Which of the following was mentioned in the text as a way to control nervousness? (a) arrive just a few moments before your speech, (b) act as if you are already poised and confident, (c) encourage listeners to ask questions throughout the speech, (d) look at a fixed point on the wall in the back of the room   **36**

a ____ 3.   The greatest amount of anxiety in a speech is usually experienced in the (a) introduction, (b) body, (c) conclusion, (d) question-and-answer period   **29**

c ____ 4.   To avoid memory lapses during a speech, (a) memorize basic facts before the speech, (b) prepare a word-for-word script, (c) prepare a card with key information on it, (d) learn to eliminate nervousness   **35**

d ____ 5.   A public speaker who tries to eliminate all fear is pursuing a goal that is (a) desirable, (b) impossible, (c) unimportant, (d) undesirable   **25**

b ____ 6.   To gain rapport with their audiences, some comedians (a) pretend to have stage fright, (b) deliberately make mistakes, (c) go out into the audience to shake hands, (d) playfully "insult" some listeners   **38**

c ____ 7.   Switching your thoughts from "I'm going to fail" to "I will give the audience some good information" is a technique known as changing your (a) opinion, (b) perception, (c) self-talk, (d) outlook   **29**

b ____ 8.   The text says that worrying about yourself and your image in a speech is a kind of (a) motivation, (b) vanity, (c) self-defense, (d) awareness   **29**

a ____ 9.   The term used by the text to describe "a zesty, enthusiastic, lively feeling with a slight edge to it" is (a) positive nervousness, (b) focused enthusiasm, (c) managed anxiety, (d) heightened sensitivity   **26**

b ____ 10.   If you flub a sentence or mangle an idea during a speech, you should (a) stop and apologize for your blunder, (b) pause and correct yourself without apologizing, (c) apologize and sit down immediately, (d) make a joke about hating speechmaking   **34**

Name _____

Fill in the missing words or phrases.

page

cucumber   1.   The text cites an old saying, "Speakers who say they are as cool as a cucumber usually give speeches about as interesting as a _____."   **26**

imagery   2.   Positive _____ is a technique used by golfers as well as public speakers to visualize success.   **28**

the introduction   3.   Of all parts of the speech, you should devote extra practice time to _____.   **29**

the unknown   4.   Of all the fears engendered by public speaking, the fear of _____ usually disappears as a speaker gets more experience.   **25**

preparation   5.   According to the text, the very best precaution against excessive stage fright is _____.   **27**

confident   6.   Pretending to be confident can sometimes cause you to become a _____ speaker.   **36**

poor   7.   Making a joking, lighthearted comment about your nervousness is a _____ technique for a speaker to use.   **34**

unaware   8.   Concerning most speakers, the audience is _____ of their physical symptoms such as pounding heart and trembling knees.   **33**

mistakes   9.   Some comedians deliberately plan _____ as a technique for gaining rapport with an audience.   **38**

performance   10.   Speakers can control nervousness and enhance their speeches if they think of speechmaking as communication, rather than as _____.   **31**

KEY

Name _____

True or False If the statement is true, circle T; if false, circle F.   **page**

F   T F   1.   In taking notes, a listener should try to record the speaker's exact words.   **47**

T   T F   2.   It is more important for a listener to remember the main points of a speech than to remember support materials.   **44**

F   T F   3.   If you whisper, it is okay to talk on a cell phone while attending a presentation.   **50**

F   T F   4.   If good listening skills are used, listening to a complex lecture should require no more mental effort than listening to a comedian tell jokes.   **44**

T   T F   5.   In some countries, whistling by listeners is a sign of approval.   **48**

T   T F   6.   In Japan, listeners who close their eyes during a speech might be showing respect.   **48**

F   T F   7.   The Golden Rule of Listening is "Listen wisely and well."   **49**

F   T F   8.   When a speaker makes a point with which you disagree, immediately prepare a rebuttal in your mind to use later in the question-and-answer period.   **49**

F   T F   9.   In giving a speaker an evaluation of a speech, you should always note any indications of the speaker's nervousness.   **54**

F   T F   10. Listening occurs when your ears pick up sound waves being transmitted by a speaker.   **43**

KEY

Name _____

Multiple-Choice Questions Each question has only one correct answer.

			page
d	___	1.	**47**

d ___ 1. Ned is trying hard to pull up his grades in a class. When the instructor lectures, he furiously writes down virtually every word that is said. Which listening mistake is Ned making? (a) not being prepared, (b) mentally arguing with the speaker, (c) making prejudgments, (d) failing to take notes correctly   **47**

d ___ 2. In what country do listeners sometimes close their eyes to show respect for the speaker's ideas? (a) Nigeria, (b) Brazil, (c) India, (d) Japan   **48**

a ___ 3. Reading background material on a speaker's topic is something the listener should do (a) before the speech, (b) during the speech, (c) immediately after the speech, (d) several days after the speech   **44**

b ___ 4. Which of these comments would be helpful for an evaluator to make to a speaker? (a) "You looked as if you were scared of the audience," (b) "Try to speak in a conversational manner"   **54**

d ___ 5. In most speeches, listeners can process information at about _____ words per minute, whereas most speakers talk at 125 to 150 words a minute. (a) 150, (b) 200, (c) 300, (d) 500   **48**

c ___ 6. Taking notes on a laptop computer during a speech is discouraged unless (a) the laptop has a noiseless keyboard, (b) the monitor is raised only when notes are being taken, (c) the listener gets permission from the speaker beforehand, (d) everyone else in the room is using a laptop   **50**

a ___ 7. Two days after listening to a 10-minute oral presentation, the average person comprehends and retains _____% of the information. (a) 25, (b) 50, (c) 75, (d) 90   **43**

c ___ 8. Two groups of students at Cornell University listened to the same lecture, with one group allowed to use laptops to browse the Internet and the other group required to keep laptops closed. When tested, the group with Internet access remembered (a) significantly more information than the other group, (b) about the same amount of information, (c) significantly less information   **52**

c ___ 9. Which one of the following options does the text consider acceptable during a presentation? (a) using a laptop computer for e-mail, (b) talking on a cell phone in a whisper, (c) using the "vibrate" option of a cell phone or pager, (d) sitting in the back of the room to receive phone calls   **50**

a ___ 10. Taking notes while engaged in a one-on-one discussion with your supervisor (a) is a compliment to the superior, (b) is insulting because of lack of eye contact, (c) makes you appear as if you have a poor memory   **47**

KEY

Name _____

Multiple-Choice Questions Each question has only one correct answer.

d ____ 1. The note-taking system suggested by the text has three columns with headings for main ideas, support material, and (a) statistics, (b) examples, (c) proof, (d) response
46

b ____ 2. A headache causes which type of distraction? (a) cryptic, (b) physical, (c) alternative, (d) auditory
47

b ____ 3. Listeners who multitask (perform a variety of activities) usually retain (a) as much information as listeners who focus on just the speaker, (b) less information than listeners who focus on just the speaker
52

a ____ 4. The text quotes Keith Davis as saying, "Hearing is with the ears; listening is with the _____." (a) mind, (b) heart
43

a ____ 5. In giving a speaker an evaluation of a speech, which should be presented first? (a) positive comments, (b) negative comments, (c) neutral comments that are neither negative nor positive
54

c ____ 6. Ten minutes after listening to a 10-minute oral presentation, the average person understands and retains ____% of the information. (a) 10, (b) 25, (c) 50, (d) 75
43

b ____ 7. A speaker who asks listeners to turn off electronic devices is (a) unwisely intruding on the rights of listeners, (b) wisely improving the odds that the audience will listen to the message
50

c ____ 8. If you have the habit of engaging in fake listening, one of the best ways to force yourself to pay attention is to (a) look directly at the speaker, (b) mentally repeat the speaker's words, (c) take notes, (d) practice self-discipline skills
48

d ____ 9. To confront listeners who are immersed in their electronic devices, speakers are advised by the text to try using _____ to capture audience interest. (a) a promise of a shortened presentation, (b) a threat of revenge, (c) a quick blast of loud music, (d) an attention-getting introduction
51

a ____ 10. Hermina listened politely to a speech on zoos, but she became angry when the speaker argued for abolition of all zoos. For the rest of the speech, she tuned him out and planned the counter-arguments that she could throw at him during the question-and-answer period. What listening mistake is she making? (a) failing to control emotions, (b) giving in to distractions, (c) failing to prepare, (d) rationalizing
49

KEY

Name _____

page

Fill in the missing words or phrases.

Listen unto others as you would have others listen unto you.

1. State the Golden Rule of Listening:
   _____
   _____
   _____
   _____
   _____

50

support

2. While listening to a speech, you should focus on main ideas and _____ materials.

45

failing to control emotions

3. When a speaker starts a speech on a controversial issue, some listeners have an emotional reaction that cuts off listening. In their minds, they prepare a counterattack to be launched during the question-and-answer period. Which listening mistake are they committing?
   _____

49

fake

4. If you engage in _____ listening, you risk embarrassment and ridicule.

48

physically

5. Before listening to a difficult lecture, you should prepare yourself intellectually and
   _____.

44

take notes

6. Refrain from using a laptop computer during a speech unless you need to _____.

51

daydreaming

7. Many listeners take notes during a speech and throw them away at the end. They didn't waste their time because note taking kept them from _____.

45

auditory

8. The major types of distractions during a speech are mental, physical, visual, and _____.

47

faster

9. While listening to a speech, our brain works _____ than the speed needed for listening.

48

faster heart action OR quicker circulation of blood OR rise in body temperature

10. Because listening is hard work, a person listening to complex material might have at least three bodily reactions. Name one of them: _____

44

Chapter 4 (Form A)   **KEY**   Name _____

Page

True or False If the statement is true, circle T; if false, circle F.

F   T F   1.   It is acceptable to tell a joke about a certain ethnic group if no one from that ethnic group is present in the audience.   **70**

T   T F   2.   The most understood form of nonverbal communication in the world is the smile.   **68**

F   T F   3.   In a large auditorium, your listeners are more likely to be responsive if they are sparsely seated throughout the hall than if they are tightly packed together.   **76**

T   T F   4.   "Taboo" is the term used to describe an act, a word, or an object that is forbidden on grounds of morality or taste.   **67**

T   T F   5.   If you cannot persuade skeptical listeners to adopt your views, you should at least try to move them closer to your position.   **73**

T   T F   6.   If you have handouts, it is a good idea to give one to a blind listener.   **71**

T   T F   7.   If your audience knows little or nothing about your topic, you should limit the number of new ideas you discuss.   **72**

F   T F   8.   Elderly members of an audience will feel stigmatized and offended if a speaker explains the meaning of terms that are popular among young people and unlikely to be known to older listeners.   **65**

T   T F   9.   Listeners might get upset if your speech topic varies from what they had anticipated.   **76**

F   T F   10.   For blind or visually impaired listeners with a seeing-eye dog, it is a good idea for a speaker to be friendly with the dog before the speech by talking to it in a soft voice.   **71**

KEY

Name _____

Multiple-Choice Questions Each question has only one correct answer.

Page

d   ____   1. Which question is the major concern of the audience-centered speaker? (a) "Am I doing a good job?" (b) "Does everyone like me?" (c) "How do I look?" (d) "Am I getting my message across to the listeners?"

    60

d   ____   2. According to advice given in the text, a speaker who is addressing hearing-impaired listeners doesn't need to (a) emphasize consonants, (b) emphasize final syllables, (c) speak loudly, (d) exaggerate words

    71

d   ____   3. Some audience members know a lot about your speech topic; others know nothing. Your best approach is to (a) keep audience attention through a highly enthusiastic delivery, (b) ignore those audience members who are extremely knowledgeable about the topic, (c) ignore those audience members who know virtually nothing about the topic, (d) begin simply and add complexity throughout the presentation

    72

c   ____   4. In preparing for a speech next week, you discover that one member of the audience has a visual disability. To find out how to meet her needs, whom should you consult? (a) her closest relative, (b) the person who invited you to speak, (c) the woman herself, (d) her health-care provider

    70

c   ____   5. Horace noticed some listeners looking confused when he used a certain term in his speech, so he backed up and explained the term in greater detail. Horace exhibited (a) catering to an audience, (b) using demographic analysis, (c) adaptation during a speech, (d) audience analysis

    61

b   ____   6. The belief that one's own cultural group is superior to other groups is known as (a) superiority complex, (b) ethnocentrism, (c) power tripping, (d) judgmentalism

    69

a   ____   7. In working with an interpreter, which of the following is NOT recommended by the text? (a) Talk directly to a sign-language interpreter instead of to the audience, (b) Provide the interpreter with your outline in advance, (c) Ask the interpreter to rehearse with you, (d) Introduce the interpreter to the audience

    67

c   ____   8. In the business world, the term for adapting to consumers' special needs is (a) matching, (b) accommodating, (c) customizing, (d) retrofitting

    61

b   ____   9. A speaker who interviews a few members of an audience before a speech is (a) wasting time because the number of listeners is unrepresentative, (b) gaining a good sample of what the audience is like

    62

c   ____   10. If listeners are already favorable toward your ideas, your task is to (a) entertain them with colorful stories, (b) heap scorn on those who don't agree with you, (c) reinforce your listeners' positive views, (d) praise the listeners for their insight

    73

KEY

Name _____

Multiple-Choice Questions Each question has only one correct answer.

page

a ___ 1. For listeners who are deaf or hearing-impaired, the text recommends which of the following? (a) slow your rate of speech slightly, (b) exaggerate your words, (c) look at them constantly — **71**

c ___ 2. If a blind listener brings a guide dog into the room where a speech will be delivered, what should the speaker do? (a) Greet the listener and speak to the dog in a soft voice to befriend it, (b) Assist the listener and the dog in finding a place in the rear of the room, (c) Do nothing unless the listener needs assistance, (d) Ask the listener to station the dog outside the room so it doesn't frighten or disturb listeners — **71**

c ___ 3. In analyzing an audience, which one of the following variables should NOT be considered? (a) age, (b) educational background, (c) personal appearance, (d) gender — **65-70**

d ___ 4. The textbook notes that many _____ persons prefer to think of their condition as a cultural difference rather than a disability. (a) learning-disabled, (b) mobility-impaired (wheelchair), (c) blind or visually impaired, (d) deaf or hearing impaired — **71**

c ___ 5. For a presentation, which approach do most international audiences prefer? (a) humorous, (b) emotional, (c) serious, (d) informal — **68**

a ___ 6. What is the most understood and useful form of nonverbal communication in dealing with people from all parts of the world? (a) a smile, (b) a handshake, (c) eye contact, (d) a soft voice — **68**

c ___ 7. Tailoring your speech to fit audience needs and interests is described in the text as (a) form-fitting, (b) shaping, (c) customizing, (d) altering — **61**

a ___ 8. A taboo is (a) a prohibition, (b) an insult, (c) a mystery, (d) a mistake — **67**

b ___ 9. An open-ended question on a questionnaire involves (a) filling in blanks, (b) writing out a sentence or paragraph, (c) answering yes or no, (d) ranking items from first to last — **64**

c ___ 10. The text recommends that an invitation to company employees should be worded as: a) "You and your husband or wife are invited to the company picnic." (b) "You and your spouse are invited to the company picnic." (c) "You and your guest are invited to the company picnic." — **65**

KEY

Name _____

Page

Fill in the missing words or phrases.

ask the disabled listeners 1. How can speakers know what accommodations to make to meet the special needs of listeners with disabilities? _____ **70**

analyze 2. To be an audience-centered speaker, your first step in preparing a speech is to _____ your listeners. **61**

adapt 3. Your second step is to _____ your speech to the needs and interests of the audience. **61**

taboo 4. A cultural prohibition is called a _____. **67**

brief 5. President Franklin D. Roosevelt's formula for speechmaking: "Be sincere. Be _____. Be seated." **76**

attitudes 6. The emotional baggage—the favorable or unfavorable predispositions—that a listener brings to a speech is called _____. **73**

smiles 7. The text quotes a Mexican-American proverb, "Everybody in the world _____ in the same language." **68**

ethnocentrism 8. The belief that one's own cultural group is superior to other groups is known as _____. **69**

nonverbal 9. Eye contact, facial expressions, and other types of _____ communication vary from country to country. **68**

time 10. A speaker who is asked to speak for 20 minutes but talks for 45 minutes has failed to respect _____ limits. **75**

Name _____

True or False If the statement is true, circle T; if false, circle F.   **page**

T   T F   1.   A good way to find speech topics is to explore the Internet.   **86**

F   T F   2.   The central idea of a speech should begin with an infinitive.   **89**

F   T F   3.   Brainstorming means doing thorough research in the library.   **84**

F   T F   4.   The key concept that you want your listeners to remember if they   **92**
                     forget everything else is called the specific purpose statement.

T   T F   5.   The three most popular types of speeches are informative,   **88**
                     persuasive, and entertaining.

F   T F   6.   Hidden objectives in a speech are always undesirable.   **91**

T   T F   7.   Jokes are not necessary in an entertaining speech.   **89**

F   T F   8.   In the informative speech, your overriding concern is to win the   **88**
                     listeners to your way of thinking.

T   T F   9.   The specific purpose statement should be limited to one major idea.   **90**

F   T F   10. "I will discuss robots as surgeons" is an effective example of a   **89**
                     central idea.

KEY

Name _____

Multiple-Choice Questions Each question has only one correct answer.   **page**

c ___ 1. The most important task in a speech is to communicate the (a) general   **92**
purpose, (b) specific purpose, (c) central idea, (d) topic

a ___ 2. What is the maximum number of major ideas that can be included in a   **90**
specific purpose statement? (a) one, (b) two, (c) three, (d) four

d ___ 3. The textbook says that a central idea should be phrased as (a) an opinion,   **94**
(b) an announcement, (c) an eternal truth, (d) an assertion

c ___ 4. "A parent who reneges on child-support payments should be forced to pay   **92**
or be sent to prison." This is an example of (a) a general purpose, (b) a
specific purpose, (c) a central idea, (d) a topic

b ___ 5. Hidden objectives in a speech (a) are always undesirable, (b) sometimes   **91**
sabotage a speaker's primary goal, (c) are a necessary component of all
speeches, (d) are always detected by intelligent listeners

b ___ 6. "To explain how the pyramids in Egypt were constructed." According to the   **90**
text, this item is (a) correctly written, (b) incorrectly written

d ___ 7. Ed's objective for his speech is to get listeners to stop a certain behavior.   **88**
What is his general purpose? (a) to inspire, (b) to entertain, (c) to inform,
(d) to persuade

a ___ 8. A verb form beginning with "to" is called (a) an infinitive, (b) a preposition,   **89-90**
(c) a gerund, (d) a participle

c ___ 9. Which one of the following is NOT listed by the text as part of overall   **95**
speech design? (a) introduction, (b) transition, (c) question-and-answer
period, (d) body

a ___ 10. "Parrots as pets" is an example of (a) a topic, (b) a general purpose, (c) a   **83**
specific purpose, (d) a central idea

| KEY | Name _____ |

Multiple-Choice Questions Each question has only one correct answer. **page**

c ___ 1. According to the text, we should eliminate hidden purposes that (a) reveal our central idea, (b) divulge our personal secrets, (c) sabotage our true goal, (d) embarrass our listeners **91**

c ___ 2. Which of the following should give the essence of your speech? (a) introduction, (b) conclusion, (c) central idea, (d) specific purpose **92**

a ___ 3. "To entertain" is an example of a (a) general purpose, (b) specific purpose, (c) central idea, (d) target **88**

b ___ 4. Which one of the following is a synonym for central idea? (a) specific purpose, (b) thesis sentence, (c) conclusion, (d) agenda **92**

a ___ 5. "Food-borne illnesses" is an example of (a) a topic, (b) a general purpose, (c) a specific purpose, (d) a central idea **83**

b ___ 6. The three most popular types of speeches are informative, entertaining, and _____. (a) inspirational, (b) persuasive, (c) motivational, (d) introductory **88**

b ___ 7. "To explain to my listeners the chemical composition of vegetable oils." According to the text, this item is (a) appropriate for a classroom speech, (b) too technical for a classroom speech **91**

b ___ 8. "How to Make a Home Burglar-Proof" is an example of which kind of speech? (a) persuasive, (b) informative, (c) inspirational, (d) entertaining **88**

c ___ 9. A verb form beginning with "to" is called (a) a gerund, (b) a preposition, (c) an infinitive, (d) a participle **89**

d ___ 10. In brainstorming, you should (a) critically examine each idea as it springs forth, (b) deliberately avoid writing down words and phrases, (c) carefully plan the path that your mind will follow, (d) produce a flurry of ideas without any initial criticism **84**

KEY

Name _____

Fill in the missing words or phrases.   **page**

an infinitive   1.   A verb form that begins with "to" is called   **89**
_____.

behavior   2.   The goal of a persuasive speech is to change listeners' minds   **88**
and/or their _____.

central idea   3.   The basic message of the entire speech is called the   **92**
_____.

a reference to   4.   "To explain how Egyptian pyramids were constructed" is a   **90**
the audience   defective purpose statement because it lacks
_____.

brainstorming   5.   _____ is a technique for generating   **84**
ideas by writing down whatever comes to your mind without
censoring or criticizing.

one   6.   A specific purpose statement should be limited to how many major   **90**
ideas? _____

persuade   7.   The three most popular general purposes for speeches are to   **88**
inform, to entertain, and to _____.

only one   8.   How many central ideas should each speech have?   **94**
_____

assertion   9.   A central idea should make a/an _____   **94**
rather than an announcement or a statement of fact.

technical   10.   A speech on the chemical composition of vegetable oils would be   **91**
too _____ for a classroom speech.

KEY

Name _____

True or False If the statement is true, circle T; if false, circle F.   **page**

F   T F   1.   A vlog is a Web option that specializes in international news and   **108**
                    opinions.

T   T F   2.   According to the text, e-mail is a good tool for interviewing experts.   **108**

F   T F   3.   A blog has limited value for researchers because it covers only the views **108**
                    of individuals.

T   T F   4.   Field research means gathering information first-hand, for example, by   **108**
                    observing an event.

F   T F   5.   When interviewing people on controversial subjects, it is a good idea to   **110**
                    record their comments secretly, so that they are candid and
                    unconstrained in giving their true views.

F   T F   6.   With so much information available on the Internet, traditional library   **102**
                    resources are typically not needed.

T   T F   7.   While advising you to set up a lifetime filing system, the text says that you **107**
                    need not worry about accumulating too many notes.

T   T F   8.   You should take notes in an interview even if you are using a video or   **110**
                    audio recorder.

T   T F   9.   If you are using a computer database to search for articles on exploration **104**
                    of Mars, the computer can be instructed to exclude Mars articles that
                    mention Venus and Saturn.

T   T F   10. A good research technique is to turn your specific purpose statement into   **101**
                    a research question.

KEY   Name _____

Multiple-Choice Questions Each question has only one correct answer.   **page**

a ___ 1. An abstract is a (a) summary, (b) mystery, (c) Web address, (d) research   **105**
              question

b ___ 2. A vlog specializes in (a) virtual reality, (b) video files, (c) verbatim reports,   **108**
              (d) vintage news

c ___ 3. The main disadvantage of interlibrary loan is that (a) you have to pay for   **105**
              any book ordered, (b) only a few large libraries have this service, (c) you
              cannot be certain of a book arriving quickly, (d) you must be an expert
              computer user to take advantage of this service

a ___ 4. Before starting your research, you should decide on your (a) specific   **101**
              purpose, (b) central idea, (c) title, (d) introduction

d ___ 5. "What percentage of registered voters actually voted in the last   **111**
              presidential election?" is an example of _____ type of
              question. (a) an imprecise, (b) a follow-up, (c) an open, (d) a closed

c ___ 6. To find out if patients using a new headache remedy are pleased with the   **106**
              drug, your best approach is to use (a) expert sites, (b) search engines, (c)
              discussion forums, (d) subject directories

b ___ 7. For researchers, one of the most valuable resources in blogs is (a)   **108**
              corporate views, (b) links to other sites, (c) personal opinions, (d) live
              video

b ___ 8. In most libraries, the person who is best able to help you with your   **104**
              research is called (a) an information librarian, (b) a reference librarian, (c)
              a database librarian, (d) a search-and-find librarian

d ___ 9. The _____ for an article gives the title, author's name,   **105**
              magazine, date, and page numbers. (a) abstract, (b) summary, (c) listing,
              (d) citation

d ___ 10. The formats of MLA and APA are designed to help you to (a) find Web   **113-**
              sites, (b) verify accuracy of information, (c) contact online libraries, (d)   **114**
              cite sources

KEY Name _____

Multiple-Choice Questions Each question has only one correct answer. page

c ___ 1. For hard-to-find information, use (a) Google (b) Yahoo, (c) several different search engines, (d) ObscureInfo.com **106**

a ___ 2. An Internet catalog that starts off with broad categories, which are then subdivided into smaller categories, is known as (a) subject directory, (b) search engine, (c) newsgroup, (d) Usenet **106**

c ___ 3. If you are looking for a book that is not available in your library, the text recommends that you (a) visit other libraries, (b) consult the World Wide Web, (c) use interlibrary loan, (d) explore discussion forums **105**

d ___ 4. Basic bibliographical facts about a source, such as title and date, are contained in the (a) abstract, (b) bulletin, (c) tipsheet, (d) citation **105**

a ___ 5. "Do Democrats outnumber Republicans in this state?" is an example of the _____ type of question. (a) closed, (b) open, (c) imprecise, (d) follow-up **111**

d ___ 6. In research, which of the following resources is likeliest to yield the most up-to-date information? (a) a just-published book, (b) an article in the current issue of a magazine, (c) a computer database of articles and summaries, (d) an interview with an expert **108**

b ___ 7. The three major research options are libraries, the Internet, and _____. (a) search engines, (b) field research, (c) reference works, (d) catalogs **108**

a ___ 8. If you want to ask dog experts on the Internet about their experiences with electronic fences, your best strategy is to post a query via (a) discussion forums, (b) Web sites, (c) search engines, (d) subject directories **106**

a ___ 9. The text says that interviewing an expert via e-mail is (a) an acceptable method, (b) an unacceptable method **108**

b ___ 10. For a speech, your own personal experiences and observations (a) can suggest avenues of research but should not be used as source material, (b) might provide valuable material that can be used in a speech **108**

KEY

Name _____

Fill in the missing words or phrases.   page

subject directory	1.	On the Internet, a _____ is a catalog that begins with a broad subject area, which is then subdivided into smaller categories.	**106**
abstracts	2.	Electronic databases often offer brief summaries of articles; these summaries are called _____.	**105**
before	3.	Should library research be done *before* or *after* an interview? _____	**110**
catalog	4.	In most libraries, the library _____ lists the titles and authors of books owned by the library.	**104**
open	5.	In an interview, questions that give the interviewee wide latitude for responding are called _____ questions.	**111**
vlog	6.	A blog that specializes in videos is known as a _____.	**108**
closed	7.	In an interview, questions that require only "yes" or "no" answers are called _____ questions.	**111**
expert sites	8.	Web sites that enable you to get information from authorities on a subject are called _____.	**107**
sources	9.	MLA and APA formats offer ways to cite _____.	**114**
field	10.	Interviewing experts and using your own investigations are examples of _____ research.	**108**

KEY

Name _____

True or False If the statement is true, circle T; if false, circle F.   **page**

F T F   1.   Researchers can trust claims that are based on testimonials.   **126**

F T F   2.   "I got my information from the Internet" is an acceptable way to assure   **139**
                  audiences that the information in your speech is valid.

T T F   3.   Anything published before 1923 is no longer protected by copyright law.   **139**

T T F   4.   Plagiarism in public speaking can cause public humiliation and loss of a   **135-136**
                  job.

F T F   5.   If you make changes in copyrighted material, it is no longer protected   **140-141**
                  under copyright law.

T T F   6.   The Internet domain suffix ".com" is the least objective of all domains.   **133**

T T F   7.   Some Internet domain names include the country of origin.   **134**

T T F   8.   To avoid plagiarism, you must give credit to the sources of your   **135**
                  information.

F T F   9.   Widespread appearance on the Internet is a strong indication that a   **130**
                  report is accurate.

F T F 10.   Almost all people are honest when they reply anonymously to questions   **128**
                  posed by pollsters.

KEY

Name _____

Multiple-Choice Questions Each question has only one correct answer.

Page

a ___ 1. Which one of the following is on the textbook's list of criteria for high-quality information? (a) current, (b) widely believed, (c) appearing in Wikipedia, (d) receiving at least 1,000 hits on a search engine   **125**

d ___ 2. The _____ loophole in copyright laws lets scholars, writers, and public speakers disseminate information without having to get permission for small amounts. (a) public domain, (b) scholarly exemption, (c) royalty-free, (d) fair use   **140**

b ___ 3. To reassure an audience that his information is accurate, a speaker says, "I got my information from Google." The speaker is (a) citing a reliable source, (b) giving a vague reference, (c) injecting unnecessary humor, (d) falsifying the entire speech   **139**

c ___ 4. The Internet address "www.etw.org" indicates (a) a government agency, (b) a commercial operation, (c) a non-profit entity, (d) a military unit   **133**

b ___ 5. If you make changes in copyrighted material (a) the material is no longer protected by copyright, (b) the material retains its copyright status, (c) the material becomes your property, (d) the material reverts to public domain   **140-141**

c ___ 6. A group called "Mothers for Honest Government" issues a report on campaign financing. A researcher (a) can trust the report because of the obvious integrity of the group, (b) should consider the group reliable if it is a nonprofit organization, (c) should find out who is in the group and what motives it has, (d) should reject the group because it represents ordinary citizens instead of economic experts   **129**

c ___ 7. According to the text, results of polls often depend upon (a) whether individuals are paid to participate, (b) the time of day the poll is conducted, (c) how a question is asked, (d) the gender of the person conducting the poll   **128**

d ___ 8. Skepticism, as defined by the text, is equivalent to (a) sour negativity, (b) rejection of new ideas, (c) cynicism, (d) open-minded inquiry   **126**

b ___ 9. A spoken acknowledgment of the source of one's material is known as (a) an oral citation, (b) an oral footnote, (c) an oral credit, (d) an oral attribution   **138**

d ___ 10. If you want to reproduce a U.S. Weather Bureau pamphlet on how to protect oneself in a tornado, you are required to (a) write for permission to reproduce, (b) pay a fee, (c) write for permission and pay a fee, (d) do nothing   **140**

KEY

Name _____

Multiple-Choice Questions Each question has only one correct answer.   **page**

d ___   1. Testimonials should be handled with care because (a) they are used only for commercial gain, (b) they are by definition dishonest, (c) they are all absurd, (d) they do not constitute proof   **126-127**

c ___   2. Which one of the following can be reprinted without getting permission? (a) a Quaker State booklet on how to change oil in a car, (b) a Microsoft booklet on how to operate a software program, (c) a U.S. Department of Agriculture booklet on how to raise bees, (d) a Yale University booklet on how to apply for admission to the school   **140**

b ___   3. Which one of the following citations during a speech is inadequate? (a) "I got my information from Dr. Kathleen Bronson of Harvard Medical School." (b) "I got my information from the Google search engine on the Internet." (c) "I got my information from this month's issue of *Scientific American* magazine." (d) "I got my information from *Cancer Prevention*, a book published by the American Medical Association."   **139**

b ___   4. Sites at which Internet domain tend to be the least objective? (a) .edu, (b) .com, (c) .net, (d) .org   **133**

c ___   5. A book or magazine published before _____ is no longer protected by copyright and may be reproduced and distributed by anyone without violating the law. (a) 1893, (b) 1900, (c) 1923, (d) 1953   **139**

a ___   6. Until recently, the text reports, most medical experts were wrong in their understanding of the correct (a) sitting position, (b) treatment of migraine headaches, (c) stretching technique, (d) cure for eczema   **129**

d ___   7. In a survey of American attitudes, the American Jewish Committee found that a large number of respondents had a low opinion of (a) Muslims, (b) Scientologists, (c) Rastafarians, (d) Wisians   **128**

a ___   8. A speaker says, "In the latest issue of *American Health,* Dr. Emily Sanchez says that ..." This is an example of (a) an oral footnote, (b) an abstract, (c) full disclosure, (d) fair play   **138**

a ___   9. Which is the most reliable type of material? (a) evidence, (b) testimonial, (c) opinion, (d) anecdote   **125**

c ___   10. A conclusion or judgment that remains open to dispute but seems true to one's own mind is (a) a testimonial, (b) an anecdote, (c) an opinion, (d) an intuition   **127**

KEY

Name _____

Fill in the missing words or phrases.

			page
plagiarism	1.	Passing off someone else's words or ideas as your own is called _____.	**135**
asked	2.	Polls are sometimes unreliable because results often depend upon how a question is _____.	**128**
.org	3.	What is the Internet domain suffix denoting a non-profit organization? _____	**133**
.com	4.	What is the Internet domain suffix used by the vast majority of sites? _____	**133**
honestly	5.	One reason for the unreliability of polls is that some people do not respond _____.	**128**
fair use	6.	The legal loophole that allows researchers to use small amounts of copyrighted material without getting permission or paying a fee is known as the _____ doctrine.	**140**
oral footnote	7.	The _____ is the equivalent of a footnote in a written document and its purpose is the same: to give credit for information or ideas that did not originate with the speaker.	**138**
public	8.	Material that was copyrighted before 1923 is now in the _____ domain.	**139**
infallible	9.	Experts can be a valuable source of information on any subject, but it is a mistake to think that they are _____.	**129**
truth	10.	Conscientious, ethical researchers are more interested in finding _____ than in espousing a cherished cause or winning an argument.	**125**

KEY

Name _____

True or False If the statement is true, circle T; if false, circle F.   **page**

T T F   1.   Dictionary definitions are generally less effective than informal definitions.   **149**

T T F   2.   In a speech, you should round off long numbers.   **157**

F T F   3.   To paraphrase means to quote someone's words exactly.   **152**

F T F   4.   If we show that two sets of data are correlated, we prove a cause-and-effect relationship.   **156**

T T F   5.   If a story fails to develop the key ideas of a speech, it should not be used.   **150**

F T F   6.   Support materials always constitute proof of an assertion.   **148**

T T F   7.   Abbreviations such as FTC should be explained in a speech.   **149**

F T F   8.   The more statistics used in a persuasive speech, the better the speech will be.   **157**

F T F   9.   A narrative in a speech must always be factual.   **150**

T T F   10.   Sometimes one single example is enough to support a point.   **150**

KEY

Name _____

Multiple-Choice Questions Each question has only one correct answer.   **page**

c ___ 1. In a speech, which is the best use of statistics? (a) "In the last election,   **157**
96,274,564 Americans voted." (b) "In the last election, millions of
Americans voted." (c) "In the last election, more than 96 million Americans
voted."

a ___ 2. Paraphrasing a quotation is (a) acceptable, (b) unacceptable, (c)   **152**
unnecessary, (d) unethical

c ___ 3. "The college's course catalog resembles a gigantic buffet table." The   **151**
speaker is using which type of support material? (a) example, (b) contrast,
(c) analogy, (d) definition

b ___ 4. A high correlation between two sets of data (a) proves a cause-and-effect   **156**
relationship, (b) does not prove a cause-and-effect relationship

a ___ 5. "Jazz is a form of American music that grew out of African-American   **149**
musical traditions." This sentence is (a) a definition, (b) a comparison, (c) a
contrast, (d) an analogy

b ___ 6. A speaker says, "According to historian Barbara Tuchman, 'Every   **152**
successful revolution puts on in time the robes of the tyrant it has
deposed.'" This sentence illustrates the use of (a) contrast, (b) testimony,
(c) example, (d) definitions

b ___ 7. "Manufacturers such as Ford, General Motors, and Toyota make sports   **149**
utility vehicles." This sentence illustrates the use of (a) testimony, (b)
examples, (c) comparisons, (d) definitions

c ___ 8. Imagine five people of the following ages: 32, 28, 20, 18, and 17. The 20-   **154**
year-old has the _____ age. (a) mean, (b) standard, (c) median, (d)
statistical

d ___ 9. The statistical device that identifies a portion of 100 is called the (a)   **155**
correlation, (b) average, (c) mean, (d) percentage

b ___ 10. "Sleet is harsh and icy, whereas snow is soft and fluffy" is an example of (a)   **151**
comparison, (b) contrast, (c) hypothetical narrative, (d) statistics

KEY

Name _____

Multiple-Choice Questions Each question has only one correct answer.   **page**

d ___   1.   "Punctuation marks are like traffic signs." This sentence is (a) a statistic, (b)   **151**
                  testimony, (c) proof, (d) an analogy

b ___   2.   A speaker who says, "France is 212,000 square miles—roughly the size of   **154**
                  Texas," is using (a) testimony, (b) statistics, (c) contrast, (d) narrative

c ___   3.   A speaker says, "Fresh pizza and store-bought frozen pizza are so different   **151**
                  that I think the only thing they have in common is the name pizza. Fresh
                  pizza is tangy, tasty, and easy to chew, whereas store-bought pizza is flat,
                  bland, and hard to chew." This speaker is using (a) statistics, (b)
                  comparison, (c) contrast, (d) hypothetical narrative

c ___   4.   The success of vivid images as support material depends upon the good   **149**
                  use of (a) flowery words, (b) poetic pictures, (c) specific details, (d) visual
                  aids

a ___   5.   "A feast is a meal that is rich and abundant and includes many guests." This   **148**
                  sentence is (a) a definition, (b) a comparison, (c) a contrast, (d) an analogy

c ___   6.   "Companies such as Canon, Nikon, and Olympus make digital cameras."   **149**
                  This sentence illustrates the use of (a) comparisons, (b) testimony, (c)
                  examples, (d) definitions

b ___   7.   A speaker says, "Former Israeli prime minister Golda Meir said, 'To be   **152**
                  successful, a woman has to be much better at her job than a man.'" This
                  sentence illustrates the use of (a) vivid images, (b) testimony, (c) example,
                  (d) definitions

c ___   8.   The term percent means "out of _____." (a) 1, (b) 10, (c) 100, (d) 1,000   **155**

c ___   9.   Support materials _____ prove a point. (a) always, (b) never,   **148**
                  (c) sometimes

a ___   10.   Imagine five people of the following ages: 45, 37, 26, 20, and 18. The 26-   **154**
                  year-old has the _____ age. (a) median, (b) mean, (c) statistical, (d)
                  balanced

KEY

Name _____

Fill in the missing words or phrases.   **Page**

statistics   1. Numerical ways of expressing information are called   **153**
                        _____.

comparison   2. Showing how two or more things are alike is called   **151**
                        _____.

dictionary   3. Avoid _____ definitions because they   **149**
                        tend to be tedious and hard to grasp.

paraphrasing   4. Taking a quotation expressed in the form of jargon and turning it into   **152**
                        plain English is called _____.

hypothetical   5. A _____ narrative tells the audience   **150**
                        about an imaginary situation.

contrast   6. Showing how two or more things are different is called   **151**
                        _____.

correlation   7. The term _____ is used to show the   **156**
                        relationship between two sets of data (for example, the relationship
                        between IQ scores and grade-point averages).

analogy   8. A special type of comparison that explains a concept or an object by   **151**
                        likening it to something that is—at first glance—quite different is
                        known as _____.

words   9. Quoting verbatim means replicating a person's exact _____.   **152**

middle   10. Regarding averages, the median is derived by listing the numbers,   **154**
                        ranging from highest to lowest, and then locating the number that
                        falls in the _____.

KEY

True or False If the statement is true, circle T; if false, circle F.   **page**

T   T F   1.   Research shows that speakers are better off using no visual aids   **167**
             than using poor ones.

T   T F   2.   If you find a photo on a Web site and want to use it in a classroom   **175**
             speech, you can use it without asking permission from the Web
             site.

T   T F   3.   Even the simplest, most easily understood visual aid should be   **184**
             discussed with the audience.

T   T F   4.   A "thumbnail" on a Web site is an image with very low resolution.   **176**

F   T F   5.   A lengthy set of handouts can be distributed during a speech if you   **178**
             tell your listeners to stay with you and not read ahead.

T   T F   6.   The device known as a "visual presenter" can be used to show   **178-**
             three-dimensional objects such as coins.   **179**

F   T F   7.   The more visual aids used, the stronger your speech.   **180**

F   T F   8.   Creating a graphic on a whiteboard or chalkboard during a speech   **177**
             is an effective way to hold the audience's attention.

F   T F   9.   If a visual aid is small, it should be passed among the listeners   **183**
             during the speech so that everyone can get a good look.

T   T F   10. Research shows that people who are taught orally and visually can   **167**
             recall far more information after a presentation than those who are
             taught only orally.

KEY

Name _____

Multiple-Choice Questions Each question has only one correct answer.   **page**

b ___ 1. The text advises that you "aim for back-row comprehension." This   **182**
means that you should (a) focus your attention on people in the back
of the room, (b) make sure all visuals can be clearly seen by people in
the back of the room, (c) speak loud enough to be heard by people in
the back of the room

c ___ 2. Another name for an information chart is (a) fact sheet, (b) information   **168**
schematic, (c) list of key ideas, (d) text file

c ___ 3. In a bar graph, the bars should be (a) horizontal, (b) vertical, (c) either   **168**
horizontal or vertical

b ___ 4. In the business world, paper handouts are (a) rarely used, (b) very   **178**
popular, (c) never used

b ___ 5. Labels on visual aids should be (a) vertical (b) horizontal, (c) either   **181**
vertical or horizontal

a ___ 6. It is legal to download multimedia files from the Internet if they are to   **175**
be used in (a) classroom speeches, (b) business presentations, (c) TV
commercials, (d) Web anthologies

a ___ 7. Most international audiences prefer (a) visuals prepared in advance,   **182**
(b) visuals prepared spontaneously during a presentation, (c) a
mixture of both types of visuals

b ___ 8. For a pie graph in a speech, the text recommends no more than   **168**
_____ wedges. (a) 3, (b) 8, (c) 16, (d) 20

d ___ 9. For a speech, the best time to distribute a five-page handout is (a)   **178**
before you begin speaking, (b) during the body of the presentation, (c)
during the conclusion, (d) after you finish speaking

c ___ 10. The textbook says that good models for visual aids in public speaking   **181**
are (a) television commercials, (b) cereal boxes, (c) outdoor signs, (d)
CD album covers

KEY Name _____

Multiple-Choice Questions Each question has only one correct answer. **page**

d ___ 1. In considering whether and how to use PowerPoint slides, your first step is to (a) decide the ideal number of slides, (b) investigate the availability of photos on the Internet, (c) compile a list of potential slides, (d) create the outline for your speech | **173**

c ___ 2. How many PowerPoint slides should you use in a speech? (a) only three, (b) no more than five, (c) as many as are needed to make key points | **180**

a ___ 3. The _____ is a device that can show three-dimensional objects such as jewelry. (a) visual presenter, (b) overhead projector, (c) image enlarger, (d) multimedia projector | **178-179**

b ___ 4. Regarding a speaker's credibility with an audience, which one of the following statements is true? (a) The more visual aids a speaker uses, the greater the credibility. (b) A speaker is better off using no visual aids at all than poor ones. | **167**

c ___ 5. It is legal to download an image from the Internet without asking for permission if the use of the image is limited to (a) a sales presentation for a pharmaceutical company, (b) a Web site for a car dealer, (c) a student speech in a college classroom, (d) a brochure for a beauty salon | **175**

d ___ 6. Posters are often preferred to PowerPoint slides in (a) corporate presentation rooms, (b) Army training rooms, (c) hotel conference rooms, (d) courtrooms | **177**

a ___ 7. If your multimedia projector stops working during a PowerPoint presentation, your best option is to (a) distribute paper copies of the slides and continue your presentation, (b) give the audience a five-minute break while you try to fix the equipment, (c) give a summary of points covered so far and end the presentation, (d) describe the contents of the remaining slides | **186**

b ___ 8. Most international audiences prefer (a) a visual that is prepared spontaneously during a presentation, (b) a visual that is prepared in advance, (c) a mixture of both types of visuals | **182**

d ___ 9. The technique whereby a visual is displayed one part at a time is known as (a) gradual revelation, (b) piece-by-piece revelation, (c) incremental revelation, (d) progressive revelation | **185**

b ___ 10. During a presentation, you should _____ look at your visual aids. (a) constantly, (b) occasionally, (c) never | **185**

KEY

Name _____

page

Fill in the missing words or phrases.

bad
1. Circulating visual aids during a speech is a _____ idea.   **183**

low
2. Do thumbnail images have *high* or *low* resolution?   **176**

touch
3. Whenever possible, appeal to the senses—sight, hearing, taste, smell, and _____.   **187**

progressive
4. The technique of revealing only one part of a visual at a time is known as _____ revelation.   **185**

100
5. A pie graph is a circle representing _____ percent and divided into segments of various sizes.   **168**

pictorial
6. Of all graphs, a _____ graph is perhaps the easiest to read, because it visually translates information into a picture that can be grasped instantly.   **168**

see
7. According to the text, the most frequent audiovisual mistake is creating a graphic that is difficult for everyone to _____ clearly.   **182**

horizontal
8. In books, labels on visuals can be either horizontal or vertical. In a speech, they should be _____.   **181**

unpreparedness and/or disrespect
9. For most international audiences, a spontaneously prepared visual aid during a presentation is interpreted as a sign of _____.   **182**

key
10. An information chart is also called a list of _____ ideas.   **168**

KEY

Name _____

True or False If the statement is true, circle T; if false, circle F.   page

T   T F   1. Organizing material from north to south is an example of the spatial pattern.   **204**

F   T F   2. Your main points should be created before you formulate your central idea.   **199-200**

T   T F   3. If you use the topical pattern, you should divide your central idea into components or categories.   **207**

T   T F   4. In the cause-effect pattern of organization, it is permissible to discuss effects first and then causes.   **205**

F   T F   5. Bridges and internal summaries should never be used together.   **212**

F   T F   6. In an outline, all main points should have the same number of supporting points.   **210**

T   T F   7. If you plan to give a speech to several different audiences, you might need to have different main points for each audience.   **203**

F   T F   8. Each main point should make an announcement rather than an assertion.   **202**

T   T F   9. For a long speech, most experienced speakers cover only two or three main points.   **202**

T   T F   10. Telling what happened before, during, and after an event is an example of the chronological pattern.   **204**

KEY

Name _____

Multiple-Choice Questions Each question has only one correct answer.   **page**

c ___   1. Which of the following organizational pattern is a TV news reporter most   **198**
            likely to use in a report of an event? (a) topical, (b) cause-effect, (c)
            chronological, (d) analytical

d ___   2. Discussing your speech's key ideas with a knowledgeable source is called   **212**
            (a) double checking, (b) an insurance policy, (c) a confirmation, (d) an
            expert check

a ___   3. In a speech on redwood trees, a speaker begins by discussing the roots,   **204**
            proceeds to the trunk, then the branches, and finally the leaves. Which
            organizational pattern is being used? (a) spatial, (b) chronological, (c)
            cause-effect, (d) problem-solution, (e) topical

d ___   4. A speaker says, "Now we come to the most important thing I have to tell   **213**
            you." Which device is the speaker using? (a) bridge, (b) internal summary,
            (c) signpost, (d) spotlight

a ___   5. A speaker says, "Now that we have looked at the problem, let's turn our   **211**
            attention to the solution." Which device is the speaker using? (a) bridge, (b)
            internal summary, (c) signpost, (d) spotlight

a ___   6. Which one of the following statements is true? (a) All main points need   **208**
            supporting materials. (b) Each main point should have the same number of
            supports as every other main point. (c) It is impossible to have too many
            supports. (d) Transitions are the most important type of supports.

c ___   7. The cause-effect pattern of organization (a) must explain causes before   **205**
            effects, (b) must explain effects before causes, (c) can explain either
            causes or effects first

b ___   8. For a speech on the history of a Native American family in Arizona, which   **204**
            organizational pattern would you be most likely to choose? (a) spatial, (b)
            chronological, (c) cause-effect, (d) problem-solution, (e) topical

c ___   9. Which part of the speech does the text recommend that you create first?   **199-**
            (a) title, (b) introduction, (c) body, (d) conclusion   **200**

a ___ 10. When you are organizing your material, each note card should be limited to   **213**
            how many ideas? (a) one, (b) two, (c) three, (d) four, (e) five, (f) six

KEY

Name _____

Multiple-Choice Questions Each question has only one correct answer.   **page**

d ___ 1. Which organizational pattern is especially popular in persuasive speeches?   **206**
(a) topical, (b) chronological, (c) spatial, (d) problem-solution

a ___ 2. A speaker describes the safety features of a new car, starting at the front   **204**
bumper and progressing to the rear bumper. Which organizational pattern is
the speaker using? (a) spatial, (b) chronological, (c) cause-effect, (d)
problem-solution, (e) topical

b ___ 3. For a speech explaining how to bake bread, which organizational pattern   **204**
would be used? (a) spatial, (b) chronological, (c) cause-effect, (d) problem-
solution, (e) topical

d ___ 4. Main points are designed to help the audience understand and remember (a)   **200**
the general purpose, (b) the specific purpose, (c) the introduction, (d) the
central idea

c ___ 5. A speaker discusses three types of work dogs. Which pattern is the speaker   **207**
using? (a) spatial, (b) chronological, (c) topical, (d) problem-solution

b ___ 6. A speaker says, "So far, we have seen that carelessness is the main cause   **212**
for industrial accidents." Which device is the speaker using? (a) crossroad,
(b) internal summary, (c) traffic light, (d) barrier

d ___ 7. A speaker says, "What I am going to explain now will help you understand   **213**
the rest of the speech." Which device is the speaker using? (a) crossroad, (b)
internal summary, (c) external summary, (d) spotlight

a ___ 8. A speaker discusses why some people abuse animals, and then describes   **205**
the effects of abuse on the animals. Which pattern is the speaker using? (a)
cause-effect, (b) chronological, (c) spatial, (d) topical

a ___ 9. Which of the following shows a parallel grammatical form? (a) If you are   **203**
trapped outdoors in a thunderstorm, avoid being the tallest object in a field,
stay away from poles and fences, and do not touch any metal. (b) If you are
trapped outdoors in a thunderstorm, avoid being the tallest object in a field,
poles and fences should be avoided, and no metal should be touched.

c ___ 10. The first thing speakers should create for their speech is the (a) title,   **199-**
(b) introduction, (c) body, (d) conclusion   **200**

KEY

Name _____

Fill in the missing words or phrases.   page

spatial   1. If main points are organized according to the way in which   **204**
                              they relate to each other in physical space, the
                              _____ pattern is being used.

central idea   2. Main points are used to drive home the   **200**
                              _____ of a speech.

topical   3. If you speak on the federal government and create main   **207**
                              points based on the three branches (executive, legislative,
                              and judicial), you are using the
                              _____ pattern of organization.

assertion   4. Which should a main point make—an assertion or an   **202**
                              announcement? _____

2 or 3 (occasionally 4) 5. How many main points should you have for a 5-minute   **202**
                              speech? _____

cause-effect   6. If main points are organized according to a cause-and-   **205**
                              effect relationship, the _____
                              pattern is being used.

chronological   7. If main points are organized in a time sequence, the   **204**
                              _____ pattern is being used.

transitions   8. Spotlights, bridges, and signposts are examples of what   **210**
                              component of a speech?

                              _____

problem-   9. Speakers who discuss a problem in the first part of a   **206
solution**   speech and then give a solution in the second part are
                              using the _____ pattern of
                              organization.

internal summary   10. In the middle of your speech, if you give a summary of   **212**
                              what you have discussed up to that point, you are using
                              the device called _____.

KEY

Name _____

True or False If the statement is true, circle T; if false, circle F.   **page**

T   T   F   1.   In the introduction, it is acceptable to tell a hypothetical narrative (a story that   **220**
                   did not actually happen).

F   T   F   2.   In the conclusion, the speaker should never repeat ideas or information   **230**
                   contained in the introduction.

T   T   F   3.   It is possible for an introduction to be too short.   **226**

F   T   F   4.   The part of the introduction that is designed to get your audience's attention   **219**
                   and interest is called the orienting material.

F   T   F   5.   The introduction should be prepared before the body of a speech is developed.   **226**

F   T   F   6.   All members of an audience listen attentively for the first 30 seconds of a   **219**
                   speech.

F   T   F   7.   Saying "In conclusion. . ." as you wrap up your speech is not acceptable in   **227**
                   good speechmaking.

T   T   F   8.   You should never bring new main points into the conclusion.   **230**

F   T   F   9.   Rhetorical questions should be avoided in introductions.   **220**

F   T   F   10. If you didn't have enough time to prepare your speech, the conclusion is a   **227**
                   good place to apologize to the audience.

KEY

Name _____

Multiple-Choice Questions Each question has only one correct answer.   **page**

c ___ 1. Which one of the following is an acceptable option in a conclusion?   **229**
(a) discussing a new main point, (b) apologizing for inadequate preparation,
(c) referring to the introduction, (d) promising to give a better speech next time

a ___ 2. A speaker says, "How long will America continue to be plagued with child   **220**
abuse?" This is an example of _____ question. (a) a rhetorical,
(b) an overt-response

b ___ 3. Telling a story, asking a question, and using a visual aid are examples of (a)   **219**
orienting material, (b) attention material, (c) evidence, (d) enticement

c ___ 4. Which one of the following is an acceptable option in an introduction? (a) a   **220**
convincing clincher, (b) a sincere apology, (c) a hypothetical narrative

c ___ 5. Most attorneys believe that courtroom battles are won because of the   **218**
effectiveness of (a) the opening statement, (b) the closing argument, (c) both
the opening statement and the closing argument, (d) the supporting evidence

a ___ 6. It is _____ for an introduction to be too short. (a)   **226**
possible, (b) impossible

b ___ 7. In a speech, which one of the following is a mistake if used in the conclusion?   **230**
(a) a quotation by a reputable authority, (b) a new main point, (c) a repetition
of key points, (d) a reference to the introduction

c ___ 8. You can signal the end of a speech with (a) verbal signals, (b) nonverbal   **227**
signals, (c) both verbal and nonverbal signals

c ___ 9. For the first few sentences in a speech, which one of the following options   **223**
would be a mistake? (a) a rhetorical question, (b) a surprising statistic, (c) an
announcement of the topic, (d) a narrative

b ___ 10. Issuing an appeal or a challenge at the end of a speech is an example of (a) a   **228**
summary, (b) a clincher, (c) orienting material, (d) attention material

KEY

Name _____

Multiple-Choice Questions Each question has only one correct answer.

page

c ___ 1. According to most attorneys, courtroom battles are usually won on the effectiveness of (a) the opening statement, (b) the closing argument, (c) both the opening statement and the closing argument — **218**

a ___ 2. A speaker says, "Please raise your hands to answer this: How many of you know how to swim?" What kind of question is this speaker using? (a) overt-response, (b) rhetorical — **220**

b ___ 3. The best place to reassure your listeners that you are well-prepared and that you are not going to waste their time is in (a) the attention material, (b) the orienting material — **223**

a ___ 4. Which one of the following options fails to serve as orienting material? (a) grabbing the listeners' attention, (b) previewing the body of the speech, (c) giving background information, (d) establishing credibility — **223**

c ___ 5. The text quotes the old speechmaking formula, "Tell 'em what you're going to tell 'em. Tell 'em. Then tell 'em what you told 'em." The last sentence refers to (a) the clincher, (b) the orienting material, (c) the summary, (d) the attention material — **228**

b ___ 6. In career speeches, a few words spoken before your attention material is called (a) a prologue, (b) an icebreaker, (c) a welcome, (d) an opener — **226**

b ___ 7. "Today I'd like to tell you how to grow vegetables." This sentence is most appropriate for (a) attention material, (b) orienting material — **223**

b ___ 8. The best way to indicate that you have finished with a quotation is to (a) say "End of quotation" (b) pause as an "oral" punctuation device, (c) use both hands to make "finger quotes" in the air, (d) crumple the card on which the quotation is written — **222**

b ___ 9. Informing the audience of your qualifications to speak on a topic is (a) a form of bragging to be avoided, (b) recommended to build credibility, (c) not advised unless you are an expert — **224**

d ___ 10. The text says, "Quotations usually work best when they are _____." (a) cryptic, (b) from an ancient philosopher, (c) risqué, (d) short — **222**

KEY

Name _____

Fill in the missing words or phrases.   **page**

credibility   1.   Telling the audience about your expertise on your topic is a   **224**
                              good way to establish _____.

rhetorical   2.   If you ask your listeners a question, but you don't want them to   **220**
                              answer overtly by raising their hands or speaking, you are
                              asking what kind of question?

                              _____

orienting material 3.   The part of the introduction in which you prepare your   **223**
                              audience intellectually and psychologically for the body of the
                              speech is known as _____.

attention material 4.   The part of the introduction in which you capture and hold your   **219**
                              audience's attention is known as

                              _____.

conclusion   5.   When is a clincher used in a speech?   **228**

                              _____

a new main point   6.   The text says that it is acceptable to use fresh material in your   **230**
                              conclusion as long as the material does not constitute

                              _____.

nonverbal signals 7.   At the end of a speech, instead of coming to an abrupt halt, a   **227**
                              speaker should use verbal signals and

                              _____.

body   8.   The text says that when you prepare a speech, you should   **226**
                              work on which part first: the introduction, the body, or the
                              conclusion? _____

pause   9.   If you use a quotation in a speech, what oral punctuation   **222**
                              device does the text recommend that you use at the end of the
                              quotation? _____

weak (bad)   10.   "I guess that's all I have to say" is a _____   **230**
                              ending for a speech.

KEY Name _____

True or False If the statement is true, circle T; if false, circle F.   **page**

F   T F   1.   Speaking notes should be written in complete sentences.   **247**

F   T F   2.   The textbook recommends that you make a fresh set of speaking notes on   **248**
                the eve of your speech.

T   T F   3.   Main points in outlines are represented by Roman numerals (I, II, III, and so   **239**
                on).

T   T F   4.   According to the text, the body of a speech should have its own numbering   **242**
                sequence in the outline, independent of the introduction and conclusion.

T   T F   5.   An outline has a title, but the speaker does not actually say it in the speech.   **241**

T   T F   6.   It is acceptable to write quotations in full on your speaking notes.   **247**

T   T F   7.   In an outline, transitions should be placed between each main point.   **242**

T   T F   8.   In an outline, one of the places where you should put a transition is   **243**
                between the body of the speech and the conclusion.

F   T F   9.   A topic outline has more words than a complete-sentence outline.   **238**

F   T F 10.   Although you can use notes if you need them, the most desirable technique   **247**
                for public speaking is to use no notes.

KEY

Name _____

Multiple-Choice Questions Each question has only one correct answer. **Page**

a ___ 1. Roman numerals (I, II, III, and so on) should be used in an outline for (a) major divisions, (b) first-level subdivision, (c) second-level subdivision, (d) third-level subdivision — **239**

d ___ 2. For speaker's notes, the text recommends that _____ should be written in large letters and contrasting colors. (a) the introduction, (b) main points, (c) transitions, (d) delivery reminders — **247**

b ___ 3. A disadvantage of using a full sheet of paper for speaking notes is (a) a sheet can contain notes for an entire speech, (b) a sheet can cause a speaker's eyes to glide over key points, (c) a sheet is larger than an index card, (d) a sheet can appear to be a computer printout — **249**

c ___ 4. An outline should include (a) delivery reminders, (b) every word that you will say during the speech, (c) transitions, (d) an audience analysis — **242**

b ___ 5. Donald Macleod of Princeton Theological Seminary tells his seminarians that the maximum time for an effective sermon is (a) 8 minutes, (b) 18 minutes, (c) 28 minutes, (d) 38 minutes — **240**

c ___ 6. Using notes in a speech (a) is a sign of weakness in communicating, (b) shows a lack of confidence in speaking ability, (c) shows preparedness and respect for the audience — **247**

a ___ 7. A good time to use a topic outline is (a) in the early stages of preparation, when you are brainstorming and putting down your ideas, (b) in the later stages, when you are refining and polishing your ideas — **238**

a ___ 8. "Czech It Out! Why You Should Visit Prague" is an _____ title for a speech. (a) acceptable, (b) unacceptable — **241**

a ___ 9. For your speaking notes on a piece of paper or note card, you should (a) write on only one side, (b) write on both sides — **247**

c ___ 10. A speech should have _____ the complete-sentence outline. (a) about the same number of words as, (b) fewer words than, (c) more words than — **239**

KEY

Name _____

Multiple-Choice Questions Each question has only one correct answer.   **page**

a ___ 1. An outline helps you to see the relationship between (a) ideas, (b) subjects and   **238**
verbs, (c) formats, (d) topics

d ___ 2. In an outline, which of the following places would be unnecessary for inserting a   **243**
transition? (a) between each main point, (b) between the introduction and the
body, (c) between the body and the conclusion, (d) between the conclusion and
documentation

d ___ 3. For an outline, which one of the following is unnecessary? (a) title, (b)   **241-**
bibliography, (c) list of visual aids, (d) speaker's notes   **243**

a ___ 4. In an outline, it is incorrect to have _____ under a   **240**
heading. (a) only one subheading, (b) more than 10 subheadings, (c) a
subheading labeled "example"

b ___ 5. Writing complete sentences in your outline (a) will guarantee a better speech   **239**
than if you write phrases, (b) will make it easier for another person to help you
than if you write phrases, (c) will help you memorize the speech, (d) will be
necessary in order for you to read your speech

a ___ 6. When no time limit is set for a speech, the speaker should talk (a) briefly, (b) as   **240**
long as the speaker wants

b ___ 7. When you deliver your speech, you should use (a) your outline, (b) your   **247**
speaking notes, (c) both your outline and your speaking notes

a ___ 8. "Ouch! How to Treat a Bee Sting" is an _____ title for a speech. (a)   **241**
acceptable, (b) unacceptable

c ___ 9. A topic outline uses (a) complete sentences, (b) only one word per line, (c) key   **238-**
words or phrases, (d) a topic analysis   **239**

b ___ 10. Concerning a complete-sentence outline and the speech itself, which one of the   **239**
following statements is true? (a) The speech itself should have about the same
number of words as the outline. (b) The speech itself should have more words
than the outline. (c) The speech itself should have fewer words than the outline.

KEY

Fill in the missing words or phrases.

			page

saying the title   1. A speaker begins by saying, "The title of my speech is 'How to Lose Weight Permanently.'" What mistake is the speaker making? _____   **241**

roman numerals   2. In the standard system of subdivisions in an outline, you mark your main points with _____.   **239**

two   3. In an outline, each heading should have at least _____ subdivisions or none at all.   **240**

trim   4. If you practice your speech and discover that you are running four minutes over the time limit, what should you do? _____   **240**

complete-sentence   5. The text says that the two most popular formats for outlines are the topic outline and the _____ outline.   **239**

mental   6. Some people have the mistaken notion that using notes is a sign of _____ weakness.   **247**

outlining   7. The text says that _____ is a common-sense way of arranging information in a logical pattern.   **236**

outline   8. You should make indentations in your speaking notes that correspond to those in your _____.   **247**

actual speech   9. Which should have more words—the outline or the actual speech? _____   **239**

shorter   10. Are speeches today generally shorter or longer than in the past? _____   **240**

Name _____

True or False If the statement is true, circle T; if false, circle F.   **page**

F   T F   1.   "The deafening din of dynamite" is an example of antithesis.   **267**

F   T F   2.   "Her and me went to Chicago" is grammatically correct.   **262**

F   T F   3.   "Just between you and I" is grammatically correct.   **262**

T   T F   4.   If your listeners share your specialized vocation, you can use jargon in a   **265**
                    speech.

F   T F   5.   Abstract words are more likely to be remembered by an audience than   **263**
                    concrete words.

T   T F   6.   Oral language requires more amplification and elaboration than written   **268**
                    language.

T   T F   7.   Words like *new, improved,* and *easy* in advertising can cause an increase in   **257**
                    sales of a product.

F   T F   8.   The best way to convey complex ideas is to use complex language.   **262**

T   T F   9.   "Passed away" instead of "died" is an example of a euphemism.   **263**

F   T F 10.   "A deferred dream dries up like a raisin in the sun" is an example of a   **266**
                    metaphor.

KEY

Name _____

Multiple-Choice Questions Each question has only one correct answer.

a ___ 1. If the person who sends your car through a car wash is called "a corrosion control specialist," what type of language is being used? (a) doublespeak, (b) cliché, (c) mixed metaphor, (d) simile, (e) metaphor | **263**

d ___ 2. "This is a government by the people, of the people, and for the people." This is an example of (a) a euphemism, (b) jargon, (c) a metaphor, (d) parallel structure | **268**

c ___ 3. "The Indonesians have a tough row to hoe to keep their economic heads above water." This is an example of a (a) euphemism, (b) jargon word, (c) mixed metaphor, (d) simile | **266**

d ___ 4. "They don't care about people, but they do care about possessions." This sentence illustrates (a) alliteration, (b) metaphor, (c) euphemism, (d) antithesis | **267**

a ___ 5. Friendship is (a) an abstract word, (b) a concrete word, (c) a phony word, (d) a meaningless word | **263**

b ___ 6. "The stars are diamonds in the sky." This is an example of (a) a simile, (b) a metaphor, (c) a euphemism, (d) jargon | **266**

b ___ 7. Which one of the following is incorrect grammatically? (a) He and Mary strolled on the beach. (b) This news is just between you and I. (c) For me and Jack, the raise was welcome. (d) Please give the files to me and Susan. | **261**

c ___ 8. "Last, but not least" is an example of (a) a euphemism, (b) jargon, (c) a cliché, (d) parallel structure | **266**

b ___ 9. The emotional meaning attached to a word is its (a) denotation, (b) connotation | **260**

c ___ 10. The text says that grammatical errors in a speech distract the audience and can cause the speaker to lose (a) self-confidence, (b) an aura of expertise, (c) credibility with the audience, (d) a tone of seriousness | **261**

KEY

Name _____

Multiple-Choice Questions Each question has only one correct answer.

				page
a	___	1.	"After you open a can of worms, they always come home to roost." This is an example of (a) mixed metaphor, (b) euphemism, (c) jargon, (d) simile	**266**
c	___	2.	"The sad sister sat on a silver seat" is an example of (a) antithesis, (b) euphemism, (c) alliteration, (d) metaphor	**267**
b	___	3.	"The stars are like diamonds in the sky." This is an example of (a) a metaphor, (b) a simile, (c) jargon, (d) a euphemism	**266**
d	___	4.	Which one of the following is incorrect grammatically? (a) Please give the files to me and Susan. (b) He and Mary strolled on the beach. (c) For me and Jack, the raise was welcome. (d) This news is just between you and I.	**261**
c	___	5.	"Blind as a bat" is an example of (a) euphemism, (b) jargon, (c) cliché, (d) parallel structure	**266**
b	___	6.	When politicians raise taxes, but call their action "revenue enhancement," they are using (a) jargon, (b) a euphemism, (c) poor grammar, (d) parallel language	**263**
a	___	7.	Honesty is (a) an abstract word, (b) a concrete word, (c) a phony word, (d) a meaningless word	**263**
a	___	8.	If a funeral director is called a "grief therapist," what type of language is being used? (a) doublespeak, (b) cliché, (c) mixed metaphor, (d) simile, (e) metaphor	**263-264**
b	___	9.	A dictionary definition of a word is its (a) connotation, (b) denotation	**260**
d	___	10.	"We want justice for ourselves, for our friends, and for our children." This is an example of (a) euphemism, (b) jargon, (c) metaphor, (d) parallel structure	**268**

KEY

Name _____

Fill in the missing words or phrases.   page

deceive (or confuse)   1.   A euphemism is harmful when it is used to _____ the listener.   **264**

metaphor   2.   If you say, "Your bread and butter will be snatched from under your feet," you are guilty of using mixed _____.   **266**

clichés   3.   Trite, worn-out words or phrases are called _____.   **266**

emotional   4.   The connotation of a word is the _____ meaning that is associated with it.   **260**

inflated language   5.   When the person who sends your car through a car wash is called a "corrosion control specialist," what kind of doublespeak is being used? _____.   **264**

jargon   6.   When people use the specialized language of a group or profession—for example, using terms such as AWOL—they are using _____.   **265**

an eye   7.   The text quotes an Arab proverb, "The best speaker is one who can turn the ear into _____."   **265**

alliteration   8.   "The tame tiger teased the tiny tot" is an example of the rhetorical device known as _____.   **267**

intelligent   9.   The text says that poor grammar can hurt you because it makes you sound (to some people) as if you are not _____.   **261**

grammatical   10.   A person who says, "You was late" has made a _____ error.   **261**

KEY

Name _____

page

True or False If the statement is true, circle T; if false, circle F.

T   T F 1.   If you are not feeling enthusiastic about giving a speech, you should pretend to be enthusiastic.   **284**

F   T F 2.   When you speak into a microphone, you should raise your voice slightly.   **280**

F   T F 3.   Pauses in speeches should be avoided because they make you look indecisive.   **283**

F   T F 4.   The extemporaneous method of delivery involves speaking on the spur of the moment with no chance to prepare.   **277**

T   T F 5.   When speaking to a small audience, you should establish eye contact with every listener.   **285**

F   T F 6.   If you don't receive any questions during the question-and-answer period, you must have failed to stimulate the audience's interest in the topic.   **291**

T   T F 7.   Some speeches call for few or no gestures.   **289**

T   T F 8.   The memorized method of delivery has the virtue of allowing the speaker to figure out exact wording ahead of time.   **275**

F   T F 9.   It is a good idea to speak fast at the beginning of your speech so that the audience doesn't get bored.   **289**

T   T F 10.   A speech should be practiced point by point, not word for word.   **293**

KEY Name _____

Multiple-Choice Questions Each question has only one correct answer.   **Page**

c ___ 1.   Which aspect of nonverbal communication is considered a "figurative   **285**
handshake?" (a) personal appearance, (b) gestures, (c) eye contact, (d)
posture

d ___ 2.   The key to effective delivery is (a) good eye contact with each member of the   **275**
audience, (b) effective use of gestures and body movement, (c) a winning
smile and enthusiastic attitude, (d) a strong desire to communicate with the
audience

a ___ 3.   If nonverbal communication contradicts verbal messages, listeners will accept   **284**
_____ as the true message. (a) the nonverbal, (b) the
verbal, (c) neither the nonverbal nor the verbal

b ___ 4.   A speaker's clothes should be (a) about as dressy as the listeners' clothes, (b)   **285**
a bit dressier than the listeners' clothes, (c) less dressy than the listeners'
clothes

b ___ 5.   If you fear that you will cry while telling a painful personal story in a speech,   **279**
you should (a) omit the story to avoid embarrassment, (b) tell the story after
alerting the audience that you might cry, (c) videotape yourself telling the story
and play the video during the speech, (d) put the story on a handout that is
distributed at the end of the speech

a ___ 6.   A few audience members are rudely chatting among themselves during your   **290**
speech, distracting other listeners. Which one of the following solutions is
unacceptable? (a) Ignore the talkers. (b) Ask the talkers to please give you
their attention. (c) Stop speaking and look directly at the talkers.

d ___ 7.   "Uh" and "um" are examples of what the text calls (a) meaningless pauses, (b)   **283**
impromptu utterances, (c) oral distracters, (d) verbal fillers

a ___ 8.   During a question-and-answer session, which one of the following responses is   **292**
undesirable? (a) "That's a good question." (b) "I don't know." (c) "I don't
understand your question." (d) "I'll find out the answer and get back to you
soon."

a ___ 9.   If you practice your speech and find that you are two minutes over the time   **293**
limit, you should (a) cut out material by using your outline and speaking notes,
(b) practice your speech with a faster rate of speaking, (c) do nothing about it
because the information is the priority, (d) plan on delivering your speech as
quickly as possible

b ___ 10. "Cannahepya?" for "Can I help you?" is an example of poor   **280**
(a) vowelizaton, (b) articulation, (c) intonation, (d) sound production

KEY

Name _____

Multiple-Choice Questions Each question has only one correct answer.

page

a ___ 1. Which one of the following statements about pauses is false? (a) Pauses should last a minimum of ten seconds. (b) Pauses give audiences a chance to digest what you have said. (c) Pauses give you a moment to think of what you are going to say next. (d) Pauses let the listeners know when you have finished one thought and are ready to go to the next. (e) Pauses can be used to emphasize an important statement.   **283**

d ___ 2. Which method of delivery involves speaking on the spur of the moment with no chance to prepare? (a) extemporaneous, (b) manuscript, (c) memorized, (d) impromptu   **276**

d ___ 3. In a manuscript speech, the text recommends inserting slanting lines to indicate (a) a louder voice, (b) a softer voice, (c) a glance at the audience, (d) a pause   **275**

c ___ 4. If you as a speaker do not know the answer to a listener's question, you should (a) give as strong an answer as you can manage under the circumstances, (b) deflect the question by telling the audience that there is not enough time to answer the question adequately, (c) admit that you do not know the answer   **292**

d ___ 5. The text recommends that you look at the audience what percentage of the time? (a) 50%, (b) 75%, (c) 85%, (d) 95%   **285**

c ___ 6. The PREP (Position, Reason, Example, Position) template is recommended for _____ speeches. (a) manuscript, (b) extemporaneous, (c) impromptu, (d) memorized   **276**

c ___ 7. If you are asked to speak impromptu in five minutes, the first thing you should do is decide (a) your introduction, (b) your main points, (c) your conclusion, (d) your opening joke.   **276**

b ___ 8. In an oral presentation, if you say, "I'm happy to speak to you today," but your facial expression shows unhappiness, your audience is most likely to assume that (a) you are happy to be speaking, (b) you are unhappy about speaking, (c) you are happy in some ways and unhappy in others, (d) you are a troubled and deceitful person   **284**

c ___ 9. Which method of delivery is a person most likely to use in delivering a paper at a scientific conference? (a) extemporaneous, (b) memorized, (c) manuscript, (d) impromptu   **275**

a ___ 10. "Watchadoin?" for "What are you doing?" is an example of poor (a) articulation, (b) vowelization, (c) intonation, (d) sound production   **280**

KEY

Name _____

Fill in the missing words or phrases.

			page
voice	1.	To sound conversational in a speech, you should be yourself but intensify the emotional tones and vibrancy of your _____.	**284**
words	2.	The text recommends that you follow the maxim "Practice ideas, not _____."	**293**
four	3.	The text recommends that you practice your speech at least _____ times.	**293**
pretend	4.	If, before a speech, you do not feel confident, the text recommends that you _____ to be confident.	**284**
in the introduction	5.	If you don't want your speech interrupted by questions but you do want questions in the question-and-answer period, you should advise your audience of your desire. When should you make your announcement? _____	**291**
a strong desire to communicate with listeners	6.	The text says that the key to good speech delivery is _____.	**275**
nonverbal	7.	If the verbal signals and the nonverbal signals in your speech contradict each other, which will the audience accept as the true message? _____	**284**
extemporaneous	8.	The _____ method of speaking is the most popular style of speaking in America today.	**277**
impromptu	9.	Speaking on the spur of the moment—without a chance to prepare—is called the _____ method of delivery.	**276**
looking at notes too much	10.	The text says that the biggest spoiler of eye contact is _____.	**285**

KEY

Name _____

True or False If the statement is true, circle T; if false, circle F.   **page**

T   T F   1.   One of the goals of informative speaking is to convey fresh information.   **299**

F   T F   2.   A definition speech focuses on giving a dictionary definition of a concept.   **299-300**

F   T F   3.   In a process speech, the goal is always to teach the listeners how to   **301-302**
                      perform the process themselves.

F   T F   4.   "To explain to my listeners the meaning of capitalism in modern society"   **304**
                      is a specific purpose statement for a process speech.

F   T F   5.   "To tell my audience about the life of Malcolm X" is an example of a   **300**
                      specific purpose statement for a definition speech.

T   T F   6.   "To inform my audience how a thunderstorm forms" is an example of a   **301**
                      specific purpose statement for a process speech.

F   T F   7.   In a speech to a graduating high school class, you can assume that all   **308**
                      the students know basic information, such as the fact that Alaska and
                      Hawaii were the last states admitted to the United States.

F   T F   8.   Of the three main channels for learning information, the visual is the   **302**
                      strongest.

F   T F   9.   An explanation speech is not appropriate for a college classroom speech.   **304**

T   T F   10. Calling on people at random is a technique that the text recommends for   **307**
                      long presentations.

KEY

Name _____

Multiple-Choice Questions Each question has only one correct answer.   **Page**

c ___ 1. Which one of these channels for learning information is the strongest? (a)   **302**
auditory, (b) visual, (c) physical activity

d ___ 2. "To inform my audience of the reasons for the near extinction of mountain   **304**
gorillas" is a specific purpose statement for which type of speech? (a)
analytical, (b) topical, (c) process, (d) explanation

b ___ 3. "To tell my audience about the life of Florence Nightingale" is a specific   **300**
purpose statement for which type of speech? (a) definition, (b) description,
(c) process, (d) topical

c ___ 4. "To tell my listeners how porpoises are trained to do out-of-water stunts" is   **301**
a specific purpose statement for which type of speech? (a) definition, (b)
analytical, (c) process, (d) spatial

a ___ 5. "To explain to my listeners the meaning of feminism in modern America" is   **299**
a specific purpose statement for which type of speech? (a) definition, (b)
description, (c) process, (d) topical

a ___ 6. Which one of the following specific purpose statements is appropriate for   **299**
an informative speech? (a) "To demonstrate to my listeners how to build
kites." (b) "To prove to my listeners that they should stop drinking soda." (c)
"To help my listeners see that they should buy cars made in Detroit." (d)
"To talk my listeners into voting for Republican candidates."

b ___ 7. The text says that for a long presentation that lasts all afternoon, it is best   **307**
to give a coffee or stretch break after every ___-minute period. (a) 30, (b)
45, (c) 60, (d) 90

c ___ 8. To provide variety during a long presentation, you can ask questions of   **307**
listeners. The best technique is to (a) ask for volunteers, (b) call a listener's
name before you ask the question, (c) call a listener's name after you ask
the question, (d) pull a name from a hat

b ___ 9. Explaining Adolf Hitler's identity to a college audience (a) is insulting to the   **308**
intelligence of the listeners, (b) can be carried out indirectly, without
insulting anyone's intelligence, (c) is unnecessary for listeners at the
college level, (d) is necessary for about 60 percent of a typical college
audience

b ___ 10. A speech recounting the history of the attack on Pearl Harbor would be   **299**
which type of speech? (a) persuasive, (b) informative, (c) entertaining, (d)
demonstration

KEY

Name _____

Multiple-Choice Questions Each question has only one correct answer. **page**

b ___ 1. According to the text, one of the goals of informative speaking is to convey what kind of information? (a) substantial, (b) fresh, (c) unusual, (d) indisputable **299**

c ___ 2. In a first aid class, a nurse says, "To control bleeding, remember RED, which stands for Rest, Elevation, and Direct pressure." Which learning device is the nurse using? (a) shortcut, (b) linguistic trick, (c) acronym, (d) alliteration **310**

c ___ 3. "To inform my listeners how a guitar makes music" is a specific purpose statement for which type of speech? (a) definition, (b) description, (c) process, (d) spatial **301**

c ___ 4. "A tornado's funnel is like the vortex you see when you let water go down a drain." This is an example of which principle? (a) Relate the speech to the listeners' self-interest. (b) Assess the knowledge of the listeners. (c) Use the familiar to explain the unfamiliar. **308**

c ___ 5. Nina Totenberg, a nationally known TV and radio reporter, says the most important element in an effective speech is _____ information. (a) humorous, (b) controversial, (c) interesting, (d) timely **306**

d ___ 6. A speaker explains why most car thieves steal 10-year-old cars rather than new cars. The speaker is likely to use the _____ pattern of organization. (a) problem-solution, (b) chronological, (c) spatial, (d) statement-of-reasons **304**

b ___ 7. "To inform my audience about living conditions in an institution for autistic children" is a specific purpose statement for which type of speech? (a) definition, (b) description, (c) process, (d) topical **300**

c ___ 8. "To inform my audience about the dangers of quicksand" is a specific purpose statement for which type of speech? (a) innovative (b) topical, (c) explanation, (d) analytical **304**

d ___ 9. The text quotes Voltaire as saying, "The secret of being tiresome is in _____." (a) repeating yourself, (b) talking only about yourself, (c) recounting boring stories, (d) telling everything **308**

a ___ 10. An ancient Chinese proverb says, "I hear, and I forget. I see, and I remember. I do, and I _____." (a) understand, (b) enjoy, (c) ask questions, (d) appreciate **302**

KEY

Name _____

Fill in the missing words or phrases.   page

informative   1.   A teacher is an example of a(n) _____   299
                       speaker, not a persuasive speaker.

difficult steps 2. In a process speech, you should give advance warning of   303
                       _____.

understand   3.   The text quotes an ancient Chinese proverb that applies to modern   302
                       communication: "I hear, and I forget. I see, and I remember. I do, and
                       I_____."

spatial   4.   If you describe a robot from top to bottom, you are using the   300
                       _____ pattern of organization.

process   5.   "To explain to my listeners how to refinish furniture" is a purpose   301
                       statement for which type of informative speech?
                       _____

extended   6.   The kind of definition that is richer and fuller than a dictionary definition is 299
                       a(n) _____ definition.

specifics   7.   Many speeches are boring because speakers deal primarily with   306
                       generalities instead of _____.

unfamiliar   8.   The text advises you to "use the familiar to explain the   308
                       _____."

**physical   9.   Of the three main channels for learning new information, the auditory is 302
action**   weakest, the visual is stronger, and _____ is
                       strongest of all.

self-interest 10. To motivate listeners to pay attention to your speech, you should relate 305
                       your remarks to their _____.

KEY

Name _____

True or False If the statement is true, circle T; if false, circle F.   **page**

F   T   F   1.   In a speech of refutation, deeply held beliefs are easier to demolish than a set of erroneous facts.   **324**

T   T   F   2.   The statement-of-reasons pattern is a good method of organization when the audience leans toward your position but needs some justification for that leaning.   **331**

F   T   F   3.   The text advocates applying pressure to those listeners who are reluctant to take action on a proposal.   **326**

T   T   F   4.   Role play can be used to change people's behavior.   **331**

F   T   F   5.   According to the text, petition drives are almost never successful in persuading lawmakers to change their positions.   **326**

T   T   F   6.   The speech to motivate action can try to stimulate either positive or negative action.   **324**

T   T   F   7.   Persuasion in one's career often requires weeks, months, or even years.   **332**

T   T   F   8.   Speakers should ask for a show of hands only when they are sure that most listeners will be eager and unembarrassed to make a public commitment.   **326**

F   T   F   9.   Implying what you want your listeners to do is more effective than asking for precisely what action you want them to take.   **325**

T   T   F   10. A leave-behind is a handout distributed at the end of a meeting.   **338**

KEY

Name _____

Multiple-Choice Questions Each question has only one correct answer.   **page**

c ____ 1. In which one of the following situations is the problem-solution pattern a bad   **330**
choice? (a) when listeners don't realize the existence of a particular problem,
(b) when listeners don't realize the seriousness of a problem, (c) when
listeners already accept your solution

b ____ 2. A good persuasive speech _____ contains sections that look like   **323**
sections of an informative speech. (a) never, (b) often

c ____ 3. According to the text, whether you succeed in persuasion often comes down   **332**
to one key question: (a) Are you sincere? (b) Are you likeable? (c) Are you
trustworthy?

a ____ 4. In a speech of refutation, you are more likely to demolish opposing arguments   **324**
if (a) the opposing arguments are based on a set of erroneous facts, (b) the
opposing arguments are based on deeply held beliefs

b ____ 5. To encourage listeners to call the Red Cross to volunteer for blood donation,   **325**
you should try to get them to use their cell phones (a) before the speech is
finished, (b) at the end of the speech, (c) as soon as they leave the room, (d)
sometime before they go to sleep that evening

c ____ 6. The first step in the motivated sequence is (a) need, (b) satisfaction, (c)   **326**
attention, (d) action, (e) motivation, (f) visualization

d ____ 7. The final step in the motivated sequence is (a) need, (b) satisfaction, (c)   **329**
attention, (d) action, (e) motivation, (f) visualization

b ____ 8. Persuasion in one's careers (a) usually demands high-pressure sales   **332**
techniques, (b) often requires weeks, months, or even years

c ____ 9. The visualization step of the motivated sequence offers a scenario that can be   **329**
(a) positive, (b) negative, (c) either positive or negative

a ____ 10. Which of the following would be a mistake if offered as take-home material?   **338**
(a) a transcript of the speech, (b) a summary of key ideas, (c) a list of new
points, (d) a bibliography of sources, (e) a printout of graphics

KEY Name _____

Multiple-Choice Questions Each question has only one correct answer.   **page**

b ___ 1. Convincing your audience that democracy is expanding in China is an example   **323**
of a (a) speech of curtailment, (b) speech to influence thinking, (c) speech to
motivate action

a ___ 2. It is _____ for a persuasive speech to include sections that   **323**
seem identical to sections of an informative speech. (a) acceptable, (b)
unacceptable

b ___ 3. Persuading people to stop smoking is an example of a (a) speech to influence   **324**
thinking, (b) speech to motivate action, (c) speech of curtailment

b ___ 4. In the motivated sequence, the first step is "attention" and the second step is (a) **326**
visualization, (b) need, (c) satisfaction, (d) action

b ___ 5. If you explain the three factors that contribute to the rise in asthma cases, you   **331**
are using which organizational pattern? (a) motivated sequence, (b) statement-
of-reasons, (c) chronological, (d) problem-solution

d ___ 6. If you show the audience the impact of brain injuries in child athletes and then **330**
tell how to improve the situation, you are using which organizational pattern? (a)
spatial, (b) statement-of-reasons, (c) chronological, (d) problem-solution

a ___ 7. In a persuasive speech, you should reveal to the audience (a) your true goals   **323**
and motives, (b) the weaknesses in your argument, (c) your feelings about
those who disagree with you, (d) your difficulty in preparing the speech

c ___ 8. A DVD about your speech topic, given to listeners at the end of your speech, is **338**
an example of what the book calls (a) a hidden persuader, (b) an enticement, (c)
a leave-behind, (d) a gimmick

b ___ 9. The technique of changing one's behavior by performing scenarios and   **331**
receiving critiques is called (a) sensitivity training, (b) role play, (c) peer
modeling, (d) assertiveness skill building

b ___ 10. "To convince listeners to reject the idea that tornadoes are incapable of striking **324**
large cities." This is an example of a specific purpose statement for (a) a speech
to motivate action, (b) a speech of refutation, (c) a speech of argumentation

KEY

Name _____

Fill in the missing words or phrases.

page

motivated sequence 1. The speech that has five steps—attention, need, satisfaction, visualization, and action—uses a pattern that is known as _____. | 326

statement-of-reasons 2. If you list three reasons why zoos should be preserved, you are using the _____ pattern of organization. | 331

comparative-advantages 3. If you show the advantages of alternative sentences over prison terms, you are using the _____ pattern of organization. | 331

problem-solution 4. A speaker who describes a problem and then advocates a solution is using the _____ pattern of organization. | 330

ask for action 5. Many speakers fail to move an audience to take action because they are reluctant to _____. | 325

speech of refutation 6. The _____ is the type of speech in which your main goal is to knock down arguments or ideas that you feel are false. | 324

stop 7. In the speech to motivate action, you can urge listeners to start doing certain things or to _____ doing certain things. | 324

leave-behinds 8. Handouts that are distributed at the end of a meeting are called _____. | 338

years 9. In your career, persuasion is often a long-term process requiring weeks, months, or even _____. | 332

persuasion 10. The process of influencing or changing attitudes, beliefs, values, or behavior is known as _____. | 322

KEY

Name _____

True or False If the statement is true, circle T; if false, circle F.   **page**

F   T F   1. The text recommends using deductive reasoning when your audience is skeptical or hostile to your central idea.   **355**

F   T F   2. Inductive reasoning is never used by scientists.   **354**

F   T F   3. Aiming sarcastic remarks at listeners who disagree with you will make them defensive at first, but will eventually increase their respect for your courage and integrity.   **347**

T   T F   4. Deductive reasoning is convincing only if both the major and minor premises are accepted by the audience as true.   **353**

T   T F   5. According to the text, some emotional appeals are inherent in pieces of evidence.   **362**

T   T F   6. Most people are more deeply influenced by one clear, vivid personal example than by an abundance of statistical data.   **352**

F   T F   7. In persuasive speaking, it is unethical for the speaker to stir up both positive and negative emotions.   **360**

T   T F   8. Explaining your expertise on your subject matter is a good way to build credibility with an audience.   **348**

T   T F   9. In a persuasive speech, your credibility is strengthened if you concede that your ideas sometimes do not work.   **350**

T   T F   10. In Maslow's hierarchy of needs, physiological needs must be met before a person can try to satisfy esteem needs.   **359**

KEY

Name _____

Multiple-Choice Questions Each question has only one correct answer.   **page**

b _____ 1. "Everyone is drinking strawberry lemonade for good health, and so should you."   **356**
This is an example of which type of logical fallacy? (a) either-or reasoning, (b)
bandwagon, (c) red herring, (d) deduction

d _____ 2. A pediatrician sees five children in her office one winter morning. Because all five   **354**
have symptoms of influenza, the pediatrician concludes that her community is
experiencing an influenza epidemic. The pediatrician has used (a) faulty
reasoning, (b) deductive reasoning, (c) emotional reasoning, (d) inductive
reasoning

a _____ 3. In Maslow's hierarchy of needs, the highest level of needs is (a) self-   **359**
actualization, (b) esteem, (c) love and belonging, (d) physiological

d _____ 4. A speaker wants to persuade an audience to stop engaging in unhealthy   **361**
behavior. Which level of fear is most effective in accomplishing this objective? (a)
no fear, (b) a small amount of fear, (c) a moderate amount of fear, (d) a high
level of fear

b _____ 5. In a persuasive speech, conceding that your ideas do not work in all cases (a)   **350**
undermines your credibility, (b) strengthens your credibility

a _____ 6. "Because Germans are the smartest engineers in the world, you should buy a   **357**
German-made car." This speaker is guilty of using what kind of fallacy in
reasoning? (a) building on an unproven assumption, (b) either-or reasoning, (c)
attack on a person, (d) straw man

b _____ 7. A speaker says, "We must adopt a vegetarian diet, or we will all die of cancer."   **358**
This speaker is guilty of using which fallacy in reasoning? (a) straw man, (b)
either-or reasoning, (c) attack on a person, (d) induction

d _____ 8. A speaker says, "Jackson says he believes that there is intelligent life on some   **357**
other planet in the universe, but how can you believe him? He's not an
astronomer; in fact, he is not a scientist at all. The only degree he has is a
masters in business administration." This speaker is guilty of using which kind of
fallacy in reasoning? (a) false cause, (b) either-or reasoning, (c) hasty
generalization, (d) attack on a person

a _____ 9. A speaker says, "People who favor gun control want to turn our society over to   **358**
the criminals. Therefore, we must ignore these gun-control advocates." This
speaker is guilty of using which kind of fallacy in reasoning? (a) straw man, (b)
either-or reasoning, (c) false cause, (d) induction

b _____ 10. A speaker says, "I knew a red-headed kid in third grade who was always getting   **356**
into fights on the playground. And I know two red heads who are easily angered.
I guess you can say that red heads are quick-tempered people." The speaker is
guilty of using which kind of fallacy in reasoning? (a) straw man, (b) hasty
generalization, (c) attack on a person, (d) either-or reasoning

KEY

Name _____

Multiple-Choice Questions Each question has only one correct answer.   **page**

c ___ 1. Which type of logical fallacy diverts listeners from the real issue to an unrelated matter? (a) either-or reasoning, (b) induction, (c) red herring, (d) deduction   **356**

c ___ 2. A speaker says, "I owned a Ford and had nothing but trouble with it. My cousin had a Ford that was a lemon. And my best friend is unhappy with her Ford. I tell you, Ford is a lousy automobile." What fallacy in reasoning is the speaker using? (a) straw man, (b) false cause, (c) hasty generalization, (d) attack on a person   **356**

a ___ 3. A speaker says, "Because the Japanese make the best stereo sound systems in the world, you should consider buying a Japanese-made sound system." This speaker is guilty of using which kind of fallacy in reasoning? (a) building on an unproven assumption, (b) straw man, (c) either-or reasoning, (d) attack on a person   **357**

a ___ 4. A speaker says, "Scientists who perform operations on animals in laboratories are not interested in getting scientific knowledge—they enjoy inflicting suffering on animals. Therefore, we must stop the use of animals in experiments." This speaker is guilty of using which kind of fallacy in reasoning? (a) straw man, (b) either-or reasoning, (c) false cause, (d) induction   **358**

b ___ 5. Which type of logical fallacy asserts an argument that is based on popularity rather than on evidence and reasoning? (a) either-or reasoning, (b) bandwagon, (c) red herring, (d) deduction   **356**

d ___ 6. In Maslow's hierarchy, the human need to help others falls into the _____ category of needs. (a) physiological, (b) safety, (c) esteem, (d) self-actualization   **359**

a ___ 7. According to research, which is the more persuasive type of evidence? (a) a clear, vivid personal example, (b) an abundance of statistical data   **352**

a ___ 8. Reasoning that moves from a generalization to a specific conclusion is (a) deductive reasoning, (b) inductive reasoning   **353**

c ___ 9. A speaker says, "We must change to the metric system or we will fall behind the rest of the world in science and industry." This speaker is guilty of using which kind of fallacy in reasoning? (a) straw man, (b) attack on a person, (c) either-or reasoning, (d) induction   **358**

d ___ 10. A speaker says, "There is no need for me to refute Senator Smith's ideas about regulating professional baseball. Senator Smith is unqualified to speak on baseball because he has never played any sport on the high school, collegiate, or professional level." This speaker is guilty of using which type of fallacy in reasoning? (a) false cause, (b) either-or reasoning, (c) hasty generalization, (d) attack on a person   **357**

KEY

Name _____

Fill in the missing words or phrases.   page

induction   1. In reasoning, the chain of logic that goes from specific instances   **354**
                              to a generalization is called _____.

credibility   2. _____ is the degree to which a speaker is   **348**
                              perceived to be believable, trustworthy, and competent.

attack on a person 3. Some speakers try to win an argument by attacking a person   **357**
                              rather than the person's ideas. This fallacy in reasoning is known
                              as _____.

high-fear   4. In a speech, which appeal—high-fear or low-fear—has been   **361**
                              found by researchers to be the more effective?
                              _____

rational   5. Emotional appeals should always be combined with   **361**
                              _____ appeals.

self-actualization 6. In Maslow's hierarchy of needs, the highest level is called   **359**
                              _____.

inductive   7. When your audience is skeptical or hostile to your central idea,   **355**
                              which form of reasoning should you use—inductive or
                              deductive?

red   8. The _____ herring fallacy occurs when a speaker tries to   **356**
                              divert listeners from the real issue to an irrelevant matter.

deduction   9. In reasoning, the chain of logic that carries you from a   **353**
                              generalization to a specific instance to a conclusion is called
                              _____.

either-or reasoning 10. When a speaker states that there are only two alternatives, when   **358**
                              in fact there are many, the speaker is using which fallacy in
                              reasoning? _____

KEY

Name _____

True or False If the statement is true, circle T; if false, circle F.   **page**

T   T F   1.   Humor can sometimes be used in a eulogy.   382

F   T F   2.   To be successful, an entertaining speech must have at least three jokes.   374

F   T F   3.   Overstating a speaker's credentials is common and acceptable procedure in   377
                    speeches of introduction.

F   T F   4.   In a speech of presentation, the name of the recipient must always be given   378
                    at the beginning of the remarks.

T   T F   5.   A eulogy should be dignified, without exaggerated sentimentality.   382

F   T F   6.   An entertaining speech should contain no elements of persuasion,   373
                    information, or inspiration.

F   T F   7.   A rule of thumb for speeches of introduction is to keep them under ten   377
                    minutes.

F   T F   8.   In a speech of tribute to a great person, it adds to your credibility if you point   379
                    out some negative features of the person.

F   T F   9.   In a wedding toast, it is acceptable to tease the bride and groom.   381

T   T F   10. When you give a speech of introduction, you should ask the speaker ahead of   377
                    time what kind of introduction the speaker would like.

KEY

Name _____

Multiple-Choice Questions Each question has only one correct answer.　　　　　**page**

d ___ 1. In a speech of introduction, you should (a) use the speaker's full name, (b) use 　377
the speaker's first name only, (c) use the speaker's last name only, (d) use the
name the speaker prefers

e ___ 2. A key objective of the _____ speech is to get the speaker 　377
and audience interested in each other. (a) entertaining, (b) inspirational, (c)
tribute, (d) acceptance, (e) introduction

a ___ 3. The speech of introduction should (a) give background information about the 　377
speaker, (b) give no background information because that would take away
from the speaker's speech

c ___ 4. Which one of the following is inappropriate for a best man's speech at a 　380
wedding celebration? (a) reciting a poem, (b) showing a video, (c) telling a joke
about the groom's ex-girlfriend, (d) focusing the entire remarks on the bride
and groom

a ___ 5. A speech of introduction should be kept under _____ minutes. (a) 3, (b) 8, 　378
(c) 12, (d) 15

a ___ 6. A toast offered at a celebration should avoid (a) teasing, (b) wishes for 　381
happiness, (c) warm reminiscences, (d) anecdotes about the bride or groom

c ___ 7. Which kind of liquid can be used for a toast in the United States and Canada, 　381
but should be avoided in some other cultures? (a) wine, (b) champagne, (c)
water, (d) soda

b ___ 8. An important dimension of inspirational speaking is (a) sarcasm, (b) delivery, 　382
(c) grandiloquence, (d) personal appearance

b ___ 9. An inspirational speech is often similar to (a) an informative speech, 　382
(b) a persuasive speech, (c) an entertaining speech

c ___ 10. A speech of tribute is defined as a speech that praises (a) only a living person, 　379
(b) only a dead person, (c) either a dead or living person

KEY

Name _____

Multiple-Choice Questions Each question has only one correct answer.   **page**

c ___ 1. The safest kind of joke is (a) satirical, (b) a play on words, (c) self-deprecating,   **375**
(d) ironic

a ___ 2. According to the text, a rule of thumb is that a speech of introduction should be   **377**
(a) under three minutes, (b) at least five minutes, (c) one-tenth of the estimated
length of the speech that is about to be delivered, (d) no more than ten minutes

a ___ 3. Which kind of speech would you be most likely to deliver to an evening   **373**
banquet? (a) entertaining, (b) acceptance, (c) tribute

b ___ 4. A speaker says, "It is easy to quit smoking. I have done so a thousand times."   **374**
This is an example of what the text calls _____ humor. (a) witty (b) low-
key, (c) perceptive, (d) indirect

a ___ 5. A spine-tingling tale of adventure would be most appropriate for which kind of   **373**
speech? (a) entertaining speech (b) speech of introduction, (c) speech of
acceptance, (d) inspirational speech

d ___ 6. Before you give a speech of introduction, you should coordinate your remarks   **377**
with the speaker's. The primary reason for doing so is to avoid (a) divulging
embarrassing personal details, (b) inadvertently antagonizing the audience, (c)
pretending you know more about the subject than the speaker, (d) stealing the
speaker's material

a ___ 7. To introduce a speech filled with humor, what kind of speech of introduction   **377**
would be appropriate? (a) a humorous speech of introduction to set a light tone,
(b) a serious speech of introduction to avoid upstaging the speaker

a ___ 8. A speech of tribute should (a) focus on the significance of a person's life and   **379**
deeds, (b) give a comprehensive history of the person's biographical events, (c)
focus on the person's career achievements, (d) focus on the person's family and
friends

c ___ 9. A speech designed to formally bestow an award of honor is known as the   **378**
speech of (a) acceptance, (b) honor, (c) presentation, (d) entertainment

d ___ 10. A coach giving a pep talk to her team is delivering which type of speech? (a)   **382**
entertaining, (b) introduction, (c) tribute, (d) inspirational, (e) acceptance

Fill in the missing words or phrases.

page

significance   1.   A eulogy should focus on the _____ of a person's life and deeds.   **382**

yes   2.   Can humor sometimes be appropriate in a eulogy? _____   **382**

material   3.   If you are giving a speech of introduction, you should not discuss the speaker's _____ unless the speaker gives prior permission.   **377**

three   4.   A rule of thumb for speeches of introduction is to keep them under _____ minutes.   **378**

positive   5.   The goal of the inspirational speech is to stir _____ emotions.   **382**

presentation   6.   Saying a few words while giving an award to a dedicated worker is an example of the speech of _____.   **378**

tribute   7.   A eulogy is an example of the speech of _____.   **379**

move them together   8.   If listeners are spread apart in a large room, try to _____.   **376**

appropriate   9.   Are jokes appropriate or inappropriate for an entertaining speech? _____   **374**

the speaker   10.   Who should be consulted before a speech of introduction is delivered? _____   **377**

KEY

Name _____

True or False If the statement is true, circle T; if false, circle F.   **page**

T   T   F   1.   A team presentation is like a speech given by an individual except that the   **396**
                      content is divided among the team members.

T   T   F   2.   For panel moderators, open-ended questions are the best way to stimulate   **398**
                      discussion.

T   T   F   3.   A group often has an IQ (or intelligence level) that is higher than the IQ of any   **388**
                      individual in the group.

F   T   F   4.   A participant should not express views in a meeting if they are clearly contrary   **392**
                      to the views of the majority.

F   T   F   5.   Meetings should not begin until all participants have arrived.   **390**

T   T   F   6.   At the beginning of a meeting, the leader should review the purpose of the   **389**
                      meeting and the scope of the group's power.

T   T   F   7.   In a meeting, the leader should periodically summarize the group's work.   **391**

T   T   F   8.   Members of a small group can catch and correct errors that might slip past an   **388**
                      individual.

F   T   F   9.   A hidden agenda is an effective technique for small group meetings.   **392**

T   T   F   10. Minutes of the preceding meeting should be reviewed at every meeting.   **391**

KEY

Name _____

Multiple-Choice Questions Each question has only one correct answer.

page

a ___ 1. A speech that is divided into parts, with each part delivered by a different person, is known as a (a) team presentation, (b) symposium, (c) panel, (d) split speech
396

a ___ 2. A group spends all its time on minor issues and never gets around to the major issues. The group could solve the problem by (a) establishing and following an agenda, (b) choosing a forceful leader, (c) allotting extra time for each meeting
389

b ___ 3. If you are part of a team and one of your team members is speaking to an audience, what signal would you send the audience if you review your notes? (a) "I want to be well-prepared when I get my turn to speak." (b) "What's being said is not very important."
397

c ___ 4. What is the first step in the reflective-thinking method? (a) Establish criteria for evaluating solutions. (b) Decide how to implement the solution. (c) Define the problem. (d) Analyze the problem. (e) Choose the best solution. (f) Decide how to test the solution. (g) Suggest possible solutions.
393

b ___ 5. A series of brief speeches on a common topic is known as (a) a panel, (b) a symposium
397

c ___ 6. Alterations to an agenda should be made by participants (a) one day before the meeting, (b) one hour before the meeting, (c) at the start of the meeting, (d) at the end of the meeting
389-390

b ___ 7. A written record of the group's activities during a meeting is called the (a) agenda, (b) minutes, (c) record, (d) dossier
391

b ___ 8. In a meeting, the group leader should forbid (a) spontaneous ideas from participants, (b) attacks on people or ideas, (c) disagreements between members of the group, (d) efforts to add new items to the agenda
391

a ___ 9. Brainstorming by a small group resulted in which successful product? (a) Image-capture chips in digital cameras, (b) Nike Air Max shoes, (c) Hershey's Candy Kisses, (d) YouTube video clips
394

d ___ 10. Writer H.L. Mencken is quoted as saying that for every human problem, "there is always an easy solution—neat, plausible, and _____." (a) ingenious, (b) workable, (c) hopeless, (d) wrong
393

KEY

Name _____

Multiple-Choice Questions Each question has only one correct answer.

c ___ 1. The secret of a successful team, says Dean Kamen, "is not to assemble the largest team possible, but rather to assemble a team that can _____." (a) reach goals quickly, (b) operate without disagreements, (c) work well together, (d) follow the directives of the leader — **392**

a ___ 2. A document that summarizes what transpired at a meeting is known as the (a) minutes, (b) agenda, (c) synopsis, (d) draft — **391**

b ___ 3. When you are a participant in a panel discussion, you should (a) stand firm on your position, (b) be willing to alter your position. — **400**

b ___ 4. Jack Smith works hard on a committee preparing a plan for action. At the sixth meeting, he finds out that the committee can only advise; it does not have the power to take action. Jack is distraught because he feels that much of his work has been in vain. Whose fault is it that Jack has labored under a misconception? (a) Jack himself, for not inquiring about the scope of the group's power, (b) the group leader, for not making clear the scope of the group's power — **389**

a ___ 5. Ideally, participants in a meeting should receive the agenda (a) well before the meeting, (b) at the start of the meeting, (c) in the middle of the meeting, (d) at the end of the meeting — **389-390**

d ___ 6. In a team presentation, the text says, the most important part is (a) the introduction, (b) the visual aids, (c) the conclusion, (d) the question-and-answer period — **396**

b ___ 7. In an agenda, items should be rank ordered (a) from least important to most important, (b) from most important to least important — **389**

a ___ 8. Meetings are sometimes sabotaged by participants who have (a) a hidden agenda, (b) a private vendetta, (c) a legitimate grievance, (d) an unwillingness to work closely with others — **392**

c ___ 9. In the famous Coca-Cola fiasco involving "New Coke" in the 1980s, the soft drink maker erred by choosing a solution that was _____ but wrong. (a) clever, (b) lucrative, (c) easy, (d) radical — **393**

a ___ 10. Meetings should always begin (a) at the designated time, (b) five minutes after the designated time, (c) 10 minutes after the designated time, (d) only when all the participants have arrived — **390**

Name _____

page

Fill in the missing words or phrases.

team presentation | 1. | What do you call a speech that is divided into sections, with each section delivered by a different person? | 396

notes | 2. | In a panel discussion, should panelists use notes or a written statement? _____ | 399

open ended | 3. | The moderator of a panel should ask what type of questions? _____ | 399

agenda | 4. | A list of items that need to be covered in a meeting is called the _____. | 389

reflective-thinking | 5. | The _____ method is the problem-solving technique derived from the writings of the American philosopher John Dewey. | 393

hidden agendas | 6. | Unannounced private goals that conflict with the group's goals are called _____. | 392

brainstorming | 7. | In group meetings, one of the best ways to generate ideas is _____, a technique wherein participants rapidly throw out ideas and the group leader writes them on a chalkboard. | 394

start the meeting | 8. | At the designated time for a meeting, if some group members have not arrived yet, what should the chairperson do? _____ | 390

minutes | 9. | A record of what was discussed and accomplished during a meeting is known as the _____. | 391

symposium | 10. | A _____ is a series of brief speeches on a common topic. | 397